SLIM BY DESIGN

*Marketing Nutrition: Soy, Functional Foods,
Biotechnology, and Obesity*

Asking Questions: The Definitive Guide to Questionnaire Design
(with Norman Bradburn and Seymour Sudman)

Consumer Panels (with Seymour Sudman)

SLIM

| BY |

DESIGN

MINDLESS EATING SOLUTIONS
FOR EVERYDAY LIFE

BRIAN WANSINK, Ph.D.

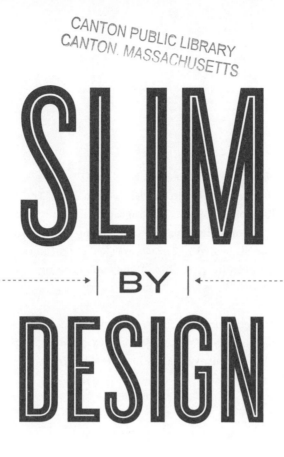

WILLIAM MORROW
An Imprint of HarperCollins*Publishers*

HarperCollins books may be purchased for educational, business, or sales promotional use. For information please e-mail the Special Markets Department at SPsales@harpercollins.com.

FIRST EDITION

Designed by Paul Kepple and Ralph Geroni at HEADCASE DESIGN

Illustrations by Mitch Blunt

Library of Congress Cataloging-in-Publication Data has been applied for.

ISBN 978-0-06-213652-7

14 15 16 17 18 OV/RRD 10 9 8 7 6 5 4 3 2 1

To my passionate, restless, tireless past, current, and future coauthors, colleagues, and students. To the trusting sponsors and donors who have believed in this mission since 1987. And to bold, insightful, and generous academic journal editors and reviewers who have made our work stronger and more relevant by caringly pushing it to the next level of rigor and impact.

CONTENTS

Introduction

. . . .

THIS BOOK IS BASED ON a very basic concept: Becoming slim by design works better than trying to become slim by will-power. It's easier to change your eating environment than to change your mind. *Slim by Design* is about changing your eating environment—what I call your *food radius*—so that you, your kids, and even your neighbors eat less and eat better. These are simple actions you can take to become permanently slimmer without really working at it. And you can get others to help.

NABISCO HEADQUARTERS, SPRING 1996. Two dozen Nabisco executives are staring at me with their mouths frozen open—like I was Medusa with snakes for hair or like I had just finished yodeling. Instead, I had just told them that if they sold "mini-packs" of their snacks, they'd make more money and help make people skinnier. Sell less food—make more money. Just like in a cartoon, I could see a big collective thought bubble above their heads: SELL LESS AND MAKE MORE?

Why was I so sure of my theory? Because I had made a mistake. But one of those good kinds of mistakes that lead to a nice surprise, and not one of those bad kinds that lead to a viral YouTube video with "Epic Failure" in the title.

For two years, my graduate students and I had been tweaking food package sizes and shapes to see how they changed how much food people ate, how much they liked it, and how much they threw away. Although we were originally interested in sustainable packaging that reduced waste, we just kept seeing the same thing over and over. The bigger the package, the more people ate and the more they liked it. This was true for everyone we tested, and it's probably true for everyone from competitive hot dog eaters in Coney Island to desperate housewives in Beverly Hills.[1]

Then came the Philadelphia Experiment. We were giving Philadelphia moviegoers free food—Wheat Thins and M&Ms—to see if they realized how much more they were eating from big packages.[2] We would take 440 calories' worth of snacks and repack them in large clear zipper bags to make sure they could see all they ate and all they didn't. Unfortunately, we ran out of these big bags and had to give some moviegoers four tiny, Tinkerbell-size bags I had mistakenly bought. These each held about 110 calories—about the same amount of M&Ms that are in those "fun-size" packs that some of us give disappointed trick-or-treaters on Halloween.

Our moviegoers watched the movie and munched away. Afterward, we collected and weighed their bags. What confused us was that moviegoers with the four Tinkerbell-size bags ate about half as much as those with the full 440-calorie one. When they got to the end of their first or second 110-calorie pack, they just stopped eating.[3] Even crazier, more than half also said they'd pay 20 percent more money for snacks if companies put them in smaller packages.[4] Pay more to eat less? This should be a snack company's dream come true.

At that time, I was a consumer behavior professor at the University of Pennsylvania's Wharton School, in Philadelphia. Since Philly is only four hours away from companies like M&M/Mars and Nabisco, I called them up and said, "Hey, I found a way you could make more money by helping your customers eat less!" Within a week, I had scheduled presentations at these companies and was hopping into my Jeep Cherokee to spread the good news, feeling like the Johnny Appleseed of mini-size packs.

Sell less and make more?

About thirty executives came to each of my presentations, and the first half hour would go pretty well. I'd show them how all the people in our studies ate more from bigger packages, and they'd nod and write down the numbers. But the train wreck always happened at the climactic "ta-da" moment when I revealed my conclusion: If they sold mini-size packs, people would pay more and eat less. The same thing always happened—they just froze and stared at me with confused frowns. "If we sell smaller snack packages, people would pay more . . . and eat less? I don't understand." Every drive home was a buzz-kill disappointment.

But five months later, one of the less skeptical execs who had moved from M&M/Mars to Nabisco called and said, "Do you really think we can make more money by selling mini-size packages?" I drove back to their headquarters and described this and other studies in more detail. Eventually Nabisco/Kraft gave my theory a try and launched the 100-calorie pack. Within two years they were followed by the other companies I'd visited, including M&M/Mars, Kellogg's, and others. These mini-size packs helped about 70 percent of all tummy-conscious snack lovers to *mindlessly* eat less, without having to count out their potato chips.[5] This was a win-win mindless eating solution.[6]

WE'RE ALL MINDLESS EATERS. Each of us makes more than two hundred nearly subconscious food choices every day—soup or salad? A little or a lot? Finish it or leave it?[7] We're nudged more by our eating environment and things like 100-calorie packs than by our deliberate choices.[8] But most of these subtle nudges—the size of our cereal bowl, the distance of the candy dish, the color of our plates—push us to eat too much.

Even though I was appointed by the White House to be executive director of the U.S. Department of Agriculture's agency in charge of the 2010 United States Dietary Guidelines, and even though I am a past president of the Society for Nutrition Education and Behavior, I still don't think most nutrition education is very effective. People know that an apple is better for them than a Snickers bar, but . . . they eat the Snickers bar anyway.

> You don't need any magical skills to make these changes.

Of course, it's good to understand nutrition, but it's much more effective to change our eating environment. Once you've made the right changes to your eating environment, you'll start eating better *without thinking about it.* You can make healthy decisions even when your brain's on autopilot.

This will be hard for you to believe at first. It was just as hard for the Nabisco execs to believe that the 100-calorie pack would succeed as well as it did. I know these small changes can work because my Lab has spent the past quarter century proving this repeatedly in scientific study after study.[9] We've seen it work for people in their homes, in their favorite restaurants and grocery stores, in their offices, and in their children's

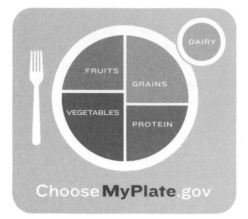

schools. Do you eat lunch at your desk, request a booth at your favorite restaurant, shop down grocery aisle 2 after you buy your vegetables, and then come home through the kitchen door? Even if you did only the last of these, our studies show you'll weigh more than your neighbor who instead comes home through their front door.[10]

The easiest, quickest, and most natural way to slim down ourselves, our families, our neighborhoods, and our country is to work with human nature and not against it. Willpower alone won't conquer bad eating habits for 90 percent of us. Fortunately, there are a lot of small, innovative, and proven solutions from behavioral economics and psychology that will help make us become *slim by design*.

This book is about taking small actions in the five places or zones that booby-trap most of our eating: our home, our favorite restaurants, our corner grocery store, our workplace, and our child's school lunchroom.[11] For each location I'll give a 100-point scorecard that uses our research-based discoveries to show whether these places are making you slim or fat, and I'll also show what you can do and how they can help to make you slim by design. Best yet, you don't need any magical skills to make these changes. All you need to know is what to do—and how to ask the people around you to help. Read on to learn the easy actions that will make us slim, hopeful, and happy.

Chapter One

MINDLESS
EATING
SOLUTIONS

ONE SENTENCE SUMMARIZES TWENTY-FIVE YEARS of my research: Becoming slim by design works better than trying to become slim by willpower. That is, it's easier to change your eating environment than to change your mind. It's easier to move your candy dish across the room than to resist it when it's on your desk. It's easier to use a small plate than to constantly remind yourself not to over-serve onto a big one. Yet while there are many solutions to mindless eating, most of them will go undiscovered because we don't look for them. Instead, we're too focused on the food and not on our surroundings. We're too focused on eating less of one thing, more of another thing, or on launching into the new "Yeast and Potting Soil Diet" we read about on the Internet.[1]

I recently spoke at a convention in Washington, D.C., along with a winner of the TV show *The Biggest Loser*. During his season, he'd weighed in at over 400 pounds and weighed out at half of that. During this over-the-top drama, he lost half his weight—200 pounds—by visualizing, sweating, and starving himself thin. Fun times.

After our speeches, we grabbed a speedy buffet lunch before heading to the airport. He's a funny, positive, interesting guy, so it seemed strange that he'd sometimes stop his animated conversation in midsentence to say things like, "Hey, did you notice that I picked out the smallest piece of chicken?" or "Look, I didn't take any bread!" After a while, it became clear that he wasn't making these comments for me. He was making them for himself. He was reminding himself that he was full-time Willpower Man. But it took so much concentration that each time he made the right choice, he wanted to announce it.

I told him I was doubly impressed with his willpower around food because I have none.[2] For me, an "all-you-can-eat" buffet is an

> # The solution to mindless eating is not mind*ful* eating—our lives are just too crazy and our willpower's too wimpy.

"eat-all-they've-got" buffet. So instead of relying on willpower, I have to change my eating environment so it helps me eat less. I take the smallest plate, serve myself salad first, move the bread basket off the table, and so on. Easy actions that help me eat less. He changed his mind. I changed my eating environment.

For 90 percent of us, the solution to mindless eating is not mind-*ful* eating—our lives are just too crazy and our willpower's too wimpy. Instead, the solution is to tweak small things in our homes, favorite restaurants, supermarkets, workplaces, and schools so we mindlessly eat less and better instead of more. It's easier to use a small plate, face away from the buffet, and Frisbee-spin the bread basket across the table than to be a martyr on a hunger strike. Willpower is hard and has to last a lifetime. Rearranging your life to be slim by design is easy. It starts with your food radius.

Your Food Radius

. . . .

IF YOU'RE A TYPICAL AMERICAN, you buy or eat more than 80 percent of all your food within five miles of where you live.[3] This is your food radius—your food neighborhood—and there are only a handful of places or zones that really matter in this food radius and in your eating life: your home, your "go-to" restaurants, your weekly grocery store, where you work, and where your kids go to school. That's it. Just five places account for more than three-quarters of what we and our families eat—so these are the places that deserve our attention.[4] Once we change the things we do in these places—or ask them to change for us—we don't have to think about them again.

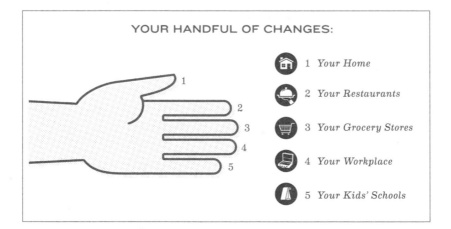

YOUR HANDFUL OF CHANGES:

1 *Your Home*

2 *Your Restaurants*

3 *Your Grocery Stores*

4 *Your Workplace*

5 *Your Kids' Schools*

Here's how to visualize your food radius. Print out a map of your town or neighborhood and put a big star where your home is. Then put a big "G" where your favorite grocery store is, put a big "R" on each of your two most frequented restaurants, a big "S" where your kids go to school, and a big "W" where you or your partner work. Using your home as the center of the circle, if you draw a circle that encompasses most of these letters, you'll see your food radius.

OUR FOOD RADIUS

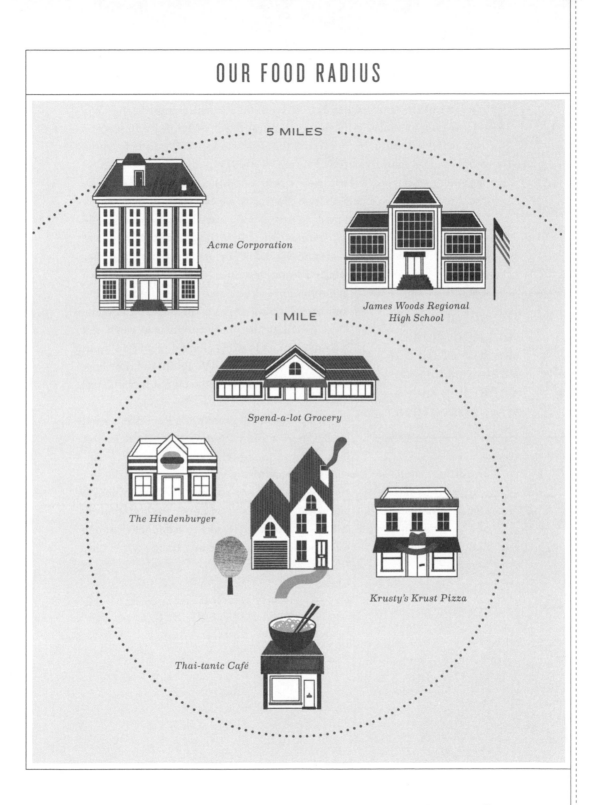

Everyone's food radius is different. It's different for a forty-five-mile BMW-driving commuter in Los Angeles than it is for someone who walks to work in Winesburg, Ohio. It's different for a working mother than her stay-at-home spouse. After analyzing hundreds of Food Radius Maps from different countries, we found that the average food radius for most people is less than five miles.[5] Again, we will buy or eat more than 80 percent of all our weekly calories within five miles of where we live. We don't need to immediately change the world; we can start close to home.

To make your life slim by design, you don't have to change the whole world. Just focus on these five miles. You can think globally, but you eat locally. This is doable for everyone—you don't need to have the willpower of the *Biggest Loser,* or a fistful of dollars for a personal chef. You don't have to fight against Safeway, Dunkin' Donuts, the East High School lunchroom, or the dingy cafeteria at work. All you need to do is to (1) change what you do in each of these places and (2) let them know how they could profitably help you eat less and eat better.

We will buy or eat more than 80 percent of all our weekly calories within five miles of where we live.

Why would they change? Because they'll make more money. Some of the changes you ask them to make will bring in new customers; other changes will keep them from losing you. A restaurant doesn't want you to eat across the street; a grocery store doesn't want you to shop down the road; and your company doesn't want you to start sending out resumes during lunchtime. Nothing can make these places change faster than believing they can help make you slim and happy while they make money.

Nobody Wants Us to Be Fat

. . . .

NOBODY WANTS US TO BE FAT. Bob's Burgers[6] or the Hindenburger doesn't give us sky-high piles of French fries because they want us to be fat. They want us to think that they are a better bargain than Burger King. Extra fries get you in the door. But once you order them, they don't care whether you eat them, toss them from a parade float, feed them to honey badgers, or throw them away. Same with the Deep-Fried Snickers Man at your state fair. He only cares that you buy from him and not from Cotton Candy Lady. If you take a teeny nibble, joke about it, sneak another bite when no one's looking, and throw the rest away, it makes no difference to him.

Places that sell food don't want to make us fat; they want to make money. If a wave of veganism washed over the land, in six months there would be Broccoli Kings, Taco Bell Peppers, and McTofu Drive-Thrus.[7] Restaurants want to make money, and we want to become slim by design. If we show them how to help us and how they can profit, it's amazing what happens—even at all-you-can-eat buffets.

Chinese Buffet Confidential

· · · · · · · · · · · · ·

RICE IS A GREAT FOOD if you're really hungry and you want to eat two thousand of something.[8] But nobody goes to an all-you-can-eat Chinese buffet for the rice. They go there to eat as if it's their last meal. A good buffet is like a massive people magnet. Some say there's only one way to not overeat at a buffet: Don't go.

Yet here's what's strange. Visit any buffet—Chinese or pizza; breakfast, lunch, or dinner—and you'll see a lot of slim people. A third might be heavy and a third average-size, but the last third will be as slim as Victoria's Secret models. So what do slim people do at buffets that heavy people don't? Well, they probably eat less, but how *exactly* do they do that? When we ask them this question, they almost all say, "I don't know." Most people have very little idea why they eat the way they eat. You can find this out only by carefully watching them. Maybe they can't tell us how they do it—but they can show us.

> Rice is a great food if you're really hungry and you want to eat two thousand of something.

After getting permission (all our studies are preapproved and people's identities are kept anonymous),[9] the researchers in my Lab found eleven cooperative Chinese buffets—from New Jersey to Iowa to California—and settled into dark corners pretending to read a book while we ate. Then we proceeded to secretly observe 213 buffet-goers from their first step into the restaurant to their last step out. We noted where they sat and what direction they faced, how they served themselves food, how many times they chewed the average bite, and practically how many times they blinked, coughed, dropped their fork, and so on. We calculated their BMI (body mass index) and categorized them as slim, average, or heavy.[10] Our goal: to secretly discover what the slim people did that heavy people didn't.

How did we get people to reveal their BMI stats and all that other info? If James Bond had been running this study, he'd have placed pressure-sensitive mats by the door so that when people walked in, their weight would be silently recorded. To get their heights, he would aim a laser beam grid at the buffet to give a reading to the nearest eighth of an inch. To time their behavior, he would have multiple Swiss stopwatches with lots of clicky buttons on them. To count how many buffet trips they made or how many times they chewed, he'd use a bunch of super-expensive precision German stadium tally counters by Zeiss or Leica.

That's how James Bond would have done it. But we didn't have a genius inventor named "Q" or a limitless high-tech British budget. So instead of being James Bond, we ended up channeling Wile E. Coyote. Remember the Road Runner cartoons? Wile E. was the somewhat dopey coyote who was always trying to catch the Road Runner with the worthless gadgets he bought from the Acme Corporation.[11] Nothing ever, ever, ever worked—every one of them was a catastrophic failure at the worst possible time. Acme Corporation—that's where we shopped.

What do slim people do at buffets that heavy people don't?

That pressure-sensitive mat? It might have been able to detect a car that rolled on it and parked overnight, but it couldn't detect a person walking over it at one mile per hour. That cool laser beam grid? After three consecutive nightmares that we were blinding people as they served themselves General Tso's chicken, I set up a sayonara eBay account to sell it. Swiss stopwatches? Neither Swiss, nor did they usually stop when necessary. German stadium tally counters? Couldn't afford anything German, so we bought one from a country I don't think had been invented when most of us were born. Worked perfectly.

Despite a bumpy first week, we finally settled into a two-month groove. We developed a cool way to match people's body shape to standardized charts that helped us classify their weight and height, and we developed detailed coding sheets to track 103 different visible characteristics and behaviors of each diner. Then we crunched the data to see what slim diners did differently from heavy ones.

Here's the first thing we discovered: Slim diners "scouted" out the buffet before grabbing a plate—before even picking up a plate, 71 percent of them walked around and scanned the salad bar, the steam trays holding fourteen seemingly identical chicken dishes, the sushi station, and the dessert bar. Only after they figured out the lay of the land did they grab their plate and swoop down to cherry-pick their favorites, with an eagle eye on the stir-fry. Heavier diners did the opposite. They were twice as likely to charge ahead to the nearest stack of plates, take one, and fill it up. They didn't skip to the foods they really liked. Instead they served themselves a bit of everything they didn't hate.[12]

Slim people even acted differently *after* taking their food. They trotted back to faraway booths along the walls, and—here's what's cool—73 percent faced away from the buffet. Heavy diners did the opposite. They sat at tables that were on average sixteen feet closer to the buffet. Moreover, they were three times more likely to sit facing the food, where they watched all the people who went back for seconds and thirds and fourths.[13] Every time they saw someone take another lap around the stir-fry, it reminded them that was "normal" behavior.

There are no twelve-step moo shu pork programs.

What else do slim people do? Besides scouting out the food, sitting farther away, and facing away, they were also more likely to use chopsticks, choose smaller plates, and chew each bite an average of fifteen times—three chews more than heavy people.[14]

Yet here's what's crazy. None of these behaviors has anything to do with counting calories or choosing the bean sprouts over the Peking duck. They instead dealt with how they scanned the food, where they sat and faced, and which plates and utensils they picked up.

So how do slim people develop these slim-by-design habits? There are no twelve-step moo shu pork programs. When we ask buffet-goers why they sat farther away, didn't face the food, chewed more, and scouted out the buffet, almost everyone said, "I don't know." Less than five minutes after they ate, they couldn't remember what they did or why they did it.

Without realizing it, these slim people had stumbled across tricks to eat less. Does where they sat, the direction they faced, or the number of times they chewed their Peking duck explain why they were skinnier than the person sixteen feet closer? No way. Yet maybe these people also do other things—at home, at other restaurants, at the grocery store, or at work—that have unknowingly helped them fat-proof their lives over the years.

AT THE BUFFET

WHAT DO SLIM AND OVERWEIGHT DINERS DO DIFFERENTLY?

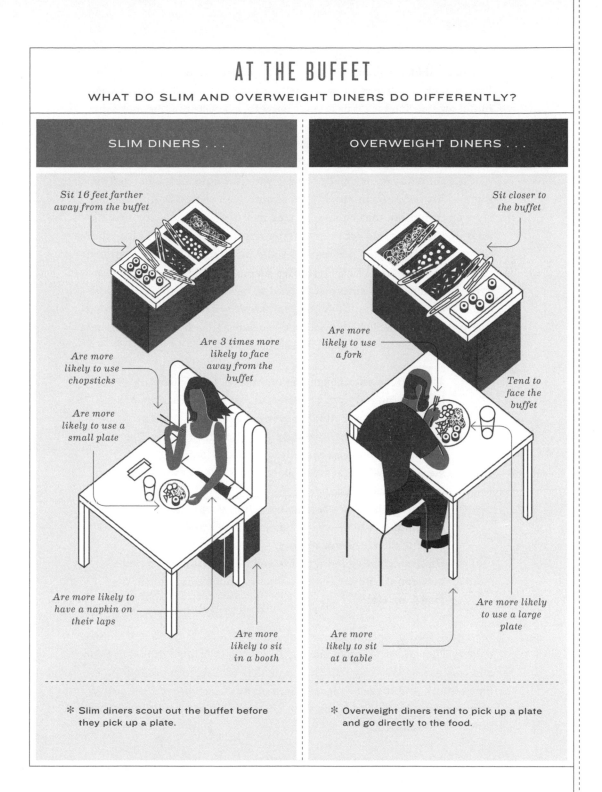

SLIM DINERS . . .

Sit 16 feet farther away from the buffet

Are more likely to use chopsticks

Are 3 times more likely to face away from the buffet

Are more likely to use a small plate

Are more likely to have a napkin on their laps

Are more likely to sit in a booth

✳ Slim diners scout out the buffet before they pick up a plate.

OVERWEIGHT DINERS . . .

Sit closer to the buffet

Are more likely to use a fork

Tend to face the buffet

Are more likely to use a large plate

Are more likely to sit at a table

✳ Overweight diners tend to pick up a plate and go directly to the food.

These hidden habits are useful if we want to avoid polishing off the Peking duck, but they're also very useful to someone else: the buffet owner. Buffet owners don't want us to gorge ourselves; it costs them money every time we belly up to the buffet. They want us to eat enough to be happy and to think this was a tasty steal of a deal. They don't want us to load our plates, waste food, and eat until we are regretful and can't breathe.

This point was made vividly one day when a young man contacted me, saying, "My father owns some Chinese buffets in central Pennsylvania." He went on to say that he and his dad heard about this study and figured that if they could get their buffet-goers to eat less—to eat like slim people—they'd save on food expenses and make more money. Sounded like a win-win plan for both the buffet-goers as well as the owner, so we agreed to help. Since slim people tend to use smaller plates, eat with chopsticks, sit far from the buffet, and scout the buffet before serving themselves, they decided to rearrange—to redesign—their buffets so that all the diners would *have* to act like slim people.

* **The buffet owner bought smaller plates for the serving line, downsized from 11 inches to just under 10. Portions looked bigger, and diners never noticed.**
* **He had the waitstaff seat people farthest from the buffet. It made the food less convenient and less tempting.**
* **He set chopsticks at every place setting. If you wanted a fork, you had to ask.**
* **He put all the plates *behind* the buffet. People had to walk around the buffet—encouraging them to scout out their favorite dishes before serving.**
* **He strategically placed plants and folding Chinese screens between the buffet and the tables to help block some of the food from sight.**

Again, the father-and-son restaurant team didn't do this out of benevolence. They did it to make money. If they could nudge diners to take and waste less food, they could bump up their profits. Suppose they own four buffets, and these changes save them $25 in food costs per restaurant per day. At the end of the year, they would have saved more than $36,000. Ka-ching.[15]

A few months later the son made a trip to my Lab to introduce himself in person. He said everything was going great, but that it had been overly time-consuming to make those changes. He'd worked on it six days a week for three months—even skipping a family vacation to finish on schedule. This seemed odd—they were only making five changes to each restaurant. Unless he was taking slow-motion pills, I couldn't see it taking more than a couple weeks. I asked, "Why do you think it took so long?"

He replied, "My dad owns sixty-three of these buffets."

That's a lot of ka-chings. Watch out, P. F. Chang's.

Buffet owners don't want us to gorge ourselves; it costs them money every time we belly up to the buffet.

A *PROFITABLE* SLIM-BY-DESIGN CHINESE BUFFET

* Seats people farthest from
  food, and facing away from
  it when possible

* Uses plants to block
  sightlines to the food

* Decreases the size of plates
  to 9¾ inches

* Offers chopsticks and
  makes people ask if they
  want a fork

* Puts plates on the far side
  of the buffet so people have
  to look at all the food first

* Gives 12-ounce (versus
  20-ounce) drinks and
  lets customers refill for
  themselves

Screen and plants
partially block the
buffet from diners.

All tables are given
chopsticks and
water.

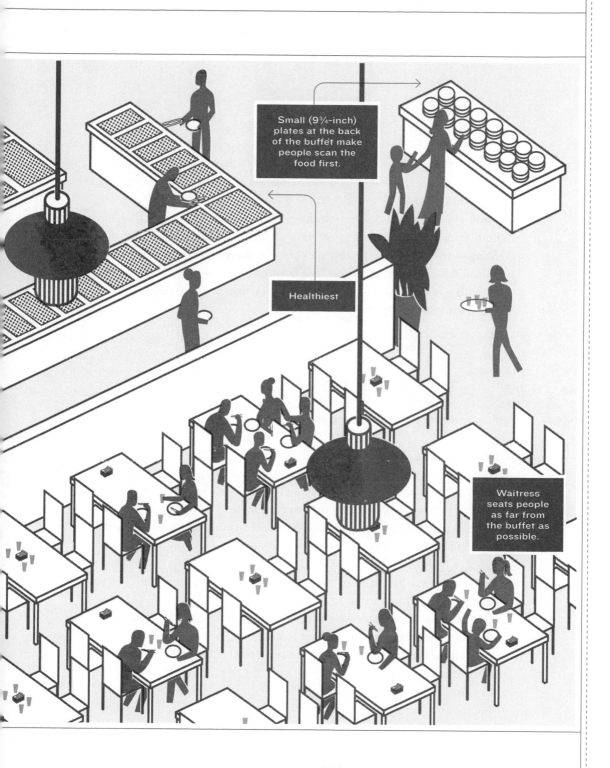

Starting Small to Get Slim

. . . .

SOME PEOPLE—LIKE MANY SLIM FANS of Chinese buffets—don't know how they stumbled across habits that either made or kept them slim. Other people are much more deliberate about finding their secret key. After *Mindless Eating* came out, people would tell me about one or two little changes or new habits that led them to mindlessly lose a lot of weight. Most people had chosen one change—using smaller plates, moving the candy dish, using the Restaurant Rule of Two, and so on. But hundreds of other people surprised me with strangely unique changes that they had invented because it fit with their unique lifestyle:

* **Eating eggs and chocolate chips every morning for breakfast**
* **Snacking only after walking the dog**
* **Eating cottage cheese after work**
* **Never using the microwave**

While these things may sound a little crazy, they all made perfect sense after they were explained: Eggs were filling and prevented a midmorning snack (and the chocolate chips made them "easier" to eat); walking the dog (and carrying the doggie bag) made snacking less appetizing; eating cottage cheese pushed dinner back and prevented late-night snacking; and not using the microwave led to smaller but better-planned meals, which used less-processed food. What is key here is that these idiosyncratic habits worked effortlessly well for these individuals because they fit with their lifestyle.

Why were these people weight losers and others not? Over the past few years we've tracked more than 1,500 struggling dieters who eventually either lost or gained weight. Some of the differences between the two groups were obvious; others weren't.[16] For example, some people made lots of dramatic changes to their eating habits and some—like

WHAT SLIM PEOPLE DON'T DO

It's not just what slim people do; it's also what they don't do. Slim people act differently from heavy people at buffets and beyond.

In 1983, Barbara Florio Graham wrote a clever article for *McCall's* titled "Thin People Don't." She explained that after living for fourteen years with a slim man who never gained weight, she came to believe it was just because he thinks differently. Here's a sample of what she observed of her husband:

Slim people:

* become so absorbed in a weekend project they forget to have lunch;

* fill the candy dish on their desks with paper clips;

* counteract the midafternoon slump by grabbing a nap instead of cookies;

* throw out stale potato chips;

* try all the buffet salads (except the white ones), leaving room for only one dessert;

* seek out interesting party conversations instead of the hors d'oeuvres;

* bring four cookies into the TV room instead of a box

There's a Slim-by-Design Registry that tracks and quantifies the secrets and habits of slim people around the world (SlimByDesign.org). Its goal is to use some of these secrets of slim people to help others become the same way—and to help the slim people stay slim. Check out what other slim people do, or add your own slim-by-design secret.

those above—made only one or two small ones. The more changes you make, the more you would expect to lose, right? Except that's not how things work.

People who most successfully lost weight made only one or two changes but stuck with them day after day—an average of at least twenty-five days a month.[17] Unfortunately, the people who didn't lose weight often tried to tackle too much all at once. They tried to change everything, and most gave

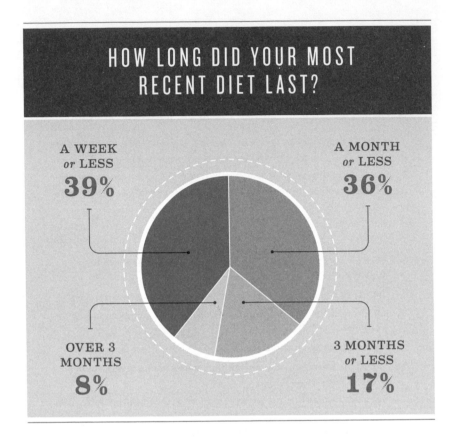

HOW LONG DID YOUR MOST RECENT DIET LAST?

A WEEK *or* LESS
39%

A MONTH *or* LESS
36%

OVER 3 MONTHS
8%

3 MONTHS *or* LESS
17%

up within a month. Making huge changes to your eating life is too tough. If we decided we wanted to start training for a marathon, we wouldn't expect ourselves to run twenty miles during our first workout. It wouldn't last. Yet that's the equivalent of what most dieters do when they start a diet. A new study of ours found that 75 percent of dieters gave up within the first month—and 39 percent didn't even make it past a week.[18] What they didn't realize is that if they'd made only one or two of the *right* changes, it wouldn't take long before they'd be a lot happier with their weight.

Sixteen Pounds from Happiness

. . . .

IN THE LAND OF SENSATIONALISTIC TV SHOWS like *The Biggest Loser* or *Bridezillas*, it's easy to believe there's little hope for our national waistline. Some claim that half the people in the United States—including our children—are overweight. Given this trend, they predict an upcoming plague-like Apocalypse of Fat. On bad days, I picture the year 2025 looking like the map on the next spread.[19]

Of course, the media fuel this fear. Some spin fat-pocalyptic stories that frighten us into believing that in ten years most of us will be spending our Saturdays riding little Wal-Mart scooters so we can be the first one to the candy aisle. The more we see these headlines, the easier it is to feel hopeless. Movie seats, stadium seats, and caskets are all bigger than they were forty years ago.[20]

But before we throw in the towel, let me ask you this: How many pounds would *you* have to lose to feel happy about your weight?

We've asked this question to thousands of people of all shapes and sizes. Some don't want to lose any weight, some a lot; some want to lose seven pounds, some seventy. What's surprising is how *little* weight the average person says they want to lose before they'd be happy. Our recent surveys of more than 1,500 women found that four out of five said they would be happy if they could lose an average of less than sixteen pounds.[21] This ranged from twenty-five-year-old hipsters in Brooklyn to sixty-five-year-old grandmothers from Topeka to all of us who skim those supermarket diet magazines while we're waiting in the checkout line.

Sixteen pounds? That's doable. We don't have to join a reality show, eat cork-flavored rice cakes, or bug our friends with a play-by-play of our latest diet. Sixteen pounds is hopeful. That's not much more than a pound a month for a year. Each day it's one less candy bar, or two fewer Cokes, or three more miles of walking—and all within your food radius.

For normal people, the winning solution is not to count calories and eat nothing but steamed fish and peas—it's just too hard to do if you're a real person with a real job.[22] We drag ourselves home at seven o'clock with seven

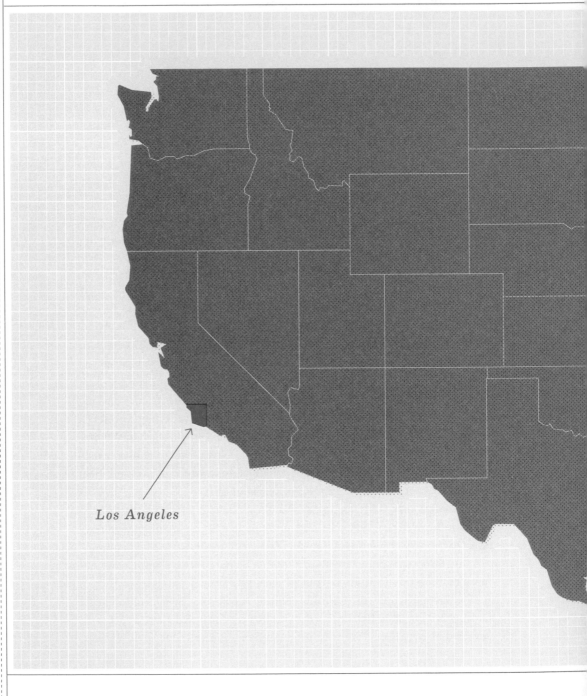

Los Angeles

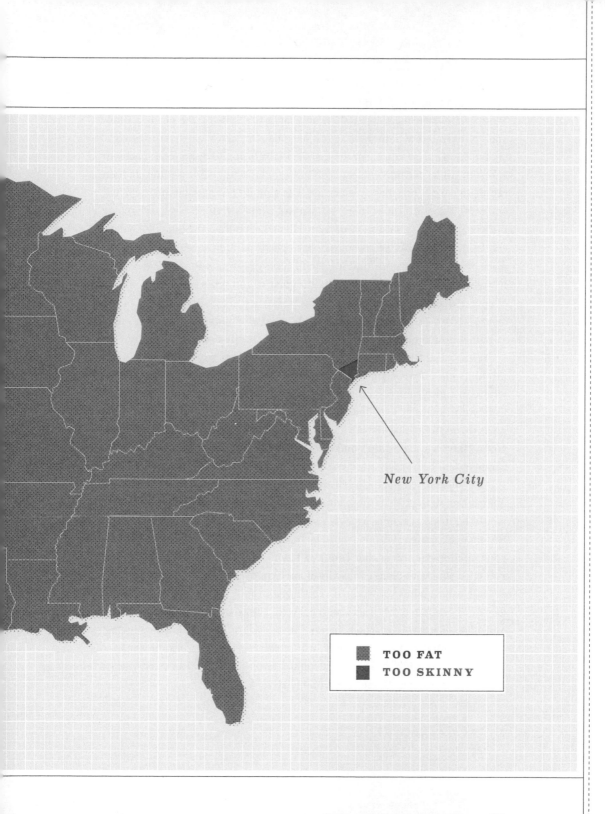

New York City

TOO FAT
TOO SKINNY

things still left on the day's to-do list. We try to change our clothes while the phone's ringing, the microwave's beeping, and the kids are turning feral. There's no way most of us can Zen out, savor the taste of one pea at a time, and contemplate whether we're full or not.[23] Our lives are just too crazy.

But here's good news. For most of us, the solution to our weight problem is not mind*ful* eating. The solution is to make a few changes in our food radius so we can mindlessly eat *better*. The ringing phone, undone to-do list, and feral kids will still be there, but we can deal with them better when our life's been set up to be slim by design. This starts with our home. It's where you inhale a handful of granola for breakfast, pack lunches for your kids, microwave leftovers for dinner, or call Krusty Krust's Pizza for delivery. It's where you might pour a late-night glass of red wine or sneak a couple of spoonfuls of Ben & Jerry's Chubby Hubby ice cream by the light of the freezer. Even if we think we eat out a lot, most of what we eat is either made at home, delivered to our home, or brought into the home for feasting.[24]

What's the first room you walk into when you get home? If it's the kitchen—*and* if you happen to have even one box of breakfast cereal anywhere in sight—our research shows you'll weigh twenty-one pounds more than your neighbor who doesn't.[25] Why? The first thing you see when you walk through the door is yummy, convenient food. Now, the kitchen door you walked through didn't make you fat, but doing so did make that free-range cereal box much more visible and reachable.[26]

One solution would be to frantically seal up your kitchen entryway with boards and nails, like in those late-night zombie movies. A second solution would be to come home through the front door (and not the kitchen door). But an even easier solution would be to vanquish all breakfast cereal from your kitchen counter so that Tony the Tiger and Count Chocula can't tempt you with their fiendish, come-hither cartoon eyes.[27]

But here's what won't work. Telling yourself, *Now that I know this, it won't happen to me.* My Lab has researched tens of thousands of people, and it's clear that even the smartest, most disciplined, calorie-counting, twigs-'n'-tofu dieters are as easily influenced by their surroundings as the rest of us—even when they know what's happening. Fortunately, there's an easier, more permanent solution for all of us.

Becoming Slim by Design

. . . .

AS WE GET OLDER, wiser, and lazier, we gradually arrange our homes to make our favorite tasty foods easier to find and eat. Meanwhile, the same thing has been happening all around us. Restaurants have made it easier to order tasty foods. Supermarkets have made them easier to buy. Workplaces have made them easier to eat at our desks. School lunchrooms have made them easier to pile onto a tray. It has all helped to make us "fat by design."

But in the same way that the 100-calorie pack helped snackers eat less (and companies make more money), and in the same way the buffet owner was able to tweak his sixty-three Chinese buffets to get diners to eat less, there are easy changes we can make to eat less everywhere in our food radius. Right now, our homes, restaurants, workplaces, grocery stores, and schools are set up in ways that lead us to pick up a cookie rather than an apple. But just as they've evolved to make us overeat, we can easily redesign them to make us slim.

Again, someone might wryly announce that the only way to not overeat at a buffet is never to go to one—but he'd be wrong. As we learned, a better solution would be to redesign the buffet visit to be slimming rather than sinning—and the buffet owner could profitably help.

This book is about solutions—concrete, actionable solutions that my Lab has developed, tested, analyzed, and tweaked in dozens of towns and cities across the United States and abroad. This book shows how you—the private citizen-muncher—can help your kids eat better, control your eating at restaurants, shop like a slim person, and eat less at home without having to think twice. In other words, it specifically shows how you can help yourself and your family become slim by design. But equally important, this book will show you how to get all of these places and people around you to help.

But let's start closer to home . . .

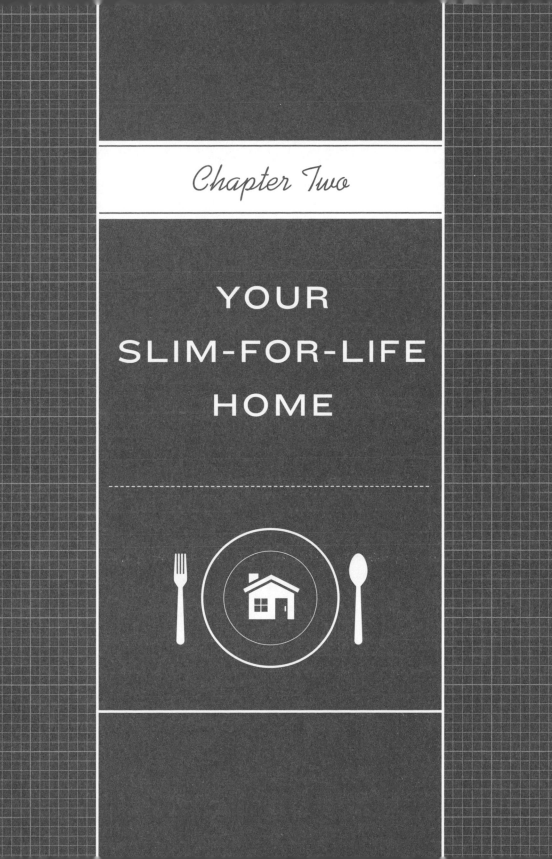

Chapter Two

YOUR SLIM-FOR-LIFE HOME

M Y EARLIER BOOK, *MINDLESS EATING*, was filled with secret studies that uncovered the hidden persuaders around our home that trick us into overeating—things like serving spoons, spouses, cupboards, and colors. But most of these (except maybe spouses) can also be reversed to make us slimmer rather than fatter. Take color: The color of your plate can make you fat. If it's the same color as the food, you'll serve yourself 18 percent more.

We discovered this one afternoon when we invited sixty lunch-goers to a free pasta lunch at Cornell's summer alumni reunion. We gave them either a red plate or a white plate and sent half the diners over to a red pasta buffet (marinara sauce) and the other half to a white pasta buffet (Alfredo sauce). After they served themselves, we secretly weighed how much they took. If they put either white pasta on a white plate or red on a red one, they piled on 18 percent more calories than those with opposite-colored plates.[1] This is news you can use: When you're eating at home, choose plates that contrast with the color of your food. Since white starches—pasta, rice, and potatoes—are the big diet busters, using darker plates is smart.

If we want to automatically eat better at home, we don't have to change our minds; all we have to do is make a few changes to our home and how we behave there. These easy changes will work for you and your kids just as they work for the rich and famous, as you'll see.

Fat-Proofing the Rich and Famous

. . . .

SHORTLY AFTER *MINDLESS EATING* WAS PUBLISHED, I received a mysterious Friday-night phone call from a stranger asking if I would be willing to do a kitchen makeover for someone he "represented." He wanted me to "fat-proof" his client's home to help her manage her weight.[2]

This had happened before, and usually the caller "represented" some rich or famous person who wanted to stay famously incognito. Who could blame them? Having some clipboard-carrying professor and his research team tiptoe through your house and risk them live-tweeting your deepest, darkest kitchen secrets is not a risk the rich or famous typically take. What if Bobby Flay's pantry were stuffed with Hamburger Helper, or if the late Orson Welles's freezer had been filled with Rosebud-brand fudge pops? Good for Gawker.com but very bad for business.

If your plate's the same color as your food, you'll serve 18 percent more.

Some of these kitchens were massively epic, but others looked like dorm kitchenettes. Some had more food booby-traps than a 7-Eleven, but others were as barren as a farmer's market seven minutes after closing time. One classic California home—two blocks from where Bob Hope and Steve McQueen used to live and complete with a retractable roof and a water fountain in the foyer—had a huge mirrored kitchen that was fully stocked, but only with salty snacks, lemons, limes, pearl onions in a bottle, and lots and lots of liquor. When I said, "This looks more like the bar on the *Titanic* than a kitchen," the representative responded, "Oh, that *is* the bar—the kitchen's way over there."

One unusual assignment involved a popular actress who set up an appointment to talk about a makeover. She didn't want me to actually *do* one, she wanted to *talk* about one—to do a verbal walk-through. Now, this actress is well over five foot six and well under 125 pounds, so it's not as if her kitchen's going to look like Willy Wonka's. She's figured out a lot on her own.[3] So I agreed to do a virtual telephone walk-through of her home and give her some basic makeover suggestions at 5 P.M. the following Monday.

Our makeovers usually start with me asking details about their typical day—for instance, what they did yesterday, from start to finish.[4] That way we can target the specific problem areas or patterns to change. But this actress was very different. She ate nicely balanced (but very low-carb) meals, and she had set up a lot of healthy eating patterns that seemed destined to keep her slim for life.[5] Why'd she want a makeover? It turned out that it wasn't for her—she wanted to discover what might accidentally trip up a teenage girl. Sometimes making changes for the ones we love is more motivating than doing them for just ourselves.

> **Our makeovers usually start with me asking details about their typical day.**

It's cool to hear about how celebrities talk about their daily food habits when they're home wearing sweatpants instead of wearing their gowns from the Oscars. It often goes a little like this: After work, they forage around the kitchen to see if anything catches their eye before they go to their bedroom and clean off their *Avatar* makeup or hang up their Iron Man costume.[6] An hour later they come back into the kitchen and poke around until dinner's ready. Later—a couple of hours after dinner—they might do a kitchen walk-through and get a drink or see if anything catches their eye to snack on. Their routine is pretty much like ours—except that we don't have to take off the *Avatar* makeup.

Celebrity or not, making a home slim by design has three parts: (1) a kitchen makeover, (2) a tablescape redesign, and (3) snack-proofing. Kitchen makeovers involve making physical changes to a kitchen that can range from quick and easy (like moving food) to more expensive and a hassle (like changing lighting or buying a new fridge). Tablescape redesigns involve making small changes at mealtime. Snack-proofing focuses on uncovering and reversing troublesome habits. It doesn't take long to come up with a basic plan to make someone's home slim by design—about three hours of Q&A, snooping, taking notes, and thinking really creatively about solutions.[7,8]

Granted, kitchen makeovers and a slim-by-design house may sound la-la-loony—like mystical food feng shui. But these fat-proofing makeovers are anything but mystical. We've nailed down the key principles, tested them in our Lab, confirmed them in homes, and published them in big-name academic journals. But before you learn how to make your home slim by design, you need to make sure you really appreciate how little things in your home could make a big difference in your life. Take our Syracuse Study, for example.

Granted, kitchen makeovers and a slim-by-design house may sound la-la-loony—like mystical food feng shui.

We've nailed down the principles, tested them in our Lab, confirmed them in homes, and published them in big-name academic journals.

The Syracuse Study

· · · · · · · · · · · · ·

WHAT DOES A SLIM PERSON'S KITCHEN LOOK LIKE? If we knew that, we could set up our own kitchens in a similar way. While it's no guarantee we'd lose weight overnight, at least it might tilt the scale in the right direction.[9]

To figure this out, you'd have to visit hundreds of homes. But you can't get the answer by visiting homes in Smallville, Gotham City, or an Inuit village—they are probably too different from ours. You need a demographically representative place—let's call it Springfield, USA. To find such a place, we looked for the cities that companies use as test markets for new products—if they're representative enough for billion-dollar companies with huge markets at stake, they're representative enough for us. Toward the top of the list was Syracuse, New York—an industrial city of 145,000 in the middle of New York State. It's distinguished by great basketball, great scenery, and great amounts of snow.[10]

If this was a movie, you could call it *Kitchen: Impossible*.

Picking the city was the easy part. The hard part was getting into people's homes. Imagine . . . would you let somebody into your house to count your cabinets and tape-measure your kitchen? No. Would you then let them take photos of everything they saw that might explain your weight: your food, appliances, televisions, radios, cookbooks, spice racks, and so on? No. Last, would you let them weigh you and measure your height with your shoes off? No. If this was a movie, you could call it *Kitchen: Impossible*. (Tom Cruise could star, since he was born in Syracuse.)

Think about it: Who in their right mind would allow a team of university researchers into their home to weigh and measure them in their socks and then take pictures of their kitchen and dining room as if it were a crime scene?[11] After being turned down by a hundred people, we found only two groups of homeowners who would agree to this. The first group was interested in food. The second was interested in money.

Once we figured this out, recruiting was easy. We told people we would help them optimize their kitchen, pay them, and give them tons of slim-by-design eating tips, and we would let them borrow a state-of-the-art digital Wi-Fi scale for six months.[12] This solved all problems. Because we had to drop off the scale, they had to invite us to their house. Check. Because we had to set up the Wi-Fi scale, we had to weigh them. Check. Because we were already there, we asked if we could photograph their kitchen—because, you know, we were already there. Check.

And we took pictures of everything: their dishes, sink, refrigerator shelves, counter, snacks, pet food dishes, tables, lighting—even the random items held up by magnets on their refrigerator. Nothing went unsnapped. We were like a busload of Elvis-obsessed tourists in the Jungle Room at Graceland. Mission accomplished.

You don't argue with misspelled tattoos.

Surprisingly, most of these home invasions went remarkably smoothly. But sometimes, when people do things for money, their heart isn't really in it. When weighing one person, he asked, "How much did that scale cost?" We said, "One hundred and eighty dollars." He was big and expressionless, and he said without blinking, "As soon as you leave, I'm selling it." You don't argue with misspelled tattoos. You just slowly back toward your getaway car.[13]

When safely locked up back in the Lab, we spent eight months coding these kitchens to see what slim people do that might make them slim by design. First we wondered if big kitchens turn us into big people. Tons of people think so, and it makes some sense. You're hanging out there, because that's where you store your thirty-six bags of Cheetos from Sam's Club and those five-pound barrels of pretzels from Costco. You hang out, you eat. You eat, you gain weight. Makes perfect sense.

It might make perfect sense, but it's not the way it is in the real world. Part of this has to do with money. Richer people have bigger kitchens, and they also have personal trainers, designer workout clothes, sparkly exercise equipment, and the leisure time to use it. If bigger kitchens make you eat more, bigger budgets can help you work it off. Big kitchens aren't the problem. It's what's *in* the kitchen.

For instance, the average woman who kept potato chips on the counter weighed eight pounds more than her neighbor who didn't. That makes perfect sense. Chips are the good-tasting bad boy of nutrition—they're irresistibly tempting, you can't eat just one, and they make you fat. But potatoes aren't anywhere near the most dangerous counter food. As was implied earlier, the most dangerous food is the meek, whole grain, vitamin-enriched food in the white box that's covered in sunshine, rainbows, and pictures of skinny smiling women with gleaming teeth. Yes, it's breakfast cereal.[14] Where do you keep your breakfast cereal? Women who had even one box of breakfast cereal that was visible—anywhere in their kitchen—weighed twenty-one pounds more than their neighbor who didn't.

> **We could roughly predict a person's weight by the food they had sitting out.**

"In sight, in stomach." We eat what we see, not what we don't. Our Syracuse Study showed that we could roughly predict a person's weight by the food they had sitting out. See on the next page how much more the average woman weighed than her neighbor who had no visible food sitting out in her kitchen.[15]

Cereal has what we call a health halo. Its boxes are covered with phrases like "Contains Whole Grain" and "Now with 11 Essential Vitamins and Minerals." This implies it's healthy, so we underestimate the calories and overeat it to reward ourselves for being so healthy. But having cereal on the counter adds weight to women more than to men. In fact, it had no impact on men—possibly because they're in the kitchen less. The more time you spend at home, the more important it is to hide the food.

Lots of other insights from the Syracuse Study will show that your kitchen makeover is the best step to making your home slim by design. Let's begin.

CLEAR THE COUNTER . . . EXCEPT FOR THE FRUIT

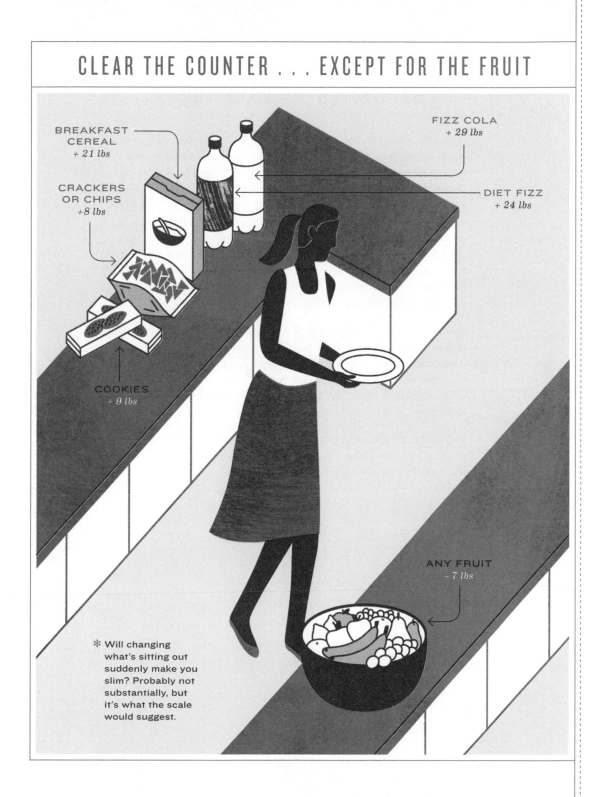

BREAKFAST CEREAL
+ 21 lbs

CRACKERS OR CHIPS
+8 lbs

COOKIES
+ 9 lbs

FIZZ COLA
+ 29 lbs

DIET FIZZ
+ 24 lbs

ANY FRUIT
- 7 lbs

✱ Will changing what's sitting out suddenly make you slim? Probably not substantially, but it's what the scale would suggest.

EMPTY KITCHENS MAKE YOU FAT

A notable gossip columnist once commissioned me to do a slim-by-design makeover for her. She had this crazy celebrity lifestyle of high-society parties, opening-night receptions, and premieres with movie stars—her workday hours ran from 6 P.M. to 6 A.M.—same as a vampire's. When I told her we'd start with her kitchen, she said, "The kitchen's not the problem. It's empty." But the empty kitchen *was* her problem; it was what was keeping her from being slim. She ate all meals out—and was usually famished because there were never any fill-in foods at home. When she did want a snack at home, she'd call and have a whole meal delivered, because most places don't want to deliver a cheese stick and eight Wheat Thins.

Empty kitchens make you fat when they cause you to overeat elsewhere. What are the hunger-busters that are best to have on hand if you hate to cook? People in our studies usually report that protein tops the list. The top mentions? Yogurt, eggs, fat-free milk, string cheese, and sliced turkey, along with canned soup, canned or cut vegetables, and finally fruit.

The next time I gossiped with the columnist, she said she now always keeps yogurt and trays of cut vegetables on hand. Probably not from the Academy Awards after-party.

Step One: The Kitchen Makeover

. . . .

AS YOU JUST DISCOVERED, big, attractive kitchens don't necessarily lead to big, unattractive waistlines—it's an urban legend. So you don't need a construction crew and a Godzilla budget to do a great kitchen makeover.[16] Based on our Syracuse Study, it's not the size of your kitchen, it's what's *in* the kitchen—and we're not just talking food. While every kitchen's different, and while some of the kitchens of the rich and famous might be more epic than ours, the same things apply. Here's the key to a kitchen makeover.

* **Make your kitchen less "loungeable."**
* **Make tempting foods invisible and inconvenient.**
* **Make it easier to cook.**

MAKE YOUR KITCHEN LESS LOUNGEABLE[17]

The more you hang out in your kitchen, the more you'll eat. The same thing happens when you hang out in nice restaurants—you eat and drink more.[18] So why do you hang out in the kitchen? Because there is a television set, an iPad, maybe a little desk computer, and comfy chairs—like the tall soft-back chairs around the island or counter. When people agree to remove televisions and comfy seating from the kitchen, they tell us they spend eighteen fewer minutes in the kitchen each day. That's less munching of cereal, chips, and Samoa cookies. Our subjects also report that their meal prep becomes more efficient, and they often bring in a radio or stream music to amp up their energy. They turn the beat around!

Here's why you start your kitchen makeover by making your kitchen less loungeable and more efficient. First, it works immediately. Second, it shows whether you're serious.

Soon after *Mindless Eating* was published in other languages, a foreign ambassador to the United States invited me to his embassy in Washington, D.C., and asked if I could do a kitchen makeover for him "as a gesture of goodwill" toward his country. Not wanting to start a nuclear calamity or a foie gras embargo, I readily agreed to take a hit for our country.

After arriving and visiting with him and a small entourage for fifteen minutes, I got down to work. I asked him questions about his eating habits and daily routines, and I took notes about his answers and about everything I saw in the kitchen, pantry, cupboards, and fridge. I asked if he wanted me to write up a plan or to just talk him through it. "Neither," he said. "Just go ahead and do it." He then excused himself to return phone calls. Although a bit stunned—I wasn't expecting to be called into action—I took off my suit jacket and jumped in feetfirst as our nation's goodwill ambassador.

He loved food, and he implied that he spent too much time lounging in the kitchen, leading him to snack on leftovers from embassy parties and accompany them with a drink. So the first change I made was to move the kitchen television set and the tall kitchen island chairs into the back hallway. From there, perhaps one of his manservants would be able to put them in storage. As I was yanking the remaining TV cords out of the wall, he returned, saying, "No, no, no, no, no! The television and chairs must stay! They must stay!"

He then quickly reverted to his ambassadorial character. At that point, he must have also realized that he wasn't really very serious about a makeover. He invited me into the dining room for a glass of Pinot before dinner, and apparently my "gesture of goodwill" was complete.

Here's the lesson from that experience: If you can't make your kitchen less loungeable, rethink how much effort you want to put into your slim-by-design makeover. In the meantime, enjoy the foie gras.

MAKE TEMPTING FOODS INVISIBLE AND INCONVENIENT

When food's out of sight, it's out of mind. For instance, when we moved candy dishes from *on* the desks of forty administrative assistants to *in* their desks, the average assistant ate 74 fewer calories every day than he or she would otherwise have—that's the equivalent of *not* gaining about five or six pounds over the next year. We find over and over that the most visible foods are the ones you eat first and eat most. The best thing you can do is not to have food sitting out in the kitchen, unless it rhymes with roots and wedgies.

This isn't always as easy as clearing cereal boxes and cookie packages off the counter. If you have open shelves, use them to display anything but food. If you have clear cupboards, make sure you put the dishware there and put the Chips Ahoy! behind closed doors, as Charlie Rich would have suggested.

FIRST SEEN, FIRST EATEN

The next stop on our kitchen makeover is to change the foods you see first. Suppose the first cereal you see in the morning is Fruity Pebbles and the next four cereals are different versions of bark-and-twig-flavored granola. Which are you going to choose?

You're three times more likely to eat the first food you see in the cupboard than the fifth one.[19] Rearrange your cupboard, pantry, and refrigerator so the first foods you see are the best for you.

In our "Reefer Madness" studies (reefer as in "refrigerator"—but you knew that) we asked people to move all their fruits and vegetables from the crisper bin to the top shelf of their refrigerator and to move their less healthy foods down into the crisper. After one week, they reported eating nearly three times as many fruits and vegetables as the week before. They might keep longer in the crisper, but the goal is to eat them, not compost them.

The tasty stuff that's visible is what you most overeat, even in walk-in pantries. A radical recommendation we sometimes make is to move your pantry to a room far from the kitchen. Some people balk at this, but others simply make it happen: Their pantry becomes their new coatroom and the coatroom becomes their new pantry. Others have put up shelving or cabinets in the laundry room. Still others use a basement utility room. Moving your pantry (which is what my family did) does three things. It makes it less browsable for a snack. It makes you think twice before you grab food off a shelf. And it gives you a few steps of exercise.

People who live in small apartments have a different dilemma. The best you can do is to store your tempting comfort foods in really inconvenient places. How often do you use your fire escape anyway?

Why not just totally vanquish all tempting foods from your house? First, it's fine to have an occasional treat yourself. Second, it's not realistic if you have growing kids who constantly forage and bring friends over to feast. Set up a designated "kids' cupboard" that's off-limits to you. One mother of teenagers even put childproof locks on the cupboard. For herself.

DOUBLE-TIME STOCKPILING

Those huge wholesale clubs like Sam's and Costco are filled with great food bargains. But once you get the forklift home, those bargains turn into a burden for your cupboards—and your diet.

In one study we found that people who had filled their cupboards with chips, juice boxes, cookies, and even ramen noodles ate half of everything they bought within the first week of buying it. They ate it twice as fast as they normally would. If you're buying it in bulk, you'll eat it faster and in greater quantities than you otherwise would.

One solution is to repackage any supersize boxes into single-serve Baggie sizes. A second solution is to store it as far away from reach as possible—in the basement or a distant cupboard. You'll get the cost saving without the calories.[20]

MAKE IT EASIER TO COOK

Making your kitchen less loungeable and making the tempting foods invisible and inconvenient will help you eat less. In this last step, you'll make your kitchen a more alluring place for you to cook more often, and to cook healthier. Now this is a part of the book where the science isn't as strong. These are weak trends we've found, and it's based on what people *say* they do—not what we see them do. So take this with a pinch of sea salt.

To begin, make it super-easy to prep food—especially vegetables—in your kitchen. One way to do this is make sure the refrigerator swings open directly to the sink (the direction in which the door opens can be switched for forty dollars unless it's a side-by-side). Then make the vegetable preparation sites seductively inviting. Here's what we found: People say they're more likely to cook vegetables if it's more convenient and fun to do so. If you're renovating, put bright halogen spotlights and overhead music speakers three feet to the left of the sink and three feet to the right. Also, create a third dedicated prep area that a helpful friend, spouse, or your little gooblet can use. Some people think having a double sink helps them make more food from scratch, because they can separate the vegetable and meat trimmings from the dishes.

We're often asked what refrigerator to buy. The best bet may be a refrigerator with the freezer on the bottom. Next best is a refrigerator with a freezer on top. Worst may be the side-by-side. You want as much of the good, healthy foods at eye level as possible. When the fridge is on the top and the freezer on the bottom, most of those fruits and veggies will be in your face. The side-by-side makes it too easy to look for something frozen to microwave. Don't want to give up your side-by-side because of the cold-water feature? Some people make this argument, but we find most people rarely use it, and would rather trade it for a few less pounds of fat.

WHAT COLOR SHOULD YOUR KITCHEN BE?[21]

Here's what we've found: Bright colors seem to agitate us and cause us to eat too quickly—and too much. Dark colors cause you to linger, eat longer, and look for more.[22] The best color may simply be the Mama Bear color, not too bright and not too dark—actually, any color seems to work other than white or cream. This color stuff is far from a science, but you can lean toward what seems right—even if it isn't proven. For instance, my kitchen is painted a pumpkin color. It's halfway between one worst and the other worst. But the best strategy yet is to eat in your dining room, if you have one. You're farther from the food, and there's no need to trick yourself with paint.

SLIM-BY-DESIGN KITCHEN MAKEOVER

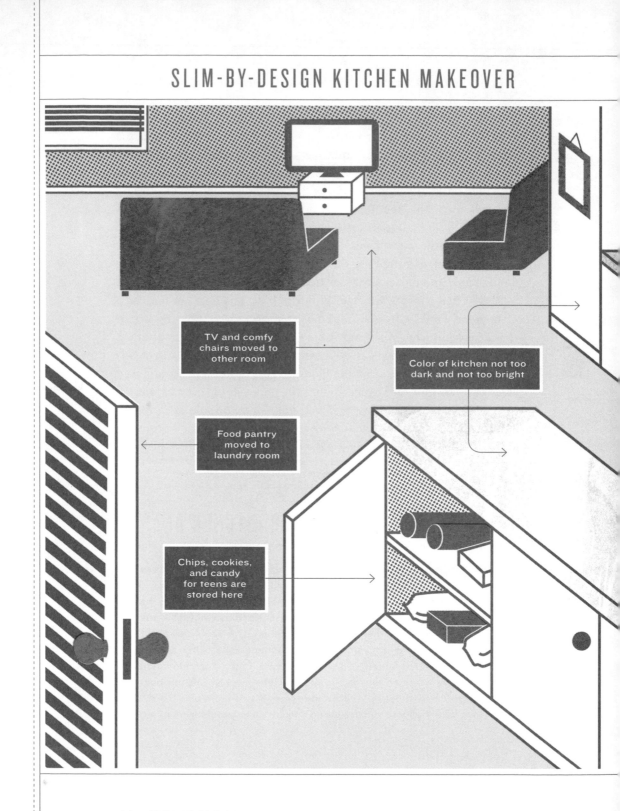

TV and comfy chairs moved to other room

Color of kitchen not too dark and not too bright

Food pantry moved to laundry room

Chips, cookies, and candy for teens are stored here

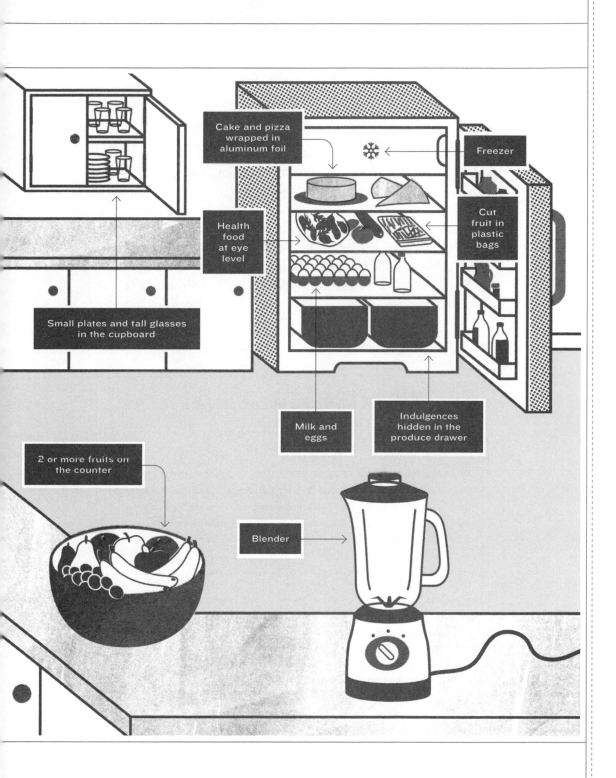

Cake and pizza wrapped in aluminum foil

Freezer

Health food at eye level

Cut fruit in plastic bags

Small plates and tall glasses in the cupboard

Milk and eggs

Indulgences hidden in the produce drawer

2 or more fruits on the counter

Blender

Step Two: Tablescape Redesign

. . . .

EVERY HOME HAS A ROOM where you typically eat your nightly dinner. It might be around a kitchen island, a scratch-proof Formica table, a coffee table in front of a saggy couch, or a nice table with uncomfortable chairs. They're all "dining rooms"—they're where we serve and eat our food. And they all have a tablescape that subtly nudges us in how much we serve and eat.[23]

Your tablescape can stack the deck against you and your family. Take your dinnerware: Two ounces of cooked pasta is about 1 cup, has around 300 calories, and looks huge on a 10-inch plate. The same two ounces on a

12-inch plate—the size most of us have—looks like a measly appetizer, so we serve ourselves another spoonful.[26] If we do this just once a day, we'll eat about 60 extra calories. If we eat off these plates for three meals a day, it quickly adds up.

It doesn't stop with just plates and forks. If you put that batch of Hamburger Helper in a 3-quart serving bowl instead of a 2-quart bowl, you'll also dish out an extra 17 percent—even though it's the exact same amount of food, just in a bigger bowl.[27] The bigger bowl makes us almost unconsciously think it's normal, appropriate, and reasonable to serve more, so we do. If you use that large serving spoon, even that will cost you 14 percent more calories.[28]

This even happens with know-it-all professors. When we invited a few dozen of my former nutritional science colleagues to an ice cream social and switched up their serving spoons, even world-renowned experts who had been given a larger scoop dished out 14 percent more ice-creamy goodness than those given a smaller scoop. They counted the number of scoops they served and not the amount of ice cream.[29]

Even your glasses get in on the action. You'll pour more juice into a bigger glass than a smaller one, and you'll pour more into a wider one than a narrow one of the same size. When it comes to setting your dining room table, think small. Small plates, serving bowls, serving spoons, and glasses.

These tablescape changes are easy. What keeps us from making them, however, is that we think we're smarter than a bowl. As a result we think, *Oh, now that I know this, it won't happen to me,* so we don't make any changes. But during the day's chaos, our automatic behaviors lead us to make the same mindless eating mistakes we've always made. We suffer—and so do our kids.

A couple of summers ago, my Lab helped sponsor a 4-H summer camp. During breakfast one week we gave our elementary-age campers huge 24-ounce cereal bowls instead of the 12-ounce ones we usually gave them. They served themselves 42 percent more than they did the other weeks. It didn't matter if it was the skinniest or heaviest kid in the group—everyone poured more Froot, more Loops, and more milk when we bumped up the size of their bowl.

At the end of the summer, we asked them to bring in the cereal bowl they usually ate out of at home. The average size? About 20 ounces. That's almost as huge as the bowl we gave them. They usually used the

WINEGLASS CLASS

Love wine, but hate headaches? Here's how to automatically drink 10 percent less.

We brought 85 wine drinkers in for happy hour and gave them different glasses and different wines and made them either sit or stand.[30] Here's what we found:

* **We tend to focus on the height of what we pour and not the width, so we pour 12 percent less wine into taller white wineglasses that hold 10 ounces than we pour into wider red wineglasses that hold the same.**

* **When we look down at a glass, it looks more full than when we look at it from the same level as the liquid.** As a result we'll also pour 12 percent less in a glass when it's sitting on the table compared to when we hold it.

* **Because red wine is easier to see than white wine, we pour about 9 percent less red wine whenever we pour a glass of it.**

same cereal bowls as their parents, and were biased in the same big ways. Big bowls lead to big children. Maybe you're the one out of 20 people who have the superhuman willpower and memory to not be influenced. Even if you do, it's unlikely your kids inherited your superpowers. Not a problem if they used kid-size 12-ounce bowls at home, but they don't. If we still think *we're* smarter than a bowl, we can at least give smaller bowls to our kids.

Guys have an even bigger problem because we're speed-eaters compared to the rest of our family. We inhale our food, then we wait around while the rest of our family picks at their food in slow motion, as though they're eating underwater. So what do we do? We take seconds of the food that's closest to us. Then it's on to thirds for our favorites. This pretty much continues until the last of the slo-mo eaters is finished.

A number of years ago, we filmed families eating dinner in their homes—simple enough. The next day, we asked them how many servings they'd eaten of those foods the night before. The result? The average person thought they ate just two-thirds as many servings as they actually did.[31] If you're off by a third for even one meal a day, your waistline will expand to accommodate the mistake. Where's the most dangerous place to have these serving bowls? Within arm's length. If it's farther than that, it's safer—at least for you.

> **People who served from the stove or counter ate 19 percent less total food compared to those serving themselves right off the table.**

Some families serve family-style meals and crowd all their serving bowls onto the table. Other families directly pre-serve their food off the stove or counter. We found that people who served from the stove or counter ate 19 percent less total food compared to those serving themselves right off the table.[32] Having to get up and walk another six feet for the food was enough for people to ask, "Am I really that hungry?" The answer's usually "Nope." On the other hand, if you want to eat more salad, plant that salad bowl right in the middle of the table.

If eating family-style—piling all of the serving dishes on the table—is a nonnegotiable must in your house, there might be a workaround. Serving out of bowls with lids might cut down on seconds or thirds. In one of our candy dish studies, simply putting a lid on a candy dish cut down

YOUR SLIM-BY-DESIGN DINNER TABLE

TV OFF

TALL OR
SMALL
DRINKING
GLASS
(30% less)

SOFT LIGHT

WHITE
WINEGLASS
(12% less)

SMALLER
PASTA BOWL
(17% less)

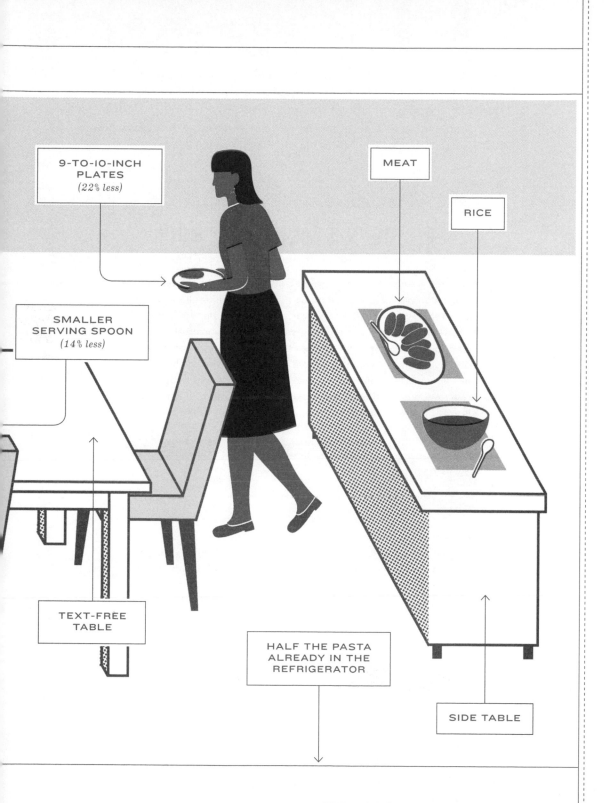

9-TO-10-INCH
PLATES
(22% less)

SMALLER
SERVING SPOON
(14% less)

TEXT-FREE
TABLE

MEAT

RICE

HALF THE PASTA
ALREADY IN THE
REFRIGERATOR

SIDE TABLE

how many Hershey's Kisses people ate by about a third.[33] When food is out of sight, it's out of mind. The same idea might work if you cover the casserole instead of temptingly leaving the top off.

The tablescape is all about meals, but once you're away from the table you need to focus on snack-proofing the rest of the house.

What You Can Do . . .

THE JOY OF COOKING TOO MUCH

Grandmothers may have invented comfort foods, but these simple basics morph every generation. So how have food recipes changed since the days when June Cleaver baked apple pie while wearing a pearl necklace on *Leave It to Beaver*? We analyzed the serving sizes and calories of all the recipes that appeared in all of the seven editions of *Joy of Cooking* from 1937 to 2006.[34] Your dishware may have gotten larger—but so has the calorie count of your recipes. Here are a few comfort-food highlights of how the number of calories per serving has increased over the years:

	1937	2006
APPLE PIE	271	353
GOULASH	267	378
CHILI	341	514

Goulash, apple pie, chili, and other classic recipes in *Joy of Cooking* have on average 44 percent more calories than when your great-grandma was serving them up. One-third of the heft is due to bigger servings, but two-thirds is due to more fat, sugar, meat, and goodies like nuts and raisins—foods that are less expensive now than they were back then.[35]

When you decide to follow a recipe, think 1937, not 2006. Plan on dividing the finished dish and storing half in the fridge for tomorrow or the freezer for next week, *before* you sit down to eat.

Step Three: Snack-Proofing

. . . .

THE LAST STEP to making your home slim by design deals with the little habits that trip us up between meals. Over the years, my Lab has gotten a lot of calls, referrals, and visits from struggling people who have an unusual or peculiar eating habit—such as drinking a twelve-pack of Pepsi every day or buying a daily mega-Slurpee at the 7-Eleven on the way home from work.

We all have our pesky little unhealthy eating habits, and we have them because we like them. Telling Mr. Slurpee "Don't drink that," "Drink it only once a week," or "Drive a different route home so you don't buy one" is not going to work. If it was that easy, he wouldn't be coming to us for advice. You break these habits by snack-proofing— not by telling somebody they can't have it. Simply make the food less convenient and less enjoyable to eat. In the case of the Slurpee lover, he was basically rewarding himself for an intense workday. We said, "Look, you can have a Slurpee whenever you want, but here's the catch: You *have* to drink it in the 7-Eleven parking lot. You can't drink it while you drive." Within two weeks he realized that instead of sitting in a parking lot for fifteen minutes and sucking on a straw until he got brain freeze, he'd rather reward himself by getting home fifteen minutes earlier.

Here's how it's done. First, you can uncover these pesky little eating traps by replaying everything you ate yesterday, step by step—even if it was just a piece of mystery candy left in the office kitchen. If you do this for three or four days, you'll start to see two or three little eating patterns you can tweak to make them less convenient.[36]

People who multitask while eating—surfing the Web, watching reality TV, or comforting a baby—have another challenge. Multitasking means one-armed eating. We gravitate to finger foods we can easily and mindlessly eat with one hand. Whether it's Cheerios, chips, or pork rinds, most of these foods have calories we don't need. In 2008, I did a Mindless Eating makeover for four glamorous *Sex and the City*–type women for *O, the Oprah Magazine*. One of these women was still breast-feeding her youngest child and found herself continually snacking on "kid foods" that she could eat with one hand. I recommended that she buy a supermarket tray of precut veggies and move her snack basket into the pantry. Five months later her photo and story were in the magazine. Precut veggies were her new staple, and she was within ten pounds of her desired weight.[37]

> ## What You Can Do . . .
>
> # JUST A BITE WILL SATISFY
>
> How much chocolate would you need to eat to be satisfied? A fourth as much as you think. When teaming with Dutch researcher Ellen van Kleef, we gave one group of 104 adults regular-size portions of either chocolate, apple pie, or potato chips, and we gave another group just a couple of bites of the same snacks—as little as a fourth of what they wanted. Fifteen minutes later, both groups were equally satisfied and happy. Almost nobody wanted anything else to eat. Here's the secret: Once you take two or three bites, put the rest of it away and distract yourself for fifteen minutes—return phone calls, straighten the room, or get a drink of water. In fifteen minutes all you'll remember—in your head, mouth, and stomach—is that you had a tasty snack.[38]

One of the snack-proofing surprises that came from our Syracuse Study dealt with the food we found outside the kitchen. We expected to find a lot of snack food squirreled away in living rooms, family rooms, and bedrooms. Instead we found almost nothing. After some investigating, here's why. Once food travels out of the kitchen, it doesn't come back. We eat it. Like a lion dragging a gazelle from a sunny plain to under a shady tree, once we transport tasty snacks from the kitchen to our comfy couch—voilà, no leftovers.

The only times we don't eat all the food we take into other rooms is when it's too inconvenient to do so. That's the secret to making these other rooms slim by design.[39] When it comes to fat-proofing between meals, the

WHY DO TV SHOWS MAKE US OVEREAT?

Your TV is making you overeat for three reasons: (I) We eat out of habit and not hunger; (2) we don't pay attention to how much we eat; and (3) we pace ourselves by the show. In one of our studies, we asked 145 Chicagoans how they knew they were through eating dinner. The third most common response was "I know I'm through eating when the TV show I'm watching is over."[40]

But it's not just TV. People overeat when they listen to radio programs and when they read. Anything distracting and enjoyable keeps you eating mindlessly longer than you otherwise would.

One solution: Put the food back in the cupboard or refrigerator or on the stove. You can have seconds, but you'll have to walk for it. And you usually won't bother.

solutions are the same regardless of the room: We need to trick ourselves into snacking less often and in smaller amounts.

Anything that makes it less convenient for you to snack will cut down on how much you eat. For instance, let's say you told yourself you'd snack only if you were sitting down at the kitchen table, with no media to distract you. Since it's pretty boring to snack if nothing else is going on, you'll probably snack a lot less. Another approach might be to tell yourself you can only have an indulgent afternoon snack if you first eat a piece of fruit. Since finding a piece of fruit (and perhaps peeling or cutting it) is a hassle, and since eating it might fill you up, you'll probably also snack a lot less—and certainly less on the indulgent goodies. In either case, you never told yourself you couldn't have the snack you wanted. You just made it more inconvenient and less appealing to do so.

A man was referred to our Lab once for advice on how to break what his doctor called a "Pepsi addiction"—twelve-plus cans a day. He was on the express train to diabetes. He even had one of those small hotel room-size refrigerators in his office—fully stocked. Any time he stretched, he was within six inches of grabbing a fix.

Telling someone in his situation to get rid of his refrigerator and go cold turkey or even just to drink half as many wouldn't work. He would have resisted, cheated, or obsessed about how many he had left in his stash. Instead, we told him he could drink all the Pepsi he wanted if he agreed to one thing: He could only keep one can in the refrigerator at any one time. When we made him decide how badly he wanted to drink a warm Pepsi, he trimmed his consumption down to about four or five a day—and two of the cans still usually ended up being warm. Without much thinking or painful self-denial, he sliced his Pepsi addiction by almost two-thirds.

If there's an in-home food that's your Kryptonite, the best thing you can do is to make it as inconvenient and unattractive as warm Pepsi. Even wrapping up a tempting food in aluminum foil can do that. An ice cream container mummified in aluminum foil and freezer burned looks a lot less tantalizing and eye-catching than when it radiates Chunky Monkey goodness. And it's a third less likely to be eaten within the first week of being wrapped up.[41]

HOW TO TRIPLE THE SHELF LIFE OF COOKIES

When you see something wrapped in aluminum, do you think, *Yum*?

After a big party in my Lab, we wrapped half the leftover food in clear plastic wrap or put it in clear plastic containers. The other half we wrapped in aluminum foil or put it in opaque containers. Within two days, all the clearly wrapped leftovers were gone. Most nonvisible leftovers were still there ten days later.

The good news was that this worked as well for carrot sticks as for cookies. The healthier a food is, the clearer the packaging you should use to store it. Plastic wrap or clear glass for the good stuff, aluminum foil for the rest.

Scoring Big at Home

. . . .

WHEN IT COMES TO MAKING HOMES slim by design, most people ask the same question: "What's your best tip?" Bummer, but there's no one best magical tip that works for all earthly inhabitants. Take Pepsi Man. His tip of keeping only one can of Pepsi in the fridge at a time led him to lose two or three pounds a month, but that's not going to work for you if you don't have his twelve-can-a-day habit.

Mindless Eating contained more than 150 proven, workable weight-loss tips we'd discovered from our studies. But most of the people who called, wrote, or visited my Lab after it was published didn't want 150 innovative ideas—they wanted the one, single customized change (like the one-can-in-the-fridge tip) that would make the big difference in their particular life. Impossible? Although everyone's pretty unique, people can still be grouped together based on whether they're a swinging single or a parent of toddlers, whether they cook or don't know how to make toast, whether they commute for ninety minutes a day or work ninety hours a week at home, and so on. If you know what works well for a few people in a particular group, it will tend to work well for many others in that group.

To help give better advice to people, we designed a Web-based program that would use their answers to twenty-six prescreening questions to statistically find three top tips based on individual lifestyles.[42] Some of these tips involved making changes in their kitchen—such as reorganizing their cupboards, pre-plating off the stove, or using smaller dishes—and many of these tips ended up becoming big favorites. Although they weren't the quickest way to lose weight, they were easy. You wouldn't lose five pounds in a month, but you'd mindlessly lose one or two without thinking about it.

Since that time we've discovered more than one hundred effective home-related tips and combined the hundred easiest ones into a Slim-by-Design Home Scorecard that we update each year with the best new tips we've discovered. When we're asked to do a slim-by-design home makeover and we can't talk with the reclusive celebrities themselves, the Scorecard is where we start. It quickly helps troubleshoot how a home is adding unwanted pounds, and it shows what changes are likely to reverse this.

You can also use this in your own home. In ten minutes you can take the Scorecard into your kitchen and check off what you do: Is the kitchen organized? Is there fruit on the counter? Is the toaster put away? After you finish, you add up the checkmarks, and that's your Slim-by-Design Home Score. Earlier, shorter versions of our Scorecard have been used by health-care companies in places ranging from Los Angeles beach communities to the state of Iowa. In one place, they even heroically claimed that it helped contribute to raising the life expectancy of a sample of 786 residents by almost three years.[43] I think that's a stretch, but it's probably in the right direction.

It all starts with taking ten minutes to fill out your Scorecard. One small step for you, one giant step toward fat-proofing your family.

If you look at the Scorecard beginning on page 60, you'll see three types of changes: (1) easy changes to make—such as filling up a fruit bowl; (2) hard changes to make—like painting your kitchen; and (3) changes you won't want to make—like getting rid of your microwave. But it doesn't matter if one change is too difficult for you—just focus on the others.

You probably won't get a score of 100 on your Slim-by-Design Home Scorecard. A score of 100 is more aspirational than possible, and the first time you fill out the Scorecard, you'll probably get between 20 and 30. As a rough rule of thumb, if your score is less than 40, your home is working against you becoming slim by design. If your score is over 60, it's working for you. Although you could raise your score to 60 within a couple of weeks, it's a bit tougher to get to 80, and even tougher to reach 90. (My home is an 83, and that's about as high as I can comfortably go without having to paint, buy a new fridge, or move the microwave.)

Almost everyone wants to be "better" than they are today—slimmer, smarter, better looking, more interesting—and they want to think they're improving. One benefit of the Scorecard is that it usually shows progress each time you fill it out. It can give you tangible evidence that you're doing the right things that will eventually make you slim by design, even if today's scale didn't budge.

When you make a few changes and bump up your score, it automatically helps your family. These same cozy kitchen, cupboard, and tablescape traps that make us overeat do the same to our kids—especially if they're extraverted and a bit hyper.[44] They grab the cookies on the counter when there's no fruit. They look at the middle shelf of the fridge and snatch a pudding cup because there wasn't any bag of cut veggies and dip sitting there instead. Many of our new research studies (and my next book) are on fat-proofing kids, and it's amazing how small changes turn bad eaters into good ones. If you don't care about making your house slim by design for yourself, do it for your kids. It all starts with taking ten minutes to fill out your Scorecard. One small step for you, one giant leap toward fat-proofing your family.

In-Home Slim-by-Design
Self-Assessment Scorecard

. . . .

Read each of the statements below as you visualize or walk through your home. For each true statement, check the box in front of it. After you've completed the checklist, tally the checkmarks. This number is your Slim-by-Design Home Score. If your score is below 40, your home is working against you. If it's above 60, it's working for you.

KITCHEN

☐ There is no television in the kitchen.

☐ There are no comfortable, "loungeable" chairs in the kitchen.

☐ Walls are painted a neutral earth tone (neither too bright nor too dark).

☐ You enter your home through a non-kitchen door (such as the front door).

☐ Counters are well organized, not cluttered.

☐ Food preparation areas are brightly lit.

☐ There is a blender on the counter.

☐ The toaster is not visible.

☐ There is no microwave (okay, this is hard to do).

☐ The kitchen has a floral scent.

☐ No breakfast cereal boxes are visible.

☐ Baked goods are not visible at all.

☐ A full fruit bowl *is* visible.

☐ The fruit bowl contains 2 or more types of fruit.

☐ The fruit bowl is within 2 feet of the most common kitchen pathway.

REFRIGERATOR

☐ The refrigerator door opens toward an adjacent food-preparation area.

☐ A favorite family photo is near the door handle.

☐ Precut fruit is on the center shelf.

☐ Precut vegetables are on the center shelf.

☐ Cut fruit and vegetables are bagged or in a see-through container.

☐ Salad and vegetable leftovers are in transparent containers or plastic wrap.

☐ Nonvegetable leftovers are in opaque containers or aluminum foil.

☐ The healthiest snacks are on the front middle shelf.

☐ The less-healthy snacks are in the back or the lower sides.

☐ Any leftover dessert is stored in the bottom produce drawer.

- [ ] Less-healthy leftovers are stored in the produce drawers.
- [ ] The refrigerator contains at least 6 nonfat yogurts (or a high-protein alternative).
- [ ] Another low-calorie, high-protein snack is available (such as low-fat string cheese or sliced turkey).
- [ ] At least 6 eggs are available (or a high-protein alternative).
- [ ] Non-, low-fat, or soy milk is in the refrigerator.
- [ ] There are no large bottles of any beverage other than milk or water.
- [ ] There is no more than I can of diet or regular soft drink per drinker.
- [ ] There is no more than I single-serve can or bottle of any fruit juice or energy drink per drinker.

FREEZER

- [ ] The freezer is located on the bottom (versus the top or side).
- [ ] There is a working icemaker.
- [ ] Cut frozen fruit or vegetables are bagged or in a container.
- [ ] Leftover vegetable dishes are in transparent containers or plastic wrap.
- [ ] Other leftovers are in opaque containers or aluminum foil.
- [ ] If there is ice cream, it is repackaged in an unbranded opaque container.
- [ ] The healthiest foods are in the front middle.
- [ ] Any frozen starches or leftovers are in the back or the lower sides.

CUPBOARDS

- [ ] Less-healthy snacks are stored together in an inconvenient "kid's cupboard."
- [ ] Food cupboards are *not* glass or transparent.
- [ ] The healthiest snacks are in the front middle.
- [ ] The less-healthy snacks are in the back or the lower sides.
- [ ] Oatmeal (in any form) is in the front center of the breakfast cupboard.

DISHWARE

- [ ] Plates are 9 to 10 inches in diameter.
- [ ] Plates have a wide, colored rim.
- [ ] Plates are *not* white or beige.
- [ ] Plates are sectioned or divided.
- [ ] Cereal bowls are smaller than 16 ounces.
- [ ] Water glasses are 16 ounces or larger.
- [ ] Non-water glasses are tall and thin (and 12 ounces or less).
- [ ] Juice glasses are 8 ounces.

PANTRY

- ☐ The pantry is *not* located in the kitchen.
- ☐ The healthiest foods are in the front middle of the shelving.
- ☐ The ready-to-eat foods are in the back or the lower sides.
- ☐ Six or more cans of vegetables are visible.
- ☐ Six or more cans of soup are visible.

COUNTERS

- ☐ No cookies are on the counter.
- ☐ No candy is on the counter.
- ☐ No regular soft drinks are on the counter.
- ☐ No diet soft drinks are on the counter.
- ☐ No nuts are on the counter.
- ☐ No breakfast cereal is on the counter.
- ☐ No bread is on the counter.
- ☐ No crackers or chips are on the counter.
- ☐ No other snacks are on the counter.

DINING TABLE

- ☐ Dinner is eaten at a kitchen or dining room table.
- ☐ If there is a television, it is turned off during mealtime.
- ☐ You use the Half-Plate Rule at dinnertime (see chapter 4, page 132).
- ☐ If there are children under 12, they use smaller plates than the parents.
- ☐ If there are children under 12, they use smaller bowls than the parents.
- ☐ If there are children under 12, they use smaller glasses than the parents.
- ☐ Salad and vegetables are served first.
- ☐ Salad and vegetables are served family-style (on the table).
- ☐ Serving bowls are small enough to have to be refilled during the meal.
- ☐ The serving bowls for starches and entrées are *not* sitting on the table.
- ☐ The serving bowls for starches and entrées are located on the kitchen stove.
- ☐ Serving spoons are tablespoon-size or smaller.
- ☐ Serving tongs are *not* used.
- ☐ At least one person at the table is drinking milk.
- ☐ Everyone has a glass of water.
- ☐ All cold beverages (except water) are served in tall, narrow glasses no larger than 12 ounces.
- ☐ No soft drinks at the table.
- ☐ No wine at the table, or if it is, it's served in narrow white wineglasses.

- [ ] No food packages (other than condiments) are on the table.
- [ ] Lights are dimmed (not at full brightness).
- [ ] Soft music is played.
- [ ] Everyone stays seated until all are finished eating.

TV ROOM

- [ ] A full glass cf water or a water bottle is always within arm's reach.
- [ ] If there are snacks, they are located at least 6 feet from the seating area.
- [ ] Any snacks are eaten out of bowls, not in bags or original containers.
- [ ] Any snacks are eaten from small bowls, 8 ounces or less.
- [ ] Any empty candy wrappers are left within view until snacking is through.
- [ ] Any beverage containers—cans or bottles—are left within view.

HOME OFFICE OR COMPUTER ROOM

- [ ] A full glass of water or a water bottle is always within arm's reach.
- [ ] If there are snacks, they are located at least 6 feet from the seating area.
- [ ] Any snacks are eaten out of bowls, not in bags or original containers.
- [ ] Any snacks are eaten from small bowls, 8 ounces or less.
- [ ] Any candy wrappers are left within view.
- [ ] Any beverage containers—cans or bottles—are left within view.

SCORING BRACKETS

- [ ] **70–100—Slim-by-Design Home—**_Gold_ ✓
- [ ] **50–69—Slim-by-Design Home—**_Silver_
- [ ] **30–49—Slim-by-Design Home—**_Bronze_

Chapter Three

RESTAURANT DINING BY DESIGN

W E CAN MAKE OUR HOME slim by design, but that's only one place we eat. Many of us eat many of our meals in restaurants. We can control our own home, but we can't control our favorite restaurant, right? Wrong. We can change what *we* do, and we can ask them to change what *they* do.

Nobody goes to a restaurant to start a diet—they go there to enjoy themselves. But small changes can let us enjoy ourselves and still eat less without resorting to an alfalfa and yak cheese salad. For instance, take our Restaurant Rule of Two—you can order any reasonable entrée you want, but you can only have two additional items with it. That could be an appetizer and piece of bread, or a dessert and coffee, or two pieces of bread—you just can't have it all. People choose what they want most, they still enjoy themselves, and they report to us that they eat about a quarter less. There are a lot of easy tricks you can use to eat better at restaurants.

There are also a lot of easy tricks restaurants can do to *help* you eat better. Why would they bother? It's simple: They make a lot of money off you, but that money disappears any time you choose to eat some-where else. You just need to know what to ask for and how to ask them. There's a one-liner about a waitress in a greasy-spoon diner who comes to the table with a full tray of coffees and asks, "Who asked for coffee in a clean cup?" If we know what to ask our favorite restaurants to do for us, they're likely to do it. If we don't ask, we have to settle for the dirty cup, or whatever they give us.

In Praise of Leftovers

· · · · · · · · · · · · ·

LET'S START WITH LEFTOVERS. Next time you're at a restaurant, start by thinking about the food you should take home. People have mixed feelings—mostly negative—about to-go boxes or doggie bags. "Doggie bag" sounds especially negative—like the sometimes-not-so-empty plastic bags people carry when walking their pooch. Only about 18 percent of dinner diners will even ask for to-go boxes after their meal.[1] After all, Styrofoam boxes don't accessorize well in the symphony lobby, they make you look cheap in front of your swoony hot date, and if you ask for one in France they'll deport you to the United States even if you're not American. Still, a lot of us would be better off if we saved part of that burrito-as-big-as-your-head for tomorrow instead of regretfully eating it all at once.

Aside from the doggie bag visual and looking like a cheap date, there's a Nobel Prize–winning reason why we don't ask for to-go boxes. It's called the endowment effect, which means that we value things more if we feel we "own" them than if we don't, according to researchers like Daniel Kahneman, Richard Thaler, Cass Sunstein, and Dan Ariely.[2] Before we order food, we don't own it. But once we order our food, we psychologically "own" it. It's harder to pry it away from us—even with a to-go box. But if a restaurant could get us to think in terms of eating half and saving the rest, we might order an appetizer, a salad, or an extra drink. In short, we might spend more money. This could be win-win. We might eat fewer calories, and they might make more money.

But how could they get you to take a to-go box? If we get possessive about our food right *after* we order it, maybe they should tell us they have to-go boxes *before* we decide what we're going to order.

> There's a Nobel Prize–winning reason why we don't ask for to-go boxes.

We tested this with a restaurant partner of ours in central Illinois that serves $20–$25 prix-fixe dinners every Tuesday. It's in a college town and the diners are mostly staff, faculty, and local townsfolk who expect to fill out a comment card about the meal at the end of the night. What they don't realize is that every dinner is really an undercover study—we might change the background music and see how fast they eat, or we might give them complimentary wine but tell them it's from North Dakota and see if it influences how they rate the taste of the food, how long they stay, and whether they come back.[3]

If restaurants could order for you, they'd probably start you off with that veggie platter or side salad.

But during this particular week we focused on how many people would ask for a to-go box. When people arrived and were seated, we had waitresses tell the people at half of the tables, "Our portions are generous. Whatever you order and don't eat, you can take home in a to-go box." They were told this *before* they ordered. The people at the other half of the tables were told the exact same thing *after* they ordered, right when their meal was set in front of them.

We've also done this a number of times in more tightly controlled situations—where the diners are a little less suspicious and aren't trying to figure out what's going on. What we usually find is that people who were told about the to-go boxes *before* they order are about 40 percent more likely to say they'll take home leftovers than those who were asked afterward.[4] Half today, half tomorrow. This was a double win. People might order more, but they tended to eat less at that sitting. Usually we find that when people eat a little less, they drink a little more, translating into extra sales of overpriced wine and lattes (but still fewer calories).[5]

> "Boy, the food at this place is really terrible."
> "Yeah, I know—and such small portions."
> —*Annie Hall (1977)*

Remember, restaurants don't want to make us fat. They want to make money. This may sound crazy, but many of them make less profit when you order $4.95 onion rings than when you order the $4.95 side salad, because the latter has only thirteen cents' worth of lettuce in it.[6] They'd love us to order the cheap-as-dirt salad, but all restaurants—whether it's Fat Boy's Burgers or the French Maiden's Delicatessen—have three goals when it comes to us:

1. They want us to eat there and not across the street.
2. They want us to spend a lot on their most profitable foods.
3. They want us to leave happy and to come back often.

If they could order for you, they'd probably start you off with that veggie platter or side salad. There's a huge profit margin on those foods. But it's just easier for them to convince you to buy the standby favorites, like French fries and Buffalo chicken wings.[7] In fact, it would be silly for most restaurants to drop their wings and rings from their menu. It's what people *think* they want, so they're highlighted on the menu, they're part of a special, and the waitstaff pushes them. They appear consistently on the menus of casual dining restaurants so people don't have an excuse to go eat across the street.

But it's not the onion rings and French fries that trip us up at our favorite "go-to" restaurants. It's what we do in the first fifteen minutes after we get there. It looks like this: We arrive without a reservation, and the hostess seats us wherever's most convenient. We listen to the specials, and skim the menu until a couple of things catch our eye. We then *imagine* which will taste best, and we proceed to order too much food. While we wait, we tear apart the bread in a way that makes zombies appear well-mannered. After our food arrives and we've picked all the meaty, cheesy, saucy portions clean, we languidly consider dessert.

From the moment we set foot in a particular restaurant, each choice —*before* we even order—adds calories to our once girlish and boyish figures: Where we sit, where our eyes land on the menu, and how we imagine the food will taste all make us eat worse than we otherwise would. But there are easy things you can do to turn this around, and easy things the restaurant can do to help. Unfortunately, even though the shrimp salad makes more profit than Buffalo wings, most restaurants don't know how to help us order the shrimp salad. Yet the answers are simpler than they might think. They start as soon as we walk in the door.

HAVE YOUR HALF-PLATE PORTION
AND EAT IT, TOO

Your restaurant du jour doesn't offer half-plate portions? If you're feeling bold, ask your server—or the manager—for a half portion for "a reduced price, so I'll have room for an appetizer or drink." It's surprising how often this works—even at the big chain restaurants. If this isn't possible, you can always have them box half of it . . . before it arrives.

But it's best to commit to the to-go bag before you start eating. Here's the plate-size rule of thumb: If *either* the portion or the plate looks big, commit to taking a to-go bag. There's more food there than you think.

Show Me to a Slim Table

· · · · · · · · · · · ·

RESTAURANTS NUMBER THEIR TABLES. Table 1 might be closest to the door and Table 91 might be farthest. This makes it easy for your server to keep track of orders. The table number gets printed on the receipt, which tells what people ordered, when they ordered, and who their server was. For instance, we might know that Table 91 is a large table in the dark back corner of the restaurant, that Sara served twelve people on June 28, and that everyone ordered fish or chicken. With enough receipts from enough restaurants, we can start to see if where you sit relates to what you eat.

```
J O E   G A N T Z   S E A F O O D

330 THE PARKWAY
SAN FRANCISCO, CA 94105


SERVER: Sara              06/28/2014
TABLE: 91/1                10:19 PM
GUESTS: 12                    10013

BLK COD                       25.96
Side Gratin                    7.50
SALMON (4 @24.95)             99.80
```

RESTAURANTS HAVE SLIM AND HEAVY ZONES

IT MATTERS WHERE YOU SIT!

Diners at high tables go for more salads and fish

Diners at regular tables order more vegetarian entrées and vegetable sides

Booth diners order more BBQ ribs and desserts

Diners at tables near a window consume fewer drinks and more side salads

Diners at tables near the TV and bar order more chicken wings and drinks

We recently visited twenty-seven restaurants across the country, and we measured and mapped out the layout of each one. We knew how far each table or booth was from the window and front door, whether it was in a secluded or well-traveled area, how light or dark it was, and how far it was from the kitchen, bar, restrooms, and TV sets. After we mapped it out and diners began arriving, we were able to track what they ordered and how it related to where they sat.

Some restaurants we visited for only one or two nights, but at one restaurant we collected every receipt for every day for three straight months. At the end of three months, our Restaurant War Room back in Ithaca, New York, looked like a recycling center. It was full of huge bags stuffed with receipts that were wrinkled or wadded, smeared with steak sauce or wine stains, and autographed with things like "Thanks, Tiffany" and smiley faces. By analyzing these A-1-smeared artifacts, we were able to figure out whether somebody at Table 91 way in back was more likely to order salad or less likely to order an extra drink than somebody at Table 7—which is way up front, next to the door and bar.

People sitting farthest from the front door ate the fewest salads and were 73 percent more likely to order dessert.

Are there fat tables in restaurants? This is preliminary, but so far it looks like people ordered healthier foods if they sat by a window or in a well-lit part of the restaurant, but they ate heavier food and ordered more of it if they sat at a dark table or booth. People sitting farthest from the front door ate the fewest salads and were 73 percent more likely to order dessert. People sitting within two tables of the bar drank an average of three more beers or mixed drinks (per table of four) than those sitting one table farther away. The closer a table was to a TV screen, the more fried food a person bought. People sitting at high-top bar tables ordered more salads and fewer desserts.

Some of this makes sense. The darker it is, the more "invisible" you might feel, the less easy it is to see how much you're eating, and the less conspicuous or guilty you might feel. Seeing the sunlight, people, or trees outside might make you more conscious of how you look, might make you think about walking, or might prompt a green salad. Sitting next to the bar might make you think it's more normal to order that second drink, and watching TV might distract you from thinking twice about what you order. If high-top bar tables make it harder to slouch or spread out like you could in a booth, they might cause you to feel in control and to order the same way.

Or this could all just be random speculation. Now, the facts are what they are, but *why* they happen is not always clear.

Does sitting in a dark, quiet booth in the back of the restaurant make you order more dessert? Not necessarily. It might be that heavy dessert eaters naturally gravitate to those tables, or that a hostess takes them there out of habit. Regardless, we know that lots of extra calories coagulate where it's dark and far from the door.

We have an expression in my Lab: "If you want to be skinny, do what skinny people do." Avoiding the fat tables may be a baby step toward being slim by design. If you want to stack the deck in your favor, think twice about where you sit. Conversely, if a restaurant knows which "skinny tables" will sell more of those high-margin salads and that expensive white wine, they can fill those tables up first, leaving the back tables empty until the onion-ring lovers rise up and demand to be seated.[8]

We have an expression in our Lab: "If you want to be skinny, do what skinny people do."

SIT WHERE THE SLIM PEOPLE SIT

Where you sit in a restaurant might relate to what you order.[9] We don't know that eating at slim tables will make you slim, but you might as well stack the deck in your favor. Here's what kind of seating to look for.

Far from kitchen or bar   Elevated tables

Well-lighted area   Far from TV sets

Near windows

Either well-lit, elevated tables near windows make you eat better, or people who eat better like to eat at well-lit, elevated tables near windows. But while you're contemplating the causality, the couple next to you just took the last elevated table by the window.

There are easy changes you can make as soon as you arrive at your restaurant, but there are also easy changes a restaurant can make to help you eat healthier. If enough people told the manager, "I'd eat here more often if it wasn't so dark and loud and if there weren't all of these annoying TVs," eventually one of the corners in the restaurant would have more light and less TV.

How Your Restaurant Can Help You . . .

FEWER TELEVISIONS AND MORE LIGHTS

Some people like restaurants with television and loud music. They make the place seem clublike, hip, and energetic. But they're not what *all* people like, and it doesn't make the place very slimming. Fortunately, restaurants can give people both. They can have a quieter, TV-free, strategically lit section for the people who want to talk more and eat less. And they can still keep the Studio 54 section for those who want to talk less and rage more.

One Antidote for Fast-Food Fever

. . . .

BUT BEFORE YOU CHARGE into a Hardee's to grab that brightly lit table by the window, you need to know that lighting and sound don't work the same way for fast-food restaurants. The lights are already so bright and the sound so loud that it jacks you up into gulping down a full meal's worth of combo-calories before you know it. Now, in nice restaurants, dark corners make us overeat because we relax more, stay longer, and order more drinks and desserts. This isn't a problem in fast-food restaurants, because most people eat quickly and leave. No waiter comes by your table every ten minutes asking if you want anything else to eat or drink. So here was our thinking: Maybe if fast-food restaurants dimmed the lights and mellowed the music, it would keep people from wolfing down food like it's their last meal. It might make them notice they were getting fuller faster.

> **People at well-lit, elevated tables near windows eat better.**

At the time, I was a professor at the University of Illinois at Urbana-Champaign, and my researchers and I would go to the local Hardee's a couple of times a week to have lunch and brainstorm new ideas. We knew the Hardee's folks by name and they knew us. We also knew this Hardee's planned to open up a large, sealed-off section that was formerly for smokers. We proposed the following: If they gave us the restaurant for a day, we would convert the sealed-off section into a fine dining room and see whether softening the lighting and music would change how much people ate and how much they liked it. Since local fast-food managers can change the music and lighting to whatever they think will sell well, this manager was game. (It probably also didn't hurt that we'd eaten there about three hundred times.)

It took the twelve of us only about three hours to black-paper all the windows in the former smoking section, replace the bright fluorescent lights with soft incandescent ones, and replace rocking Aerosmith and ZZ Top music with the mellow and eternally hip jazz album *Kind of Blue* by Miles Davis. When that day's lunch bunch came in and ordered, we ushered half into the original "bright light and loud music" part of the restaurant and the other half into the converted softer lighting and music room—Le Bec Hardee's.

Head to the darkest, quietest corner after you get your fast-food tray.

Everyone had basically ordered the same foods with the same calorie content. The only difference was how much they ate and how much they liked it. Those eating in our converted room ate 18 percent less food, and they rated it as tasting a lot better. Miles Davis delivered.[10]

Softer lights and music slowed diners down, and two things happened. First, their stomach caught up with their brain and they realized they were full. Second, although French fries and bacon cheeseburgers taste great when hot, they taste soggy when not. So what's a fast-food eater to do? Head to the darkest, quietest corner after you get your fast-food tray.

And there's also some leftover news you can take home with you: Turn down the lights and music—or TV—when you eat dinner at home. Your family will probably eat a little slower, eat a little less, and like it a little more. Maybe you could even top the evening off by using some Hardee's tray liners as place mats. "It's a good thing," I imagine Martha Stewart *not* saying.

A HEALTHY CONCESSION LESSON: BUILD IT AND THEY WILL COME

Some restaurants tell us, "We give people what they want, and they don't want healthy food." Most of these restaurants have never really tried to sell any healthy food. And if they've only halfheartedly tried selling one or two such items, how would they *know* healthier food wouldn't sell?

Few places in the world have worse food than concession stands at sporting events. All these concessionaires say the same thing: "People only want chili dogs with fries, and nachos with Cheez Whiz, so that's all we sell."

But maybe if they sold healthier food, people would come. To test this, we teamed up with the University of Iowa Medical School to do a concession-stand makeover in time for high school football season in Muscatine, Iowa—ninety miles south of the actual Field of Dreams from the movie of that name.

We added ten healthier foods, like chicken-breast sandwiches, trail mix, string cheese, carrots with dip, and even big dill pickles. We kept all of the favorites—just added some new foods.

If you offer it, they *will* come. Within a year, healthy foods were nearly 10 percent of sales, and the numbers kept rising with each game—by the last game, 175 people had even bought pickles.[11] And our surveys showed they were happier, especially parents. We built it, and they came. It's a healthy concession lesson.[12]

"Can I Take Your Order?"

· · · · · · · · · · · · ·

WHEN YOU'RE HANDED A MENU, how do you decide what to order? You probably skim over what's listed and screen out things you don't like (the eggplant and puffer fish stir-fry). Then you narrow it down to two or three finalists. You may think you made these choices yourself, but you really didn't. Your finalists were largely biased by the menu's layout.

There's an art and a science to understanding how we read menus. The world's greatest expert at doing this is my friend Gregg Rapp, an urbane but unassuming man who lives high above Palm Springs in an *Architectural Digest*–worthy midcentury home that is Frank Sinatra hip. Gregg's a professional menu engineer. He shows restaurants how to redesign their menus so they guide our eyes to the most profitable items they can sell. But the same principles can be used to help guide our eyes to the healthier foods (which, again, are often the most profitable). Most important, we can use his principles to find hidden healthy treasures and not just settle for the red-boxed, big-type-size listing for the Half-a-Bison Burger we couldn't ignore.

When it comes to what you order for dinner, two things matter most: what you see on the menu and how you imagine it will taste.

I. WHAT YOU SEE

We read menus in a Z-shaped pattern. We start at the top left, move to the top right, go to the middle, veer down to the bottom left, and end up on the bottom right. After that, we look at whatever catches our eye—boxes, bold type, pictures, logos, or icons. Basically, any item that looks different is going to get your attention and make you just a little bit more likely to order it. As Gregg says, if the shrimp salad for $8.99 is in a regal-looking burgundy font in a lightly shaded gold box and has a little chef's-hat icon next to it, even Mr. Magoo wouldn't miss seeing it. He might not buy it, but he'll consider it. He might remind himself that he had shrimp for lunch or is hungrier for beef, but he might also think, *Shrimp salad . . . that sounds good for a change.*

Still, it's a big step from reading the menu to ordering the shrimp salad. What stands in between? Just your imagination. If the words used in the menu lead you to expect this salad will be fresh, flavorful, and filling, you're a lot closer to ordering it than if they made it sound like fishing bait.

2. HOW YOU IMAGINE IT WILL TASTE

With well-engineered menus, what you *see* isn't a coincidence and what you *imagine* isn't a coincidence. Your imagination is guided. A great menu guides your imagination to build these expectations so you're tasting as you're reading. Again, it leads you to think the shrimp will be "fresh and flavorful" instead of "live bait." This can be accomplished in only two words.

A few years ago, a staid, sleepy place named Bevier Cafeteria wanted to rebrand itself by offering a bunch of healthy new foods. The problem with healthy foods is that most people don't want them. They want tasty foods—if they happen to be healthy, that's great but secondary. My buddy Jim Painter and I reviewed the menu and did nothing more than tweak the names of some of the items, adding a descriptive word here or there: red beans and rice became *traditional Cajun* red beans and rice, seafood fillet became *succulent Italian* seafood fillet, and so on. Not a single thing changed in the recipes themselves—the only difference was two descriptive words.

Not only did foods with the descriptive names sell 28 percent more, but they were rated as tastier than those with the plain boring old names.[13] When people ate a food with an "improved" name, they even liked the cafeteria better—rating it as more trendy and up-to-date.[14] They even rated the chef as having more years of European culinary training. In reality, for all we knew the guy had been fired from Arby's two months earlier.

And it didn't even matter how ridiculous the names were. We egregiously renamed chocolate cake as Belgian Black Forest Double-Chocolate Cake. This was dried-out, nasty, chocolate sheet cake—really sad stuff. Now it doesn't matter that the Black Forest isn't even in Belgium—when we asked diners what they thought of the cake, people loved it, and some

THE *Slim-by-Design* DINER

APPETIZERS

Crisp Summer Salad with Pineapple and Avocado 6
Juicy pineapple and fresh, ripe avocado paired in our lightest and easiest summer salad.

Chips and Salsa 7
Crispy tortilla chips served with homemade salsa and fresh guacamole.

Soup of the Day 5
Please ask your server for our homemade special.

Vegetables and Hummus 6
Broccoli, carrot, and cucumber platter served with a duo of homemade hummus options.

Cherry Tomatoes with Creamy Pesto Cheese 6
Plump tomatoes filled with our famous creamy pesto spread made with reduced-fat cream cheese.

Light and Fresh Roasted Beet Salad with Humboldt Fog Cheese 6
Featuring watercress, toasted pistachios, and a raspberry vinaigrette.

HOUSE FAVORITES

Grilled Steak and Harvest Stew
Tender blade steak served with a full harvest of vegetables.

London Broil in Mushroom Sauce
Thick, tender steak in an unforgettably rich sauce.
    * TRIM PORTION 7
    * FULL PORTION 10

South Island Style Pork Tenderloin with Mango-Cilantro Salad 14
Lean, delicious pork tenderloin served with lime-infused mango and sprinkled with cilantro and chilies.

Succulent Italian Cod Fillet with Whole Grain Rice 16
Whole flaky white fillets in a crispy batter served complemented by a unique Italian-inspired tomato salad.

Smoked Salmon with Broccoli 13
*Hickory-smoked salmon garnished with capers and served with a side
of sautéed spinach.*

Shrimp Gumbo
*The New Orleans classic, rich with onions, bell pepper, and diced
tomatoes and served over brown rice.*

    * TRIM PORTION 11
    * FULL PORTION 15

SIDES

Roasted Vegetables 3
Tender and caramelized carrots, broccoli, squash. and potatoes.

Chef Salad 3
*Featuring crisp greens, garden fresh vegetables, hard-boiled eggs, ham,
and Wisconsin cheddar cheese.*

Baked Sweet Potato 4
The savory favorite, topped with cinnamon and light butter.

HAPPY ENDINGS

Fruit Plate 5
Fresh grapes, strawberries, and blueberries for a light and sweet treat.

Italian Sorbet 5
*Please ask your server for our daily flavors of this classic Italian
frozen dessert.*

* **Chocolate Cake** 6
*Everybody's favorite! Rich cake with fudgy frosting, paired with
vanilla-bean ice cream.*

Place healthy items in the four corners and at the beginning of sections.

For select items, offer half-size portions for 70 percent the price of the full portion. Don't call them half-size— use words like "trim," "moderate," or "light."

Place healthy high-margin items in bold boxes or colored boxes to call them out.

Almost any notation can catch one's eye and increase consideration and choice.

raved about it. One guy went on and on, concluding with "It reminds me of Antwerp." Where in Antwerp? An abandoned food cart in a train station restroom? Adding a couple of words changed sales, tastes, and attitudes toward the restaurant. And it even reminded one person of a possibly delusional vacation.

So what kinds of words do restaurants rely on to help make a satisfied sale? We analyzed 373 descriptive menu items from around the country and found four categories of vivid names:[15]

1. **SENSORY NAMES:** Describing the texture, taste, smell, and mouthfeel of the menu item raises our taste expectations. Pastry chefs are the masters of these, using evocative names like Velvety Chocolate Mousse, but a great main menu also has Crisp Snow Peas, Pillowy Handmade Gnocchi, or Fork-Tender Beef Stew.

2. **NOSTALGIC NAMES:** Alluding to the past can trigger happy, wholesome associations to tradition, family, and national origin. Think Old-Style Manicotti, Oktoberfest Red Cabbage, and Grandma's Chicken Dumplings, or words like Classic or House Favorite.

3. **GEOGRAPHIC NAMES:** Words that create an image or sense of a geographic area associated with the food. Think Iowa Farm-Raised Pork Chops, Southwestern Tex-Mex Salad, Carolina Mustard Barbecue, or Georgia Peach Tart.

4. **BRAND NAMES:** Cross-promotions are catching on fast in the chain-restaurant world. They tell us, "If you love the brand, you'll love this menu item." That's why we can buy Jack Daniel's® BBQ Ribs, and Twix® Blizzards. For the high-end restaurants, this translates into Niman Ranch pork loin or a Kobe beef kebab.

A smart restaurant owner who wants you to eat his healthy, high-margin foods can engineer his menu so that you see these items first, and he can describe them so you taste them in your mind. Unfortunately, he could also engineer his menu for evil purposes to guide customers toward his most profitable *unhealthy* foods. You can avoid this by decoding some of these seductive names and uncovering the hidden healthy treasures instead.

Most non-chain restaurants don't list their calories, but it's still pretty easy to break their code and figure out whether their special of the day will make you fit or fat. For the past few months we've been tracking the calories on the menus of chain restaurants. Our research is far from complete, but here are some preliminary rules of thumb. On average, if a restaurant puts the word "buttery" in the name of a dish, it will have 102 more calories in it. Anything described with the word "crispy" will have 131 more calories than its non-"crispy" counterpart.

But just as there are high-calorie words, there are low-calorie words. Order something that is described as seasoned, roasted, or marinated and you won't be regretting it for as long on the treadmill. These foods have about 60 fewer calories than their unseasoned, unroasted, or unmarinated counterpart.

What You Can Do . . .

MENU WORDS THAT MAKE US FAT

Menu descriptions sell. But some words are a lot more caloric than others. We matched more than two thousand menu descriptions of items from chain restaurants with their calorie content. Here's a preliminary take on the most and least caloric words on restaurant menus.[16]

HIGH-CALORIE WORDS	LOW-CALORIE WORDS
Buttery	Seasoned
Creamed	Roasted
Crispy/crunchy	Light
Smothered	Fat-free
Alfredo or white sauce	Reduced
Fried/deep-fried/pan-fried	Marinated
Scampi	Fresh
Loaded	Broiled

Other words that didn't come up in our study—but you should also be on watch for—include "blubbery" and "911" (on the high-calorie side) and "Doesn't taste as bad as you'd expect" (on the low-calorie side).

If the description sounds too good to pass up, it might deliver more in calories than the taste is worth.

If you really want to track down the hidden healthy treasures that might be buried in the middle of the menu, just ask your server, "What are your two or three lighter entrées that get the most compliments?" or "What's the best thing on the menu if a person wants a light dinner?" If nothing catches your interest, you can always make a request. You can ask if you can get a salad with a skirt steak filet on it, or you can ask for a side of vegetables instead of the fries, or you can ask for the pan-fried fish cooked with Pam instead of oil. More often than not, they'll make what you want—even huge chains like Red Lobster and Ruby Tuesday often make adjustments. Of course, they could also say, "We're not going to make what you want," just as you could say, "And I might not be back."

Just ask your server, "What are your two or three lighter entrées that get the most compliments?"

If nothing catches your interest, you can always make a request. Of course, they could also say, "We're not going to make what you want," just as you could say, "And I might not be back."

Half-Plate Profits

· · · · · · · · · · · · ·

THERE'S A MEXICAN RESTAURANT in the Midwest that boasts "Burritos as Big as Your Head." If the United Nations had guidelines about what not to eat, this would be in the top three:

1. **Don't eat things on fire.**
2. **Don't eat things that are moving.**
3. **Don't eat things as big as your head.**

Why are restaurant portions so huge? Restaurants think that the more food—the more calories per dollar—they give us, the more likely we'll eat there and not eat across the street. But this can backfire if they go too far. When burritos become as big as your head, reasonable people either split one or they don't buy any additional side dishes or desserts. Either outcome is bad for the restaurant. They win the Largest Entrée Award but not the Largest Check Size Award.

But they could avoid this if they offered some popular entrées in both full and half sizes. Instead of selling 10 ounces of pasta for $10, they could also sell a 5-ounce portion for $5. Yet what restaurant in its right mind would want to sell less food for less money? Only the smart ones. Just as 100-calorie packs meant higher profits and new markets (sweet-tooth dieters) for the snack companies, half-size portions mean the same for restaurants.

Let's test this out in a truck stop. After all, if it can make it there, it can make it anywhere. Trail's Restaurant is a Minnesota truck stop on Interstate 35 that's hard to miss because it has a ten-foot-high chain-saw-carved wooden Viking in the lobby.[17,18] It does a solid business—half the customers are local townsfolk and half are truckers and travelers—but Trail's wanted to do better *and* help their truckers, travelers, and townsfolk eat better.

We started by recommending they offer half-size portions of some popular entrées. They did it, but instead of losing money, they made more. Whereas Lester and Grace would regularly visit the restaurant and split a $10 chicken entrée because "it was big enough for two," they now each ordered their own half-size version. For twenty years, Lester had quietly let his wife order the chicken breast. Now he could order a half-size steak, and they still had room to order an appetizer or the four-dollar salad. Trail's also made more money from the people at the table next to them. These people heard about smaller portions and lower prices and figured they'd eat here rather than ordering a flavorless turkey sandwich at the local sub shop.

Within three months, more people went to the restaurant, more total entrées were sold, and more people bought side salads. Each month they sold three times as many half-size meals. They also sold 435 more monthly side orders of salad than they did before.[19]

How Your Restaurant Can Help You . . .

OFFER HALF-SIZE PORTIONS

Won't a restaurant lose money if they offer half-size portions of their most popular entrées? No. They usually make more money.[20]

1. **People buy extra things.**

2. **Two half-size portions at 50 to 70 percent of the price of a full portion is still at least 100 percent more than if two people went somewhere else because they weren't that hungry.**

3. **Being able to eat a little less for a little less money might bring in new diners who would have stayed home.**

While offering the half-size portions was only one of a dozen restaurant makeover changes we made at Trail's Restaurant, it made a big difference. Guest counts increased, sales increased, and check averages increased.[21] Also, for the first time, they won awards for Top Sales of the Year and National Franchise Restaurant of the Year.

Asking our server or the manager for a half-size portion—or to make it a permanent part of the menu—is tough for some of us. But it becomes a lot easier if we think we're doing them a favor. It might even make them Restaurant of the Year.[22]

Smaller and Taller

. . . .

REMEMBER THE OWNER of all of those Chinese buffets in chapter 1? When he tossed his 11-inch plates and bought 9¾-inch ones, other things got smaller, too. People took less food, they wasted less, they ate less, and it cost the restaurant less. The only thing that increased was his profits.

But what if you're not serving yourself or you don't own a buffet? Small plates work great for buffets, but they also work for restaurants with table service. Here's why. That 8-ounce strip steak looks great on the 12-inch plate most restaurants serve it on, but it looks massive on a nice-looking 10-inch plate. It looks like a bigger, better value for the money ("Jeez . . . it filled the whole plate!"). In one study with a favorite colleague of mine, Koert van Ittersum, we found that when we reduced the size of plates, people rated the food as a better value—even when there was 15 percent less food.[23]

It's the same with glasses. Both their size and shape bias how much we pour and how good a deal we think it is. When pouring out of a gallon jug, you'll pour less milk or Red Bull into a small glass than a large one, but you'd also pour less into a tall, thin glass than a short, wide one that holds the same volume. But it's not just you. The same thing happens to professional pourers—to bartenders.

One winter we visited eighty-six Philadelphia bartenders—from high-end Rittenhouse Square restaurant lounges with orchids in their windows to low-end West Philly dives with iron bars on their windows. We asked them to pour the amount of alcohol they would use to make a gin and tonic, a whiskey on the rocks, a rum and Coke, and a vodka tonic. It didn't matter if they had worked there for thirty minutes or thirty years, the typical bartender poured 30 percent more alcohol into short, wide 10-ounce tumblers than into 10-ounce highball glasses. When we showed these bartenders how much they overpoured, they balked, even guffawed. They're experts—they do this all the time. We asked them to pour again two minutes later. Same result.[24]

If bartenders pour 30 percent too much alcohol into short glasses, it costs the bar money—alcohol is a lot more expensive than tonic, Coke, or ice cubes. That's bad for the bar, but it's also bad for you: If you think you're getting two drinks' worth of alcohol when you're really getting closer to three, you might not want to drive home.

This was important enough for us to take on the road. We contacted the big chains—like Applebee's, T.G.I. Friday's, and Olive Garden—and let them know there was an easy way they could make more profit on each drink while also helping their diners get less buzzed. We showed them that regardless of how super-awesome their bartenders were and how much training they had, they would always pour 30 percent more alcohol into short, wide tumblers than tall, skinny highball glasses. The easiest solution: Use only tall, skinny glasses for most of the drinks, unless somebody insists on a short one.

Bartenders would always pour 30 percent more alcohol into short, wide tumblers than tall, skinny highball glasses.

Of course, as they say in the movie *This Is Spinal Tap,* "It's a fine line between clever and stupid."[25] Some of these chains ended up jumping overboard, apparently thinking, *If tall is better than short, then the Super-Duper Tall must be best.* Visit some of these casual dining chains today and you'll find specialty drinks come in atmospherically tall glasses with ridiculously little in them—they look like two-foot-long straws. Though perhaps more stupid than clever, it still works.

SMALLER DISHWARE AND TALLER GLASSES

Buying all-new dishware costs a lot, but it can be good both for restaurants and for us. When my Lab tells restaurants that smaller plates and taller glasses save money, the restaurants that make changes do one of three things: some restaurants reduce both their plate size *and* their entrée size—smaller plates, smaller entrées, lower food costs. Some restaurants reduce their plate size, their entrée size, and the price. And some restaurants reduce plate size and keep the entrée the same size because it looks like a much better value than when on a bigger plate—"That steak totally filled the plate!"

There are also big benefits to taller glasses—since even expert bartenders pour about about 30 percent less alcohol into them than into short, wide tumblers.[26] Since water, ice, and mixers are cheaper than the cheapest alcohol, restaurants make more profit, and a customer doesn't hop in the driver's seat thinking they've had two drinks when they've really had more than two and a half.

TALLER GLASSES MEAN FEWER CALORIES... BUT THERE'S A LIMIT

THESE GLASSES ALL HOLD 12 OZ., BUT...

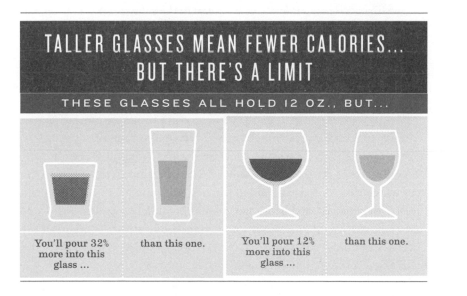

You'll pour 32% more into this glass ...

than this one.

You'll pour 12% more into this glass ...

than this one.

Bread and Water

. . . .

I N THE HISTORY OF WESTERN CIVILIZATION, no one has ever left a Mexican restaurant saying, "I wish I'd eaten more tortilla chips." Nobody has ever left an Italian restaurant pining away for more bread and olive oil. Given all the times we've eaten out, we ought to know that it's way too easy to carbo-load before our meal arrives. Restaurants pile the carb freebies on the table because they think it's a low-cost way to make us happy. They sometimes even bring these items out before the menu—which can be a silly thing to do because we eat up, fill up, and don't order the high-profit appetizers and side dishes.

Sure, we could simply turn down the bread or tortilla chips, but when your friends are famished, it's hard to be the Carb-Enforcer. However, it's easier to say no if the server *asks* whether you want it to begin with. It's easier to turn down a bread basket up front than to send it back after it arrives. Changing their bread-offering policy is a smart win-win move for restaurants—especially since they can make more money selling you other expensive items.

So a slim-by-design restaurant can help you avoid carbs, but it should also help you drink more water.[27] Most of us run around slightly dehydrated, and although our bodies know something's missing, we don't think it's water.[28] We confuse it for hunger and we overeat. It's best to overdrink water during a meal even if we don't think we need it. When we've recommended that drought-area California restaurants offer water, they've said, "But the law won't allow us to give water unless people ask." The solution's easy: Ask your customers if they want it. The number who take water will double from about 25 to 50 percent.[29]

But won't people who drink more water drink fewer Cokes or avocado margaritas? Strangely enough, they don't—they still drink what they otherwise would—plus more water. And the people who wouldn't drink anything else would have asked for water anyway.

$\longrightarrow$

BREAD BASKET CONFIDENTIAL

Butter or Olive Oil—Which Is the Slim-by-Design Choice?

Think olive oil is healthy? Not if you eat it all.

We slipped diners in Italian restaurants either butter or olive oil to see how much they would use on their bread. After they finished their meal, we weighed the remaining olive oil and the remaining bread. The verdict?

Olive oil users conveniently dunked each piece of their bread into 19 percent more calories of fat than those given butter. But here's the twist—they get tired of olive oil faster than they do butter, so they end up eating fewer pieces of bread.[30] Diners served olive oil ate 264 calories' worth of bread, compared to 319 calories for those served butter.

If you're going to eat one or two pieces of bread, butter's better. If you're going to eat until you're stuffed, olive oil will get you to eat less bread.

But the best slim-by-design solution would be to tell the waiter to hold the bread in the first place.

What You Can Do . . .

TELL SERVERS, "KEEP THE BREAD AND BRING MORE WATER"

If the bread's not in front of you, you probably won't miss it, and you'll probably enjoy your meal more. As the French say, "Hunger's the best sauce."

The opposite's true with water. It's good to have a glass of it staring at you. If you ask, it shall be yours.

CALORIE COUNTING: START WITH A FEW FAVORITES

Too much of a hassle for your restaurant to calculate calories? This could help.

First, they could calculate the calories of the bestsellers among their healthiest items. They could post these on the menu, on a table tent insert, or have laminated versions around in case someone asks. Now, it's up to us to ask. If it's important for us to know the calories and it's important for them to keep customers, they'll do this.

Second, a restaurant can easily do this because all they need is a phone. A quick call and a quick "here's-the-basic-recipe" meeting with a dietitian or nutritionist is inexpensive. A quick call to a local college with a similar student program might even be free.

Faster Food and Happier Meals

. . . .

ABOUT TWENTY-FIVE YEARS AGO, I was at my favorite Palo Alto, California, Burger King with a vegetarian friend who asked the cashier if they sold vegetarian burgers. The cashier replied, "Yep, we sure do." As we talked and waited for our order, I laughed when I saw the counter worker prepare her vegetarian burger. He efficiently unwrapped a Whopper, took off the meat, threw it away, wrapped it back up, and handed it to my friend.[31] Le Whopper sans boeuf!

Things have come a long way since then. Whether it's Taco Bell's cheese- and guacamole-free Fresco line or KFC's baked chicken sandwich, some fast-food items are getting healthier and still taste good. But most of us fast-food lovers don't know this, because we always tend to order the same three items over and over and over again.

For at least ten years, Burger King has allowed you to swap out your French fries for a side salad. But back then, only about one in thirty people reportedly ordered the salad.[32] Maybe the other twenty-nine wanted fries, or maybe they didn't know they could make the swap—it's not really advertised anywhere. The same used to be true with McDonald's Happy Meals. Before they switched to the four-piece meal (adding apple slices and subtracting most of the French fries), kids could get fat-free milk and apple slices instead of a Coke and fries.[33] Unfortunately, most kids and parents didn't know about it, so 89 percent still got the fries.[34]

There are tons of healthy fast-food options. The problem—which is as old as McDonald's failed low-fat McLean burger of 1995—is that not enough people buy them. But these companies can change this by making these new healthier options cheaper and more convenient—the two main reasons we buy fast food in the first place. Surprisingly, these options don't have to be *much* cheaper—they only need to look a tad cheaper. Americans love deals, and even a tiny deal will make some of us change direction.

←

As one part of their company wellness program, Rich Foods, a large company in Buffalo, New York, asked us to try to motivate the French fry–loving lunch-goers in their cafeteria to either order a side salad (instead of fries) with their combo meal, or to order a chicken-breast salad. To do so, we developed a Healthy Habit Loyalty Card. Every time a worker ordered a salad, his or her card was punched. After six punches, they got a free meal. This increased salad sales by 21 percent more than when they were instead given a fifty-cent discount.[38]

What about all of the money the restaurant lost by giving away every sixth meal? Many people don't remember to cash in their rewards cards, and even when they did, the cafeteria was happy they were buying five meals at the cafeteria and not at the buffalo-wing joint across the street.

These deals don't have to be very big. Even a five-cent discount can nudge a fence-sitter to order a diet soft drink instead of a regular one, or a baked chicken sandwich instead of a fried one. This works even if the restaurant doesn't cut the price but instead says that five cents goes to charity.

These healthy items could also be moved to the top of the menu board, or they could be pictured on posters or highlighted on table tents—the way McDonald's only advertises white milk in ads for Happy Meals. Just as with menus, fast-food posters and menu boards can make healthy foods more visible and more exciting, with juicy descriptions, in-your-face graphics, special fonts or colors, boxed specials, corner positioning, and so on. Even the cashier can prompt a healthier choice: "Care to start off with a salad?"

FAST-FOOD FAVORS

Here are just a few of the many ways fast-food restaurants can help you eat healthy and do themselves a favor by making you a happy repeat customer:

1. **Make it motivating.**
   * Start a Healthy Habits loyalty card—five punches and the sixth healthy item is free.
   * Give 5 percent off the healthier combo version: diet versus regular, baked versus fried.

2. **Make it easy.**
   * Move the high-margin healthy choices up on the menu board.
   * Feature these items on in-store promotions, such as table tents, tray liners, or posters.

Give away a sixth meal? Give a 5 percent discount? On a $5 meal, that's a 25-cent loss. Think of it instead as a $4.75 gain, because diners could have easily otherwise gone somewhere else. And it's a $9.50 gain if they brought a friend.

HOW TO CHANGE ALMOST ANYTHING AT BURGER KING (AND ELSEWHERE)

Burger King prides itself on letting you "have it your way"; there are 1,024 different ways you can order a Whopper.[39] But what if you wanted them to do even more . . . like sell a low-fat hamburger, a low-calorie dessert, give a five-cent discount if you order a diet soft drink, and put up posters inside encouraging kids to choose the apple slices and the milk?

You can mention this to the manager—he has some local flexibility in what he serves, how he prices food, and what he promotes in the store. Yet here's a case when you get a chance to act both locally *and* globally—you can also directly e-mail the King himself. Let him know the changes you think would be healthy, reasonable, and profitable to make. If you're not sure what to say, you can copy parts or all of the sample letter on page 256. If all you want is to photocopy it, fill in your name, and sign it, that's fine also. Have it your way.

Burger King knows you have dozens of choices about where to eat, and they won't take it lightly if they hear from you or see your #BurgerKing tweet. Nor will #McDonalds, #Taco Bell, #KFC, #Pizza Hut, or whatever fast-food restaurant you and your family visit most often. Let them know how they can help you become slim by design. Following the sample letters and beginning on page 265 are the addresses, Twitter hashtags, and e-mails for many of our favorite fast-food chains.

What Would Batman Eat?

· · · · · · · · · · · ·

MILLIONS OF PARENTS TAKE their happy kids to fast-food restaurants every day. Most of us don't even try to get our kids to order the apple slices instead of the fries or to order the white milk instead of the juice. We're there because we don't have the time, energy, or motivation to cook, and because we also don't have the time, energy, or motivation to argue with our kids—especially when *we're* the ones getting the fries with our combo meal.

My Cornell Food and Brand Lab has done about a hundred studies with little kids, and one totally "duh" finding that we see all the time is that kids can be stubbornly habitual in what they want to eat. If kids had French fries yesterday, they want them again today—it's their default and it works for them. If you ask them "Do you want apple slices or French fries?" they'll answer

What would Batman eat, apple slices or French fries?

before you finish your question. The secret solution might be in interrupting their thinking—interrupting their default answer. This way they'd have to push the reset button on the side of their brain and at least give apple slices a chance.

Here's an idea: Instead of asking them what they want, what if we ask them about someone they admire? If we ask them—without judgment or comment—what a friend, teacher, Scout leader, or their favorite superhero would choose, it might cause them to push that reset button and think again. It might cause them to think about how someone else might go about choosing. Our code name for this study was "What Would Batman Eat?"

That summer we were helping sponsor a 4-H summer camp for elementary school kids, and one week we decided to treat them to their side-order choice at a local fast-food restaurant—either apple slices or French fries. Now, if you ask twenty children ages five to ten whether they want apple slices or French fries, the score will be French fries 19, apple slices 1. But the next week we tried something different. Instead of asking what *they* wanted, we asked, "What would Batman eat, apple slices or French fries?" After they answered for Batman, we'd ask, "What do *you* want, apple slices or French fries?"[40] This time, the number of kids who ordered apple slices jumped from 1 to 9—almost half of them.

We've done this a bunch of times in a bunch of different ways, and here's what's crazy. First, it doesn't matter *who* you say: Batman, the Joker, their teacher, or their best friend. Simply having to answer for *anyone* else seems to make them think twice—and often change their order. Second, it doesn't matter *what* they answer. They could precociously say that Batman or their third-grade teacher would eat French fries, but they'll still order apple slices half the time.

It doesn't matter *who* you say: Batman, the Joker, their teacher, or their best friend.

The only thing that doesn't work is if you ask them too early. If you ask them even fifteen minutes before they place their order, only 25 percent will still order apple slices. You can plan ahead, but don't ask until you pull into the parking lot.

Within three days of discovering this, the people in my Lab changed the way we fed our kids. Anytime our kids are facing an either/or decision in a restaurant—milk or soft drink, fried or baked, green beans or macaroni—we casually ask them, "What would [_____] eat?" Of course you have to regularly change up the name, but if you ask it nonjudgmentally, it's amazing how many times they push their brain's reset button and do the right thing. And if it doesn't work this time, try using a different name next time. Now, back to the Bat Cave.

WHAT WOULD BATMAN EAT?

No kid in their right mind would choose apple slices over French fries—unless you ask. The secret is you can't ask them what *they* want to eat; you have to ask them what their favorite friend, teacher, or superhero would eat. Here are some tips our What Would Batman Eat? studies have shown work:

✳ **Be specific, nonjudgmental, and make it a decision between two choices: "What would Batman eat—apple slices or French fries?"**

✳ **Don't criticize their answer or even comment.** Then simply ask, "What do *you* want—apple slices or French fries?"

✳ **Give them what they asked for and move on.**

Crazy . . . but doing this for yourself will also help you make similar choices. Before making your choice between the salad and the cheesy bacon fries, if you ask yourself something like, "What would my cool friend Steve choose?" you'll be a lot less tempted. Thinking about what a well-liked person would do makes us less indulgently compulsive. It's somewhat in the spirit of when people wore the WWJD wristbands. When faced with a difficult decision, it was supposed to prompt them to ask themselves, "What Would Jesus Do?"

I'm pretty sure he wouldn't have ordered the Cheesy Bacon Fries.

Transforming a Town

· · · · · · · · · · · · ·

WHAT IF A WHOLE TOWN of restaurants agreed to become slim by design? Over the years we've advised the big casual dining chains to use smaller plates because it makes the food look bigger, and it makes people eat less and be more satisfied. We've advised these same chains and legions of bars to serve drinks in tall, skinny highball glasses instead of short, wide tumblers so that bartenders pour less and drinkers drink less. We've helped companies redesign their menus so diners purchase the most healthy and most profitable items. But we hadn't tried to transform an entire town of restaurants to help lead their diners to be slim by design. One evening in the fall of 2008, my chance was about to start.

No restaurateur can be expected to push healthier choices just because he's a jolly good fellow.

I got a call from a soon-to-be-friend Dan Buettner, a fellow midwesterner my exact age who had written *Blue Zones,* a book on longevity. His plan was to take a small town in Minnesota called Albert Lea and make the townsfolk healthier. He wanted me to come up with an easy checklist of what they could do in their homes, and to also develop a simple plan—a restaurant pledge—that restaurants could use to help people eat better.

At that time I was completing my White House appointment as executive director of the USDA agency in charge of the Dietary Guidelines. When you're a White House or presidential appointee, you have the gift of partially seeing into the future. You know the exact date and time you're going to be fired: 1 P.M. on the inauguration day of the next president. I told Dan I'd happily take on his challenge when I returned to Cornell, but that I'd only ask restaurants to make the changes I believed would also make them more money. Otherwise the whole plan would fail; no restaurateur can be expected to push healthier choices just because he's a jolly good fellow.

THE ORIGINAL SLIM-BY-DESIGN RESTAURANT PLEDGE

Restaurants can increase check averages and bring in new customers by making easy changes that help diners eat healthier and become slim by design.

While there's a full 100-point Restaurant Scorecard at the end of the chapter, we often recommend that a restaurant start by checking out the idea of slim by design by making only the three basic changes they think would be easiest, quickest, and most profitable. These are ten they frequently choose:

1. **Create a menu that highlights high-margin healthy options using the tips in the Slim-by-Design Restaurant Self-Assessment Scorecard (page 108).**

2. **Use serving plates no bigger than 9 to 10 inches in diameter.**

3. **Offer an option of smaller portions of selected entrées (say, half the amount for 50 to 70 percent of the price).**

4. **Develop at least two new healthy meals or side dishes.**

5. **Offer bread or tortilla chips only if asked.**

6. **Offer a salad/vegetable substitution option for French fries (or other starches).**

7. **Replace short, wide bar glasses with taller, narrower glasses.**

8. **Promote a "We'll pack half" policy—have servers let customers know that you'll set aside half a dish before serving.**

9. **Train the servers to mention only the healthy side dishes.**

10. **Create a "fruit-only" dessert option, such as a bowl of berries or a melon plate, and give it a refreshing, appealing name.**

Along with the full 100-point scorecard on page 108, there are other certification programs that encourage restaurants to make win-win healthy changes. Some focus more on encouraging healthier habits (like REAL—the United States Healthful Foods Council), some focus more on the food (like Blue Zones), and some are in between (WooFood). Find out more at SlimByDesign.org.

The rules were as follows: The changes I suggested either had to bring in more customers or increase the check size per customer, *and* these changes had to lead diners to buy either healthier food or fewer calories. I'd already suggested some of these changes to restaurant chains as executive director at the USDA, so I knew they worked.

The restaurants in Albert Lea, Minnesota, ranged from an elegant French-inspired bistro to truck stops,[41] from fast-food outlets to fish-fry roadhouses. I asked these restaurants to make any three of the changes on the original pledge (see the pledge on page 103)—whichever they thought would be easiest and most profitable for them. I thought this would be easy, but small towns are small towns. Even though I grew up only two hundred miles away in Iowa, they were still pretty suspicious—I was now a geeky, East Coast, Ivy League professor, and that's just a little too weird for everyday life.

To overcome their hesitation, I visited their restaurants, helped solve their challenges, drafted up personalized plans for their restaurants, and held small nightly workshops for them. Late in the evening after one workshop, a restaurant owner asked if I had tried some of these slim-by-design strategies on a local joint called the Nasty Habit. I said I hadn't heard of it, and four or five of them chuckled among themselves and left.

Locals call it the Nasty Habit, but its neon sign calls it "The Nasty Habit Saloon." It's a dark bar at the dark end of a short, dark street. Late one night, Dan, Nancy Graham (the editor of *AARP* magazine, who was reporting on the redesign), and I decided to check it out. A couple of days later I was again talking to some of these restaurant owners.

"Been to the Nasty Habit yet?" one of them asked, as the others chuckled.

"Yeah, I was there," I said, "but I wasn't really in the spirit of doing a makeover of the place. It was late, and it was the only place open, and about all I could see was this massive, blinding Jägermeister sign."

"Did you have one? A Jägermeister?" he asked.

"Well, yeah, of course," I said, "It was about eleven o'clock and I hadn't eaten dinner, so yeah, I had a Jägermeister and a bag of Fritos."

Small towns are small towns. Maybe it's my imagination, but things seemed to turn around with these restaurant owners. Picturing me eating Fritos for dinner next to a blinding neon Jägermeister sign might have struck a chord.

Some of these restaurant owners might have been initial doubters, but the "pick-and-choose" approach of doing only what they thought would make them money was a juicy selling point. Again, they weren't doing it for some abstract ideal of having healthier customers; they were doing it to make money. But these restaurants stepped up to the plate—and got the credit and customers they deserved. *AARP* magazine even called it the Minnesota Miracle. But then that could have also been the Jägermeister talking.[42]

The restaurant makeover (as with the household makeovers) in Albert Lea was a community effort by community leaders to try to get everyone—from restaurants to households—to make just a couple of small changes. There's good news and bad news here. The bad news is that community efforts are top-down, and they can require mountains of money, tons of time, and lots of tedious meetings. The good news is that you don't have to wait for a community movement if you focus on your own food radius. All it takes is you.

Is Your Favorite Restaurant Making You Fat?

. . . .

ASKING A RESTAURANT to start with just three small changes is one way my Lab helped restaurants take baby steps to becoming more profitably slim by design. Over the years, our studies have discovered dozens of other changes restaurants can make to profitably help customers eat healthier. They're profitable because some changes guide customers to buy the ten-dollar Shrimp Salad instead of the six-dollar Onion Rings, others are profitable because they bring in new customers looking for a restaurant that meets their healthy eating needs, and still others are profitable because they keep their loyal customers coming in a little more frequently because they know they won't have to blow their diets the way they used to.

> If restaurant owners and managers want our business, they'll listen. If not, we can always find a new favorite.

The one hundred top changes that can help you eat healthier are each awarded one point in the Slim-by-Design Restaurant Scorecard. Although it's designed for restaurants to use to become healthier and more profitable, you can use it, too. It helps you know which of your favorite restaurants will make you slimmer and which will make you fatter. Each of the action items—offering half-size entrée portions, having at least three healthy appetizers, offering bread only if requested, and so on—gets a checkmark and is worth a point. The higher the score, the more your restaurant is nudging you to be slim by design rather than fat by design. But besides helping you evaluate your favorite restaurant, you can also use the scorecard to decide what changes you'd most like *them* to make. If an unchecked action would help you eat better, ask the manager to make the change that will keep you coming back. The worst they can do is say no.

With just a few changes, restaurants can help make you healthier and themselves wealthier. Some changes cost time and money (such as buying smaller plates), but others can be done in a day. And you don't have to wait for the restaurant to change for *you* to change. Sit far away from the buffet, ask for a half-size portion or a to-go box, ask them to bring the water and hold the bread—these are mindlessly easy changes that are healthier than leaving things to fate. Think back to the diner waitress who comes to the table with a full tray of coffees and says, "Who asked for the coffee in a clean cup?" *We* can be the one who asks for our coffee in the clean cup. *We* can either wait and hope for change, or ask for it.

But the best results happen if restaurants lean in and make changes, too. Ask for the manager, and tell them what changes would make it easier for you to eat better. If you don't know what to say, you can copy one of the letters starting on page 255 and either hand it, e-mail it, or text it to them. You could also download a letter from SlimByDesign.org/ Restaurants, change it to suit your personality, and send it.

There's no one-size-fits-all change for every restaurant owner, and it's up to them to decide what will work. Chapter 7 shows what tips and strategies you can use to start your own movement. If restaurant owners and managers want our business, they'll listen. If not, we can always find a new favorite.

Slim-by-Design Restaurant Self-Assessment Scorecard

· · · · · · · · · · · · ·

Is your favorite restaurant making you slimmer or fatter? This scorecard will tell you. The higher the score, the harder they're trying to make you slim. Anything that isn't checked is one more change they can make. Pick out something they could do to make you eat a little better and to be a happier customer. Then ask them to help. These are all proven, research-based (or at least principle-based) changes that help people eat less and help restaurants make money. We update them each year with our newest findings—check them out again next year with the newest scorecard at SlimByDesign.org.

PRE-MEAL AND DÉCOR

☐ The restaurant lighting is neither too bright nor too dark.

☐ At least some tables are in well-lit locations.

☐ The restaurant is neither too loud nor too quiet.

☐ At least some dining locations are quiet.

☐ Customers are seated near the windows first; dark corners last.

☐ There are no more than two TV sets (including in the bar area).

☐ There are *no* TV sets (including in the bar area).

☐ Bread is brought only upon request.

☐ Water is provided to everyone, or each is asked if they want water.

☐ Water glasses hold at least 12 ounces.

☐ There are scales in the bathrooms.

☐ Raw vegetables or a healthy sample (amuse-bouche) are offered before dinner instead of bread.

MENU DESIGN

☐ At least 3 healthy appetizers are offered.

☐ At least 3 healthy entrées are offered.

☐ At least 3 healthy desserts are offered.

☐ At least 3 healthy beverages (other than water) are offered.

☐ At least 3 healthy side dishes are offered.

☐ A nonstarch vegetable or fruit is the default.

☐ A salad is the default.

☐ A soup option is available as a substitute.

☐ A healthy side is included with unhealthy entrées.

☐ Colored or bolded words are used to highlight healthy target foods.

- ☐ Logos or icons are used to draw attention to targeted items (but don't use "healthy" logos, which can signal bad taste and scare diners away).

- ☐ There is a healthy section of the menu labeled "Light and Fresh" or a similar taste-related phrase.

- ☐ Selected entrées are available in half-size portions (but labeled as trim, moderate, light, and so on).

- ☐ Appealing and evocative words are used to describe healthy items to make them sound mouthwatering.

- ☐ At least 5 healthy items are placed in one of the four corners or special sections of the menu.

- ☐ Salads are the default side-dish selection for lunch (as opposed to French fries).

- ☐ The healthier items are listed first in each of the menu sections (such as appetizers, entrées, desserts, and so on).

- ☐ Healthy, high-margin items are in bold or in colored boxes to call them out (when appropriate).

- ☐ Waitstaff is instructed to recommend healthy pairings.

- ☐ Appealing photos of healthy target items are highlighted on the menu or table tents (when appropriate).

- ☐ Calorie levels of selected items are on the menu or available upon request.

- ☐ A separate menu or an app with calorie listings is available.

KIDS' MEALS

- ☐ The kids' menu offers fun, healthy options (such as Broccoli Madness).

- ☐ The healthier items on children's menus are bright and appealing.

- ☐ Coloring books or interactive place mats are related to nutrition.

- ☐ There are friendly cartoons that promote healthy foods on the kids' menus.

- ☐ Fruit or vegetables are the default side item.

- ☐ Nonfat or 1 percent milk is the default beverage.

- ☐ Plates, glasses, and bowls are smaller for children than for adults.

WAITSTAFF

- ☐ Mentions at least one special of the day that is healthy.

- ☐ Mentions that to-go boxes are available *before* people order.

- ☐ Mentions a "we'll pack half" policy before serving.

- ☐ Mentions the healthiest side items first.

- ☐ Mentions healthy substitutes.

- ☐ Offers desserts to go.

- ☐ Mentions to-go containers for desserts.

- ☐ Mentions healthy desserts first.

- ☐ Knows the two or three lighter entrées that get the most compliments.

SPECIALS AND PROMOTIONS

- [ ] At least I appetizer special is healthier.
- [ ] At least I entrée special is healthier.
- [ ] At least I dessert special is healthier.
- [ ] Healthy options are displayed and dramatized as the first thing seen when entering and as point-of-purchase display, visible and accessible (for example, a salad bar by the counter, apples by the register).
- [ ] Half of any *coupons* offered promote healthier items.
- [ ] Half the items promoted on the website are healthier items.
- [ ] A frequent salad-buyer program is available (such as 5 salad punches = free salad).
- [ ] Family combos are served—kid's dish with an adult dish, or family-style dishes that can be split.

- [ ] Discounts or deals are available on healthy family meals.
- [ ] Meal bundles or combos are available that feature healthy combinations and nonfried food, and veggies with an appetizer, salad, and small dessert.
- [ ] The first specials mentioned are ones that offer salad as a course.
- [ ] Delivery or carry-out meals contain a fruit or healthier salad option.
- [ ] Meals are lower in calories than the dine-in equivalent.
- [ ] A gym, fitness, or health center is co-promoted in the restaurant.
- [ ] A discount on healthy meals is offered on a predetermined sponsor night—and the restaurant donates the savings to the targeted charity or cause.

DINNERWARE

- [ ] Plates are less than 10 inches in diameter.
- [ ] Plates are a darker color than white or beige.
- [ ] Bowls hold 16 ounces or less.

- [ ] Bar glasses are tall and narrow.
- [ ] Wineglasses are narrower at the bottom than the top.
- [ ] Plates have a wide, colored rim.

PORTION SIZE, PREPARATION, AND SUBSTITUTION OPTIONS

- [ ] A double portion of vegetables is available for a side-dish substitution.
- [ ] The entrée special is available in a half-size portion.
- [ ] At least 3 entrées are available in half-size portions.

- [ ] The dessert special is also available in a half-size portion.
- [ ] At least 3 desserts are available in half-size portions.
- [ ] Vegetable portions are 20 percent larger than in the past.

- [ ] The size of vegetables on the plate has increased and the size of the starch has decreased.
- [ ] There is the option of having your food cooked with a low-fat spray (like Pam).
- [ ] You have the option of requesting the type of cooking material you would like used (for example, cooking pasta with water instead of oil).
- [ ] There is the option of having either lightly or regularly seasoned versions.
- [ ] Dressings and sauces can be requested on the side (when appropriate).
- [ ] Extra vegetables can be substituted for the starch.
- [ ] Soup can be substituted for the starch.
- [ ] Salad can be substituted for the starch.
- [ ] Fruit or a fruit salad is available instead of traditional desserts.
- [ ] Sugar-free syrup is available.
- [ ] Sugar-free jellies are available.

BAR

- [ ] Default glasses are tall and narrow (rather than short and wide).
- [ ] Wineglasses are narrower at the bottom than at the top.
- [ ] Patrons are asked if they would like a glass of water.
- [ ] Wine flights (small 2-ounce samples) are available.
- [ ] Diet tonic water is available.
- [ ] Nonalcoholic beer is available.
- [ ] There is a wine special.
- [ ] Bar snacks are provided only when requested.
- [ ] Bar snacks are healthier, such as nuts rather than chips and Chex Mix.

SCORING BRACKETS

- [ ] 70–100—Slim-by-Design Restaurant—*Gold*

- [ ] 50–69—Slim-by-Design Restaurant—*Silver*

- [ ] 30–49—Slim-by-Design Restaurant—*Bronze*

Chapter Four

SUPERMARKET
MAKEOVERS

YOU'VE NEVER SEEN A KLEENEX CAM. That's why it works so well—it sees you, but you don't see it. It's helped us learn why the crazy things grocery shoppers do aren't as crazy as they seem.

Back in 2001, I asked some clever engineering students at the University of Illinois at Urbana-Champaign to rig up a small, remotely controlled movie camera into what looked like an ordinary box of Kleenex.[1] Using this invisible camera we could follow shoppers to learn exactly how they shop. We took our Kleenex Cams and stacked them on top of "deserted" shopping carts, hid them on shelves next to Fruity Pebbles cereal, and positioned them in our carts so we could follow shoppers as they moved through the aisles. The Kleenex Cams showed us what catches a person's eye, what they pick up and put back, why they buy things they'll never use,[2] when shopping lists don't matter, and how they shop differently in the "smelly" parts of a grocery store. Again, these studies were all university approved.[3]

But let's back up and set the stage. Our best and worst eating habits start in a grocery store. Food that's bought here gets moved into our homes. Food in our homes gets eaten.[4] If we bought more bags of fruit and fewer boxes of Froot Loops, we would eventually eat more of the first and less of the second. Although bad for the Froot Loops Corporation, it's great for us—and great for grocery stores. The typical grocery store makes more profit by selling you $10 more fruit than $10 more Froot Loops. There's a higher markup on fruit, and—unlike the everlasting box of Froot Loops—fruit spoils, and spoiled fruit spoils profits. You have to sell it while you can.

So if a grocery store makes more by selling healthy foods like fruit, why don't they do a better job of it? They try—but what they really need is a healthy dose of redesign.

Our best and worst eating habits start in a grocery store.

We've been following grocery shoppers since 1995, and some things have changed since then. For one, we no longer have to wrestle with Kleenex Cams. Our newer cameras are so small they're embedded into Aquafina water bottles with false bottoms.[5] The technology is sexier, but the results are *e-x-a-c-t-l-y* the same.[6] Wherever we've done these studies—corner markets in Philadelphia or warehouse stores in France, Brazilian superstores or Taiwanese night markets—people pretty much shop in the same time-stressed, sensory-overwhelmed way. But knowing what can be done to get them to buy a healthier cartful of food is good for shoppers, for grocers, and even for governments.

Wait. Governments?

What jump-started a lot of our recent thinking was a request we received from the Danish government. In April 2011, they sent a six-person delegation out to my Lab. Their mission: to help Danish grocery stores make it easier for shoppers to shop healthier. Our mission, if we chose to accept it: develop a healthy supermarket makeover plan that would be cheap, easy, and profitable for Danish grocery stores to implement. Our makeover plan had to be profitable for stores because that's the only way it would work. But here's the cool clincher: They'd give us an entire island on which to test our plan.

The Desserted Island of Denmark

. . . .

BORNHOLM IS A DANISH ISLAND with forty-two thousand inhabitants that sits in the Baltic Sea, one hundred miles east of Copenhagen.[7] The government of Denmark wanted us to help change the grocery stores on the entire island so they could profitably help these islanders shop healthier. They wanted to turn it from a Dessert Isle into a Salad Aisle.

Anyone who's read or seen H. G. Wells's *The Island of Dr. Moreau* knows that islands are a researcher's dream. You can do all sorts of crazy, mad scientist things on them and not worry about the rest of the world bothering you. You can change the shopping carts or layout of all the stores on the island, and if the sales of Crisco and Pixy Stix drop by 20 percent, you know it's not because people are swimming over to buy them in Lapland.

Until they came to talk with us, the Danish government was considering three types of changes: tax it, take it, or teach it.[8] But taxing food or taking it away creates pushback. Shoppers don't like it, grocers don't like it, and so it can often backfire. For instance, when we did a six-month study on taxing soft drinks in grocery stores in Utica, New York, a medium-size city in the United States, we found that the only people who bought fewer soft drinks were beer-buying households—and they just bought a lot more beer.[9] People had to drink something with their pizza and burgers, and it wasn't going to be tap water or soy milk. They changed from Coke to Coors.

And teaching doesn't work much better.[10] As shoppers, we don't behave the way we're supposed to because (1) we love tasty food, and (2) we don't like to think very hard. Because of our love for both tasty food and for mindless shopping, we don't approach grocery shopping like a nutrition assignment. We just do it and move on to the next fifty-seven items on our to-do list. With this mindless mindset, when we're shopping

at 5:45 on a Friday evening, we're not about to be fazed by there being a few more calories in pizza crust than in pita bread.

Maybe the best way we can change grocery shopping habits is to make them more mindlessly healthy—make it more convenient, attractive, and normal to pick up and buy a healthier food.[11] So here's what we did in Bornholm. Based on our "Kleenex Cam" recordings,[12] notes, stopwatch times, and data from thousands of similar shoppers, we focused on design changes in five areas of the store: carts, layouts, aisles, signs, and checkout lines. We had two criteria: (1) all the changes had to make the store more money in a month than they cost to implement, and (2) they all had to help make people slim by design. Let's start with a shopping cart.

Half-Cart Solutions

. . . .

HERE'S A TEN-WORD DESCRIPTION of how most people shop for groceries: *They throw things in their cart and they check out.* What's the right amount of fruits and vegetables to put in a cart? We don't really know because we don't really care. Yet imagine what would happen if every time we put something in our cart we had to ask ourselves whether it was healthy or not. It would be irritating—for sure—but after a while we'd think twice about what we casually threw in. Just stopping and thinking for a split second would be enough to snap us out of our mindlessly habitual zombie shopping trance.[13,14]

Back to the cart. When most of us shop, fruits and vegetables take up only 24 percent of our cart.[15] But suppose your grocery store sectioned a cart in half by taping a piece of yellow duct tape across the middle interior. And suppose they put a sign in the front of the cart that recommended that you put all the fruits and vegetables in the front and all the other foods in the back. This dividing line in the cart doesn't moralize or lecture. It just encourages shoppers to ask themselves whether the food in their hand goes in the front or back of the cart. There's nothing to resist or rage against—they're simply sorting their food . . . if they want to.

When you use duct tape at home, you become MacGyver. When it's used to divide your grocery cart, you become healthier.[16]

We made a few dozen of these divided carts to test at supermarkets in Williamsburg, Virginia, and Toronto, Canada.[17] When people finished shopping and returned their souped-up, tricked-out carts, we gave them a gift card to a local coffee shop if they would answer some questions and give us their shopping receipt.

Shoppers with these divided carts spent twice as much on fruits and vegetables. They also spent more at the store—about 25 percent more. Not only did this fruit and vegetable divider make them think twice about what they bought; it also made them believe that buying more fruits and vegetables was normal. Who knows how much healthy stuff your

→

neighbor buys? *It must be about half,* people think as they throw in some pears and three more red peppers.

TEST THE HALF-CART WATERS

Will a divided, half-cart approach be profitable? It can if it can sell more perishable produce—like fruits and vegetables. All that's needed is a visual divider in a few of your carts and a sign in the front that says, "Put your fruits and vegetables in the front of your cart."

If your grocery store doesn't want to bust out the duct tape, they can use printable mats for the bottom of the cart that make the same suggestion—fruits and vegetables in the front half and everything else in back (download at SlimByDesign.org).

THE MIRACLE OF DUCT TAPE:
A Half-Cart Solution

Do it yourself. Divide your cart with your coat, your purse, or your briefcase. Or bring your own duct tape.

HINTS FOR HALF-CART SHOPPING

Your local supermarket might not have divided carts yet, and you probably don't travel with your own. Here's what you can do . . .

✳ **Decide what you want to buy more of.** For instance, a shopper with children might want to be nudged to buy more fruits and vegetables, and a shopper with high blood pressure might want to buy more low-sodium foods. A dieter might want to be nudged to buy more low-carb foods, and a diabetic might want to buy more foods with a low glycemic index.

✳ **Physically divide your cart by putting something across the middle.** This could be a a purse, backpack, scarf, briefcase, coat, or a sleeping child you want to keep an eye on. You can then claim the front half of your cart for whatever you want to purchase more of. If that target space isn't full, you'll naturally tend to buy more to balance things out.

You're 11 percent more likely to take the first vegetable you see than the third.

When opening your cupboard, you're three times as likely to take the first cereal you see as you are the fifth.

Healthy First and Green Line Guides

. . . .

WHEN YOU WALK UP TO A BUFFET, you're 11 percent more likely to take the first vegetable you see than the third.[18] When opening your cupboard, you're three times as likely to take the first cereal you see as you are the fifth.[19] The same is true in grocery stores. When you start shopping, you can't wait to start piling things in your cart. But after it starts filling up, you become more selective. If stores could get you to walk by more of the healthy—and profitable—foods first, they might be able to get you to fill up the cart on the good stuff, and squeeze out any room for the Ben & Jerry's variety pack.

We spend less than six minutes in the fruit and vegetable section.

Most grocery stores in the United States place the fruit and vegetable section on the far right of the store. It's the first thing we see and wander over to. The bad news is that many of us spend less than six minutes there.[20] We pick up some apples and lettuce and then wander over to the next aisle. But if stores could get us to linger there a little longer, we'd buy a little bit more.

The secret might lie in the fact that we're wanderers—we're not always very deliberate. What if they put a dashed green line that zigzagged through the produce section, and what if they they put floor decals in front of food shelves that offer healthy meal ideas? Just like that dashed yellow line on the highway that keeps you mindlessly on the road and the billboards that keep you mindlessly amused, maybe putting a dashed green line and floor decals would also have us wandering the produce section a bit longer.

To test this, we proposed Operation: Green Highway on our mad scientist island in Denmark. Supermarkets could put a two-inch-wide dashed green line through the produce section—around the apples and oranges, over to the lettuce, past the onions and herbs, and back around to the berries and kumquats. They could even include some kid-friendly visuals or floor graphics. If a shopper followed this green highway, he or she might be tempted to buy more fruits and vegetables.

To test this, we had people initially trace their way through grocery stores that either did or did not have Health Highway lines. Did people stay on the line? Of course not, but they would have spent an average equivalent of three more minutes in the produce section. At about $1/minute, this would mean they could spend as much as $3 more on fruits and vegetables than they otherwise would have.[21,22]

But what about the other store aisles? Let's say that you have two favorite grocery stores: Tops and Hannaford. At Tops, the aisle after the produce section—let's call it Aisle 2—is the potato chips, cookies, and soft drinks aisle. At Hannaford, the potato chips, cookies, and soft drinks are in Aisle 15—the second-to-last aisle in the store. If you're on a diet, which store should you choose?

We followed 259 shoppers in Washington, D.C., grocery stores to see if a person shops differently depending on which aisle they're in.[23] We discovered that most people with shopping carts behave the same way: They walk through the produce section, then turn and go down Aisle 2 (which leads back toward the front of the store). It almost doesn't matter what's in the aisle—health food, dog food, or mops. At this point, shopping's still a fun adventure. But after Aisle 2, shoppers get mission-oriented and start skipping aisles as they look for only what they think they need. So, Aisle 2 gets the most love and attention from the most shoppers.

So, what's in Aisle 2 at your favorite grocery store? It's often soft drinks, chips, or cookies as in the Tops store. To make a grocery store more slim by design, managers could easily load up this aisle with whatever healthier food is most profitable for them. This might be store-brand canned vegetables, whole-grain foods, or high-margin lower-calorie foods. First in sight is first in cart.

GUIDING ANGLES, AISLES, AND LINES

One way to help shoppers fill up their carts with healthy foods is to make sure those are the aisles they visit first and stay in longest. People cherry-pick their favorite fruits and vegetables and quickly move to the center of the store, but you can keep them in the produce area longer by angling displays so they guide shoppers through the store—think of the 30- and 45-degree angles you used to see in those old-school pinball games. Also, green lines—Green Highways— seem to nudge most of us, at least occasionally, to turn in a direction we otherwise wouldn't have turned in.

Since shoppers are more likely to buy healthy foods when their carts are empty, stores should load up Aisles 1, 2, and 3 with whatever's healthiest and most profitable.

WANDER THE HEALTHY AISLES FIRST

Following the green line works well if there *Is* a green line. But if there isn't one, you can always make your own.

* **Make a point of wheeling through as many of the produce aisles as possible.** Even if it's fast and furious, simply seeing more fruits and vegetables while your cart is empty makes them more tempting.

* **Hit the other healthier aisles—like those with canned and frozen fruits and vegetables—before you head for the Crunch & Munch section.**

Wide Aisles and High Products[24]

. . . .

T HE MORE TIME YOU SPEND in a store, the more you buy. Similarly, the more time you spend in an *aisle*, the more you buy.[25] In order for us to buy a healthy food, we need to (1) see it and (2) have the time to pick it off the shelf.

But not all shelves are the same. Food placed at eye level is easier to spot and buy. For instance, kids' foods are placed at their eye level, so that they can irritate us into buying them ("I want it! I want it! I want it!").

This works for Count Chocula and our kids, but would it for kale chips and us? We returned to our "I-Spy" habits and observed 422 people purchasing thousands of products in the Washington, D.C., area. First we estimated the height of each shopper using a series of pre-marked shelves they walked by (picture those height-marker decals on the doors of convenience stores).[26] We then measured the height of each product they looked at. Based on where they looked, we could figure out what percent of the foods they bought were at eye level.[27]

If you're shopping in a narrow aisle, 61 percent of everything you'll buy is within one foot of your eye level—either one foot above or one foot below.[28] This is useful to know if you're a grocery-store owner who wants to sell us healthier foods. Smart store managers can put these profitable healthy foods at eyeball level. If the product is one that's typically bought by males, it can be placed even five inches higher, since the average male is that much taller than the average female.

One well-known finding among people watchers is that nothing causes a person to scoot out of an aisle faster than when someone accidentally brushes against their behind. In his book *Why We Buy*, Paco Underhill refers to this as the "butt brush."[29] Think of the last time this happened to you—five seconds later you had pretty much teleported yourself to another spot in the store. Since brushing against people probably happens much more in narrow grocery store aisles than wide ones, people might spend less time and buy fewer items there. Many grocery store aisles range from six to eight feet wide. In the Washington, D.C., grocery stores mentioned earlier, we measured the width of all the aisles and timed how long the average shopper spent in them. Indeed, the wider the aisle, the more they bought. It didn't matter what was there—canned Brussels sprouts, twenty-pound bags of cat food, dishwashing liquid—the more time they spent in the aisles, the more items they bought.[30]

Your grocer could put more healthy, high-margin food in wider aisles and less healthy food in narrower ones. Identifying or creating healthy food aisles that are wider would be one solution. Another solution—make sure the healthier foods are at eye level.[31]

EYE-LEVEL SHOPPING BULL'S-EYE

* 60 percent of what shoppers buy is within 12 inches of their eye height.

12 INCHES

SLIM-BY-DESIGN GROCERY SHOPPING

MEAT

FISH

LESS-HEALTHY FOODS

DIVIDED CART

CANDY-FREE CHECKOUT LANE

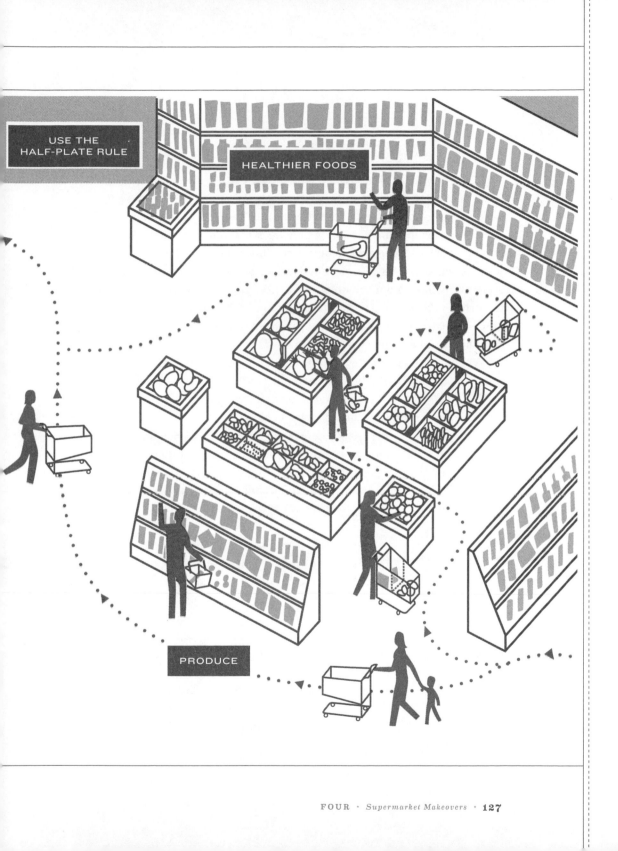

USE THE HALF-PLATE RULE

HEALTHIER FOODS

PRODUCE

Groceries and Gum

· · · · · · · · · · · · ·

MOST OF US KNOW that it's a bad personal policy to go shopping on an empty stomach. We think it's because we buy more food when we're hungry—but we don't. In our studies of starving shoppers, they buy the exact same amount of food as stuffed shoppers. They don't buy more, but they buy worse.[32] When we're hungry, we buy foods that are convenient enough to eat right away and will stop our cravings.[33] We don't go for broccoli and tilapia; we go for carbs in a box or bag. We go for one of the "Four C's": crackers, chips, cereal, or candy. We want packages we can open and eat with our right hand while we drive home with our left.

When it comes to cravings, our imagination is the problem. The cravings hit us super-hard when we're hungry because our hunger leads us to imagine what a food would feel like in our mouth if we were eating it. If your Girl Scout neighbor asked you to buy Girl Scout cookies, you'd buy one or two boxes. But if she were to instead ask you to describe what it's like to eat your favorite Girl Scout cookie, you would start imagining the texture, taste, and chewing sensation, and wind up ordering every life-giving box of Samoas she could carry. (Keep this in mind the next time your daughter wants to win the gold medal in cookie sales.)

> **Starving shoppers don't buy more, but they buy worse.**

Most food cravings—including those that occur when we shop—are largely mental. As with the Girl Scout cookies, they seem to be caused when we imagine the sensory details of eating a food we love—we start imagining the texture, taste, and chewing sensation. But if we could interrupt our imagination, it might be easier to walk on by.

One way we can interrupt these cravings is by simply chewing gum. Chewing gum short-circuits our cravings. It makes it too hard to imagine the sensory details of crunchy chips or creamy ice cream. My colleague

Most food cravings—including those that occur when we shop— are largely mental.

Chewing gum short-circuits our cravings. It makes it too hard to imagine the sensory details of crunchy chips or creamy ice cream.

Aner Tal and I discovered this when we gave gum to shoppers at the start of their shopping trip. When we reconnected with them at the end of their trip, they rated themselves as less hungry and less tempted by food—and in another study we found they also bought 7 percent less junk food than those who weren't chewing gum.[34] If you shop for groceries just before dinner, make sure the first thing you buy is gum—and our early findings show that sugarless bubble gum or mint-flavor might work best.

Lights, Stars, Numerology!

· · · · · · · · · · · · ·

SUPERMARKETS COULD MAKE US slim by design if they only told us what foods were the healthiest, right? Not really. Supermarkets and food companies have endlessly experimented with little stickers and icons that they hoped would help us to eat better. They'd say things like "Good for You," "Better for You," "Don't Have a Stroke," and so on. The United Kingdom even uses a traffic light—each food has a green (go), yellow (slow), or red (no) icon on it.

Do you remember these icons? Of course you don't. Most of us ignored them because they were too confusing, self-serving, or unconvincing. Oh, and even when people *did* pay attention to them, they often backfired. Some people believed the green and yellow foods were a lot healthier than they actually were and gorged out on them. Then food companies got tricky and took advantage of this by producing foods that barely met the minimum requirements for a green or yellow icon. Getting the healthy icon then became more important than actually coming up with a healthier product.

Most labeling systems seem to backfire because we ignore them or we game them.

One exception seems to be the Guiding Stars program. Back in 2005, an innovative, brilliant, high-end grocery store in New England—Hannaford Brothers—boldly stuck its neck out by putting bright yellow stars next to the healthiest foods on their shelves—super-healthy foods even got three stars. So, did people buy better food? Well, according to one study, they didn't initially seem to buy any more of the starred food. But they initially did buy less of the unstarred foods. They didn't buy more tofu, though this led them to think twice about the Doritos.[35]

But here's why most of these labeling systems seem to backfire: (1) We don't believe them, or (2) we game them. We know an apple gets a green light, an A-plus, or a 100 percent rating. And we know a Twinkie gets a red light, a D-minus, and a 2 percent rating. It's the stuff in the middle that turns us into nonbelievers. If a food gets a rating that doesn't line up with our intuition, it totally loses credibility. When the magic formula is too complicated or too secret, we dismiss these ratings as ridiculous and ignore them.

But worse than our ignoring them is when we game the system. We're experts at getting around something we don't want to do or believe. If one type of cracker is rated five points higher than another type of cracker, we choose it instead of an orange.[36] Then we end up rewarding ourselves by eating more of them.[37]

Using the Half-Plate Rule

· · · · · · · · · · · ·

EACH SPRING, WEGMANS, a popular grocery chain in the Northeast, does a big health promotion push called "Eat well. Live well." From time to time, we've helped develop new ideas for their stores. In 2009, they visited our Lab to see if we could help develop a program that would encourage their own employees to eat more fruit and vegetables. They were thinking of providing some sort of education or promotion program. Instead, we were thinking of giving them a simple, visual rule of thumb. What we told Wegmans worked great for them, and it can work great for you in the store and even when you get home.

In the good old days when we were kids, eating was easy. Your grandmother piled dishes of food on the table, you'd take a little of each, and— ta-da—that was nutrition! Today, the 273-page United States Dietary Guidelines tips the scale at almost three pounds. But there's an easier way for most people. When I was the executive director in charge of the

HALF-PLATE HEALTHY

✳ Follow the Half-Plate Rule

Dietary Guidelines and people asked me how they should eat, although not the official USDA-sanctioned answer, my shortcut answer was to simply encourage them to use my Lab's Half-Plate Rule.[38] Half of their plate had to be filled with fruit, vegetables, or salad, and the other half could be anything they wanted. It could be lamb, a blueberry muffin, a handful of cheese . . . anything. They could also take as many plates of food as they wanted. It's just that every time they went back for seconds or thirds, half their plate still had to be filled with fruit, vegetables, or salad.

Could a person load up half of their plate with Slim Jims and pork bellies? Sure, but they don't. Giving people freedom—a license to eat with only one simple guideline—seems to keep them in check. There's nothing to rebel against, resist, or work around. As a result, they don't even try. They also don't seem to overeat.[39] They may want more pasta and meatballs or another piece of pizza, but if they also have to balance this with a half plate of fruit, vegetables, or salad, many people decide they don't want it bad enough.[40]

> Using our Half-Plate Rule works amazingly well at home, but only if you also use it when you shop.

Using our Half-Plate Rule works amazingly well at home, but only if you also use it when you shop.[41] To use it, you need to have enough fruits, vegetables, and salad around in the first place. If as you shop you think about you and your family being half-plate healthy, you'll buy healthier and you'll also spend more. The first is good for you; the second is good for the store.[42]

Wegmans jumped on our idea. Within two years, it was rolled out to all their stores, and you can now get Half-Plate place mats, magnets, posters. (They renamed it the trademarkable Half-Plate Healthy.) You can see it in action in any of their stores, and the only place it works better than in a grocery store is in your home.

Supermarkets don't have to talk about servings of fruits and vegetables to get the point across. All they need to do is to reinforce the idea that half a plate could hold whatever fruit, vegetables, or salad a person wanted. They can do this on signs, specials, recipes, or in-store promotions—and subtly encourage people to fill their cart with slightly more fruits and vegetables than they typically do.[43]

THE HALF-PLATE RULE AT HOME

"Fill half your plate with fruit, vegetables, or salad, and fill the other half with whatever you want." We've given this simple rule to tens of thousands of people because it works. People often report back to us that they eat fewer calories and they eat a lot more "balanced" diet than they did before. They also say they eat until they're full but not stuffed.[44]

Nobody likes to be told they can't do something. With the Half-Plate Rule there's nothing you can't eat. You just have to eat an equal amount of fruit, vegetables, or salad. At some point, getting that fourth piece of pizza just isn't worth having to eat another half plate of salad. But, most important, you're the one who made that decision.

After forty-five minutes of seeing food, guess what we want?

It's not a snack-size can of lima beans.

The Three Checkouts

. . . .

G ROCERY SHOPPING ISN'T EXACTLY a trip to Fantasy Island, but the checkout line can be an exception. It's filled with guilty-pleasure rewards at the end of the ho-hum errand of shopping. There are bizarre new gum flavors like mango chutney mint, meal-size candy bars, and irresistibly tacky tabloids with headlines like "Cellulite of the Stars." These aisles are entertaining, but if you're with kids, you're doomed. Kids in grocery checkout lines are like kids in toy stores. They grab, bug, beg, pout, and scream. And if we cave in to buying pink marshmallow puff candy shaped like Hello Kitty, we also cave in to buying something with lots of chocolate—for us. There's usually nothing in the aisle that we actually need, but after forty-five minutes of seeing food, guess what we want? It's not a snack-size can of lima beans. So we buy the Heath bar we swore we'd never buy again, finish it by the time we leave the parking lot, and shake our head on the way home . . . just as we did last week.

Mothers shopping with children wanted more food-free cashier lines. Fathers shopping with children didn't exist.

One supermarket solution is to set up at least one checkout line so it's totally candy-free.[45] Just as large supermarkets have different lines for "10 items or less" or "cash only," some lines could have candy, others could have healthy snacks, and some could totally be free of food. The stores could still sell magazines and other crazy things—like eyeglass repair kits and superglue—but one or two aisles wouldn't have any food at all.

To see what tired shoppers in grocery store parking lots thought of this idea, we asked, "If your favorite supermarket had ten checkout lines, how many should be candy lines, healthy lines, or food-free lines?" Here's what we found:

* **Men shopping alone wanted all candy lines.**
* **Women shopping alone wanted more of the healthy food lines.**
* **Mothers shopping with children wanted more food-free lines.**
* **Fathers shopping with children didn't exist.**

An easier first step would be to help convince your local supermarket manager to start by simply adding a healthy line—perhaps selling fresh fruit, granola bars, and so on. It might be the one longer line shoppers wouldn't mind waiting in. When the manager sees those lines getting longer, he'll quickly make the bigger steps. If he doesn't, there are other places you can shop.

How Your Grocer Can Help You . . .

WHAT IF ALL THE AISLES WERE CANDY AISLES?

If you want that food-free checkout experience but all the aisles are loaded up with Skittles and SweeTarts, here's what you do:

1. **Tell the manager that you want to avoid impulse-buying candy while you're in the checkout line.** Ask him or her which of the open checkouts would be least tempting for a dieter or a shopper with children.

2. **While the manager is thinking, ask if they would consider putting in a candy-free aisle.** You can mention that other stores (such as Hy-Vee, Wegmans, and HEB) have at least one candy-free checkout aisle, and you've heard they're popular with both dieters and parents shopping with kids. If one of those stores you mention happens to be a nearby competitor, it might not be too many more trips before you have your candy-free aisle. That will be a good time to say "thank you."[46]

WHICH OF THESE WOULD YOU LIKE TO SEE AT YOUR GROCERY STORE?

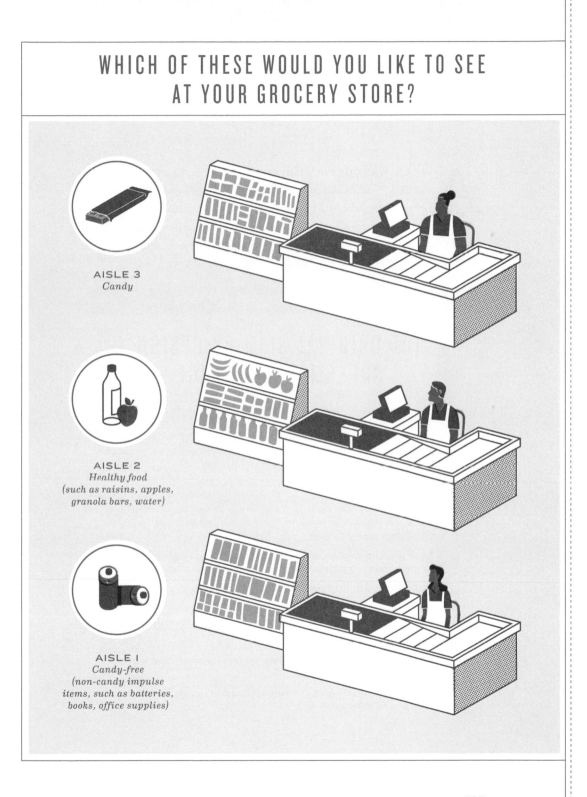

AISLE 3
Candy

AISLE 2
*Healthy food
(such as raisins, apples,
granola bars, water)*

AISLE 1
*Candy-free
(non-candy impulse
items, such as batteries,
books, office supplies)*

Back to Bornholm

· · · · · · · · · · ·

A FTER WATCHING, CODING, AND ANALYZING SHOPPERS
on the Danish island of Bornholm, we generated a small list
of changes—baby steps—these grocers could make to profitably help shoppers become slim by design. We were scheduled to present
these ideas to all nine grocery store managers at the Bornholm Island
Hall after they got off work a couple of days later at seven thirty.

How Your Grocer Can Help You . . .

THE ORIGINAL SLIM-BY-DESIGN SUPERMARKET PLEDGE

When the Danish government said they'd be willing to try almost anything we recommended, here's what we first suggested, and here's
what paved the way for the full 100-point Supermarket Scorecard
at the end of this chapter. We asked them to try the three changes
that would be easiest and most profitable for them.

1. **Provide divided half carts that encourage people to put their
fruits and vegetables in front.** The dividers can be made from
paint, duct tape, mats, etc.

2. **Angle produce displays and use floor decals (such as green lines)
to guide and keep people shopping longer in the produce section.**

3. **Place the healthiest foods in Aisles 1 through 3.**

4. **Make the healthiest aisles the widest and put healthy
products at eye level or on end-of-aisle displays (endcaps).**

5. **Use the "Half-Plate Rule" promotion.**

6. **On end-of-aisle displays, combine the regular promotion with
a healthy food complement.**

7. **Have two or three types of checkout lines: standard, food-
free, and healthy foods only.**

Unfortunately, two days later at seven thirty my five-person delegation of researchers almost equaled the six grocery managers who actually showed up. Strike one. After starting the presentation with the only Danish word I knew—"Velkommen" (welcome)—I told them the night was all about "new ways you can sell more of your healthier foods and make more money." We then went on to give a punchy presentation on seven easy changes that we knew would work well. We had photos, video clips of shoppers, cool study results, numbers, and funny stories. It was great . . . except that nobody laughed, asked a question, moved, or even seemed to blink. It was like Q&A hour in a wax museum. Strike two.

Because there were no signs of life, I idled down my enthusiasm and wrapped up our presentation a half hour early so my Danish colleagues could try to salvage the evening. Once they started talking in Danish, some sort of switch flipped in the managers. They started talking louder, started to un-Danishly interrupt each other, and then started arguing. Thinking things were getting out of control, I suggested we call it a night before they started to break furniture. My Danish colleagues waved me off and the melee continued. An hour later, things had slowed down, and the managers thanked

We generated a small list of changes these grocers could make to profitably help shoppers become slim by design.

us and cleared out. Before we started cleaning up, I asked my Danish colleagues why they were so irate. They said, "Oh, no. They like the changes and they'll make most of them. The rest of the time they were talking about the *other* changes they wanted to make, like having more produce tastings, more pre-prepared salads, and bundling meat and vegetable specials together."

After all our supermarket makeovers, does every Bornholmian look like a sleek, slim, Danish version of *Mad Men*? As I mentioned earlier, it's still too soon to say (we're posting updates at www.SlimByDesign .org/Bornholm), but with every trip I make, all signs point in the right direction.

One way to tell how well a new idea is working is by how many people want to jump in and be a part of it. The more changes we made to the grocery stores in Bornholm, the more other groups got involved. Before long, a public health advertising campaign was being rolled out, petitions were launched, and local ordinances were proposed. After the kitchen smoke clears, it will be difficult to see which of these moved the dial the most—but the people on the island are buying in to becoming slim by design.

There's a humbling expression: "Success has a thousand fathers, but failure has only one." If there are dramatic changes in the foods these Danes buy, the public health people will say it was because of their ads, the activists will say it was because of their tireless petition drives, and charismatic politicians will say it was because of their bold regulations. But if nothing happens and the whole plan ends up being a failure, which father will take the blame? It won't be the public health adviser or the politician. They'll abandon the program in a heartbeat. Unsuccessful public health campaigns cost lots of money. Unsuccessful ordinances can cost political careers.

> We projected each change would turn a profit within a month if not immediately.

Yet these supermarket makeovers were cheap and easy to make. Many were done over a weekend, and we projected each of them would turn a profit within a month if not immediately. Still, if even one works, stores will be further ahead than before. On my most recent trip, they asked me to help expand it to the mainland, so some hidden sales numbers must be looking pretty good. It's the beauty of being slim by design.

How Your Grocery Store Can Make You Slim

. . . .

THERE ARE DOZENS OF WAYS your favorite grocery store could profitably help you shop a little healthier. In April 2014, I shared the Bornholm story with some of the innovative American grocery stores that sponsored some of the studies you've read about throughout this chapter. They all had clever ideas they were trying out in their stores to help their customers shop a little healthier, but they were all doing something different—and often repeating each other's mistakes. If we could pool together all of my Lab's slim-by-design research findings with some of the ideas they were successfully experimenting with, we could make a supermarket scorecard that could help guide all of them to make profitable healthy changes.

Grocery chains are competitive—and not just for shoppers. Even though a grocery chain in Texas doesn't compete for the same shoppers as a grocery chain in Chicago, they all want to win awards for Most Popular, Prettiest, Smartest, or Most Likely to Succeed at their annual Grocery Store-a-Palooza Award Conference. Because having a scorecard means there might be yet another new award they could compete on, most

> **This supermarket scorecard tells shoppers what they should look for or ask their local grocery manager to do.**

were eager to help develop one. But more important than enabling grocery chains to compete with each other, this supermarket scorecard will transparently show them exactly *how* to compete. Also, it will tell shoppers what they should look for or ask their local grocery store manager to do. If all these changes help grocery stores make a little more money, grocers will want to make the changes. If all these changes help shoppers shop a little healthier, shoppers will want to hassle their favorite grocer until he or she makes changes.

←

Slim-by-Design Grocery Store
Self-Assessment Scorecard

. . . .

Okay, so your favorite grocery store has great prices, selection, and convenience, but it might still be making you fat and happy instead of happy and slim. This scorecard tells you what your store is doing to help you eat better. Our Lab has been working with top grocery chains around the nation to help them make you slim by design. You can use a scorecard like this to compare your favorite grocery stores, but it will also tell you what you can ask them to do to make you and your family more slim—and more loyal to their store. Some items on this scorecard might initially seem to have nothing to do with food—like having restrooms and a drinking fountain in the front of the store—but together they will make you less anxious or more comfortable, and others will slow you down and relax you. In the end, even some of these nonfood changes can lead you away from impulsively buying Chunky Monkey ice cream and more toward intelligently buying bananas. This is a start—every year this scorecard is updated with the best practices and the best research that helps us shop better (and helps stores make money). The newest can be found at SlimByDesign.org.

ENTRANCE

☐ Assign designated parking spots (similar to handicapped spots) for pregnant women and mothers with infants.

☐ Offer preprinted shopping lists of basic staples near the entrance.

☐ Provide information sheets near the entrance on healthy ways to shop.

☐ Offer healthier foods near the entrance to prime healthy shopping.

☐ Two sizes of shopping carts are available.

☐ Handbaskets are available.

☐ Divided shopping carts with a "place fruits and vegetables here" section are provided.

☐ The first area entered by most shoppers is the produce section.

☐ Free healthy samples are near the entrance.

☐ There's a small "grab and go" area in the front of the store with a small selection of milk and bread for the in-and-out, or "fill-in" shopper.

SERVICES AND SIGNAGE

☐ Signs promote seasonal combinations of fruits and vegetables.

☐ Signs provide "Did you know?" facts about the health benefits of specific foods.

- ☐ Educational posters are located around the stores to educate people about healthy eating (for example, the Half-Plate Rule).
- ☐ Local and seasonal foods are clearly promoted.
- ☐ There is a special section for organic fruits and/or vegetables.
- ☐ The organic section is boldly and clearly labeled.
- ☐ At least one produce-tasting station is near the entrance.
- ☐ A wide range of precut fruits and vegetables are available.
- ☐ There are separate in-aisle promotions for canned fruits.
- ☐ There are separate in-aisle promotions for canned vegetables.
- ☐ There are separate in-aisle promotions for frozen vegetables.
- ☐ There are specific perimeter promotions for lean meat.
- ☐ There are specific perimeter promotions for lean dairy.
- ☐ There are specific promotions for whole-grain products, such as bread and pasta.
- ☐ Calorie information is available in the meat section.
- ☐ Healthy food apps such as Fooducate and QR codes are promoted.
- ☐ A kiosk with tear-off recipes is available in the produce section.
- ☐ Combo packs are available that co-promote healthy foods (such as tomatoes and mozzarella).
- ☐ A guidance system such as Guiding Stars or a stoplight approach is used.
- ☐ A dietitian is available and visible in the store a couple of days each week.
- ☐ Unit pricing ($/oz) is available where relevant.

LAYOUT AND ATMOSPHERE

- ☐ Relaxing music is played in the produce section.
- ☐ Show price per unit along with price per weight for healthy food, for ease of calculation.
- ☐ Floor decals are used for way-finding to healthy sections.
- ☐ Lighting varies throughout the store, but is always brightest on the healthier foods.
- ☐ Healthy tear-off recipe cards are provided near the fruits and vegetables.
- ☐ Recipe ingredients for the recipe cards are located next to the cards.

AISLES AND SHELVES

- ☐ Some fruits are bundled into family-size packs.
- ☐ Some vegetables are bundled into family-size packs.
- ☐ A complementary fresh produce display is available in the meat section (such as one containing broccoli, peas, cauliflower, and peppers).
- ☐ A complementary fresh produce display is available in the seafood section (such as lemons, tomatoes, beans, and asparagus).

- [ ] A complementary fresh produce display is available in the frozen food section.

- [ ] Displays of single fruits (such as oranges, apples, pears, nectarines, and apricots) are next to desserts.

- [ ] Ready-to-eat fruits and vegetables are available in variety packs.

- [ ] Ingredients are organized by preparation type (stir-fry versus salad)—for example, put mushrooms, eggplants, and peppers in a "stir-fry" section.

- [ ] Expiration dates are visible (at front of package or on signs).

- [ ] Aisles with healthy foods are the widest.

- [ ] Less healthy foods are inconveniently placed very low or very high on the shelves.

- [ ] Healthier foods are conveniently placed at eye level.

- [ ] Aisles with healthy food are brighter than aisles with unhealthy food.

- [ ] Hard-to-decide-upon foods ("long-buy" items), such as soups, dressings, and baby foods are located in less busy aisles so people are relaxed enough to comparison shop.

PREPARED FOOD AREA

- [ ] Fruit is available in all food-service areas.

- [ ] Vegetables are available in all food-service areas.

- [ ] A mix of whole fruit options is displayed in an attractive bowl or basket.

- [ ] The "pick me up" or prepared food section has healthy default foods.

- [ ] A daily fruit or vegetable option is bundled into all grab-and-go meals.

- [ ] A salad bar is available.

- [ ] All beverage coolers have both water and white milk available.

- [ ] Alternative healthy entrée options (salad bar, yogurt parfaits, and the like) are highlighted on posters or signs within all dining areas.

- [ ] The healthy daily targeted entrée is placed as the first one seen in all dining areas.

- [ ] The healthy daily targeted entrées have creative or descriptive names.

- [ ] Posters displaying healthy foods or a guidance system (such as the Half-Plate Rule) are visible in the dining area.

- [ ] The cafeteria tracks the popularity and frequency of healthy-option orders to see what promotions work most effectively.

- [ ] All promotional signs and posters are rotated, updated, or changed at least monthly.

- [ ] Half portions are available for all entrées.

- [ ] Half portions are available for all desserts.

- [ ] Takeout boxes are available for leftovers not eaten in the cafeteria.

SHOPPER COMFORT AND SERVICE

- ☐ Restrooms are easily accessible in the front of the store.
- ☐ A drinking fountain is located in the front of the store.
- ☐ There is an area for shoppers to sit and relax.
- ☐ There is an area for shoppers to eat.
- ☐ There is a supervised playroom for children.
- ☐ Health and nutrition games dominate the playroom.
- ☐ A local fitness club is co-promoted.
- ☐ A small discount to a local fitness club is given to loyalty club shoppers.
- ☐ There is a drive-through where you can pick up your groceries, if you call ahead.
- ☐ Home delivery is available (for an extra charge).

ENGAGEMENT: EMPLOYEES AND SOCIAL MEDIA

- ☐ The produce-department manager and staff are specifically trained to suggest healthy answers to shopper questions.
- ☐ The meat-department manager and staff are trained to suggest healthy answers to shopper questions.
- ☐ The dairy-department manager and staff are trained to suggest healthy answers to shopper questions.
- ☐ The bakery-department manager and staff are trained to suggest healthy answers to shopper questions.
- ☐ All employees are trained to suggest healthy complementary products when asked about a particular item.
- ☐ There are plentiful staff in the meat and produce sections who are trained to suggest healthy upsells or substitutes.
- ☐ Store or chain has an engaging website that has a health-related blog featuring local or seasonal products.
- ☐ The website has shopper loyalty specials.
- ☐ Tips, features, or videos involving better shopping and better living (such as "Shopping with Kids") are available.

CHECKOUT

- ☐ Loyalty programs specifically reward fruit and vegetable consumption.
- ☐ Receipts are itemized in categories or otherwise coded to indicate how healthy you're shopping.
- ☐ The back of receipts feature coupons for healthy foods.
- ☐ There is at least one food-free checkout aisle.

- [ ] A discount is offered if a certain percentage of purchases are fruits and vegetables.

- [ ] Individual containers of precut fresh fruit are available next to at least one cashier.

- [ ] Healthy snack options are offered next to the cashiers.

- [ ] Receipt uses loyalty card information to show how much was spent on fruits and vegetables *compared* to past trips.

- [ ] Receipt provides an indication of what percentage of purchases were fruits and vegetables, low-fat meat, and low-fat dairy.

- [ ] A default shopping "starter" list is made available to each shopper at the front of the store with a number of the major staples preprinted on it.

- [ ] The same healthy shopping-tips brochure available at the beginning of the shopping trip is also available at the checkout register.

- [ ] "Don't Forget" signs are placed at the register to remind customers about certain healthy foods.

- [ ] A "fruits and vegetables only" self-checkout station is provided for quick purchases of produce.

SCORING BRACKETS

- [ ] **70–100—Slim-by-Design Grocery Store—***Gold*

- [ ] **50–69—Slim-by-Design Grocery Store—***Silver*

- [ ] **30–49—Slim-by-Design Grocery Store—***Bronze*

Chapter Five

OFFICE SPACE
AND
WORKPLACE

L OTS OF US SQUIRREL AWAY FOOD in our desks. If there's ever an emergency need to hibernate in our office for the winter, we want to be prepared.

Just for fun, we conducted a snack-food desk audit of 122 office workers to see how well stocked the average desk is. People would pull out granola bars, gum, a half-full container of Tic Tacs, ketchup packets, and errant M&Ms mingled in with the paper clips. The average office worker had 476 calories' worth of food *in* their desk within arm's reach.[1] One person had more than 3,000 calories—bags of Cheetos, Oh Henry! candy bars, wasabi packets, an opened granola bar in a zip-top bag, sugar-free Certs, and five cans of pop-top tuna fish. Three thousand calories and sugar-free Certs?[2] Perhaps for the tuna fish. Another desk had packets of six-year-old Northwest Airlines peanuts, two warm beers, and a piece of birthday cake. Nothing gets you over a late-morning carbo craving like stale birthday cake and a warm beer.

People who had candy in or on their desk reported weighing 15.4 pounds more than those who didn't.

Move Away from the Desk

· · · · · · · · · · · ·

BUT, HOW HARMFUL CAN EATING a few calories at your desk really be? One thing we know is that people who had candy in or on their desk reported weighing 15.4 pounds more than those who didn't. A forty-five-minute lunchtime workout can be undone in three minutes by an Oh Henry! bar and vintage collectible airline peanuts.

Yet while most people snack at their desk, there are others who eat their whole lunch there. We usually tell ourselves that we work through our lunches because we're overwhelmed with work, we need to catch up on e-mail, or because we want that gold star for being seen as a dedicated worker bee.

Really—do we honestly think we're decreasing our work stress or improving company efficiency by working during lunch? Probably not. Really—do we honestly think we're impressing our boss or our coworkers with our worker-bee "I'm skipping lunch" efforts? Probably not. Many of us are just too lazy to ask someone else to go to lunch. So what we do is grind away and feel a tad either martyr-like or resentful. We don't realize it, but we don't leave our desk because we don't think there's anything better to do.

> ## Not that long ago, companies used to pay workers to smoke.

A nice solution would be if our company offered us something more interesting to do during lunch than update our Facebook page and watch YouTube videos of skateboarding dogs. Companies could offer a brown-bag presentation series, a Pilates class, a made-over break room that doesn't look like an air-raid shelter from the Cold War, or even a lunchroom that offers foods in colors other than white and brown. These would be the first steps in a new kind of corporate wellness program: one that gets us to move a little more and eat a little better without really trying. One that's focused on the majority of us, who are already in pretty decent shape.

DESKTOP DIETS

OUT OF SIGHT, OFF OF THIGHS

✳ Our hidden-camera candy dish study showed that moving a candy dish only 6 feet away from a desk led workers to eat 125 fewer calories—half of what they would have otherwise eaten. The most dangerous candy dish is one that is close, clear, and chocolaty. How many extra calories does the candy dish cost you each year?

4 CANDIES PER DAY
6 feet away

✳ If your candy dish is going to be close and clear, don't fill it with chocolate. Replacing chocolate with something you're not crazy about—perhaps hard candy—helps you feel like a "giving" person without giving too much to your inner Orca.

9 CANDIES PER DAY
clear candy dish

7 CANDIES PER DAY
candy dish

3 CANDIES PER DAY
candy dish
[in desk drawer]

Rethinking Corporate Wellness

. . . .

NOT THAT LONG AGO, companies used to pay workers to smoke. Everyone was given fifteen-minute breaks in the morning and again in the afternoon to have their coffee and cigarette.[3] Your company basically paid you 6.25 percent of your salary to go out and smoke a filterless Camel if you wanted.

Today, company wellness is a big business—your company wants you to be healthy and productive, and the right wellness program can cut health-care costs and absenteeism by 25 to 30 percent.[4] But many wellness plans are like New Year's resolutions: They're enthusiastic and bold, but they never really seem to deliver. These plans almost always have four parts: a health education program, a company fitness component, revamped cafeteria food, and incentives.[5] Unfortunately, there just aren't as many amazing success stories as there are disappointing fizzles.[6]

Part of the reason these plans don't work is that they look suspiciously like tenth grade. Health education is like health class, company fitness is like gym, new cafeteria foods are like boring school lunches, and incentives are like grades. These programs might perk up the former valedictorian, but they don't do too much for those of us who daydreamed our way through biology class.

WELLNESS PROGRAMS AT WORK	TENTH GRADE AT HIGH SCHOOL
Health education programs	Health class
Company fitness	Gym
New cafeteria foods	Boring school lunches
Incentives	Grades

The companies we work with say that about 60 percent of their employees are healthy, another 30 percent are fairly healthy, but it's the last 10 percent that cost all the money—through absenteeism, presenteeism (being at work without really working), and higher insurance costs.[7] Ten percent might not sound like a big deal, but there's a migration: Healthy people

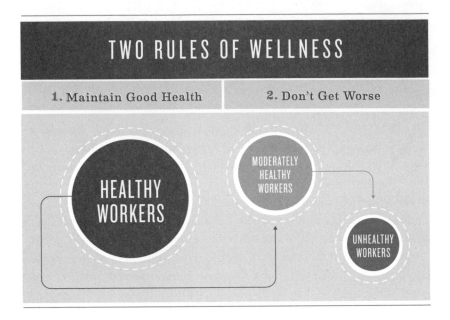

TWO RULES OF WELLNESS

1. Maintain Good Health

2. Don't Get Worse

HEALTHY WORKERS

MODERATELY HEALTHY WORKERS

UNHEALTHY WORKERS

gradually become fairly healthy, fairly healthy people gradually become unhealthy, and unhealthy people gradually leave the company. This seldom works in reverse.

Instead of focusing so much attention on the unhealthy people, it would be more forward-thinking to focus on keeping the healthy people healthy. You'll never have everyone in perfect health, but as Dee Edington, a noted University of Michigan kinesiologist, argues (1) keep the healthy healthy and (2) don't let anyone get worse.

But if corporate wellness programs are too much like going to school— health class, gym, lunchtime, and grades—they won't work very well, because most people don't want to be in school for the rest of their lives. Instead, the best wellness programs are ones people don't even know they're doing. Better to have a small program that helps most people than a glitzy one that helps only the Body for Life fanatics who were pumping it up anyway. Let's start off easy with break room and cafeteria makeovers, then move to fitness and weight loss programs. After that we'll get really radical.

Break-Room Makeovers

· · · · · · · · · · · ·

WHEN PEOPLE EAT AT THEIR DESKS, it looks like they're shackled to the oars of a galley ship. One advantage to break rooms or lunchrooms is they do just that: They give you a chance to take a break and enjoy your lunch—if they're done right.

Unfortunately, most break rooms don't have that cozy Martha Stewart feel with the yellow, soft-focus lighting. Instead, they look like the interrogation rooms you see in police movies—gray and barren with a beat-up metal table, glaring lights, and a Nick Nolte–looking guy who's growling that "you can either do it the easy way or the hard way." Of course this is an exaggeration. Unlike the interrogation room, your company break room has a Pepsi machine.

What You Can Do . . .

PACK A LUNCH OR PACK ON POUNDS?

What happens when you make a lunch from home? You generally make it on a full stomach. Either you make it after dinner the night before or you make it the next morning after breakfast. And you usually put at least a little thought into it—maybe you include a sandwich, chips, and fruit or yogurt.

But what happens when you buy your lunch at work? You're generally starving and will inevitably end up with something that's a lot less healthy and has a lot more calories.[8]

We do a lot of lunchtime intercepts, and when it comes to healthier eaters, the adult brown-baggers are usually the gold medalists. Even with the cookie and chips they often bring, they eat better and eat less.

BREAK-ROOM MAKEOVER

TV

HEALTH-RELATED MAGAZINES

BALANCED-LIVING BULLETIN BOARD

BANANA BOWL

COMFY COUCH

DOOR

PLANT

MICROWAVE

SINK

"USE THE HALF-PLATE RULE" POSTER

PANTRY

REFRIGERATOR

* What's it take to pull people away from the desk or from driving to the local fast-food drive-thru? Not much more than new paint, a flat-screen TV, some updated bulletin boards, and a refrigerator and microwave from this century.

The Dutch have a word for warm, cozy places: *gezellig*. The Russians have a word for cold, noncozy places: *gulags*. Most break rooms are less Dutch gezellig-y than they are Russian gulag-y. It's no wonder they're often empty and that people would rather sit at their desk updating their Facebook page than chatting with Mr. Nolte about the kids.

As part of a slim-by-design redesign, we worked with a midsize welding company that made a lot of large, iron, green-painted farm machinery. Their workers didn't work at desks; they did real work—they moved, welded, lifted, and painted stuff. They went home with backaches, not headaches. But many also went home overweight.

The company had three shifts and no cafeteria. What they had was more along the lines of a break room–lunchroom with a rusty refrigerator from an *Animal House* basement, a microwave with brown stains from burrito explosions, a couple of work safety signs that I imagine said things like 4 DAYS WITHOUT AN ACCIDENT, and a beat-up table with dented folding chairs that looked like they had been used in fights. Outside the room, there were four or five vending machines, including one of those 1950s-looking "Vend-o-Mat" machines where you spin the shelves around, plug in some money, and open a little door to take out your hermetically sealed egg salad sandwich with no expiration date.

Within one month, the break room was the hip place to be.

This wasn't a place where people ate lunch at their desks—there were no desks. But the lunchroom was simply too depressing to entice any workers to eat there. Instead they would drive down to the local fast-food restaurants or grab things out of the Vend-o-Mat and head out of the building to wolf it down and smoke. Who could blame them? No one wants to eat in an interrogation room.

We first focused on vending machines. We recommended that they move the Pepsi and candy machines to faraway corners on the factory floor. This way we weren't taking away any indulgences; we were just making people work a little harder for them—they would have to walk another hundred yards for their Pepsi. We also asked Mr. Vend-o-Mat if he could add a few healthier foods—turkey and cheese, mixed nuts, fruit—and put these healthy foods in the eye-level slots. Since he made higher margins from these foods anyway, he did it immediately.

The second change was a break-room makeover. Management brought in bright paint, nice lights, new appliances, tables, chairs, and a big flat-screen TV. They also put in some snappy posters,[9] an announcement bulletin board, and pamphlet holders with company newsletters and wellness brochures. Oh . . . and free fruit. Every day the company brought in bunches of bananas and put them in colorful bowls in the middle of each table. Inexpensive bananas that were great for the company and great for the workers.

Within one month, the break room was the hip place to be. The TV set helped a lot, but so did the paint, posters, and free bananas. Workers spent less time driving to the drive-thru and picked up more health newsletters and brochures. The Mr. Pepsi distributor might have made a bit less coin because some people thought the new vending machine location was a little far to walk to, but he still got to keep a profitable account.

Doing a break-room makeover isn't just for the blue-collar factory floor, however. It's also for office buildings. Making the break room a place to take a healthier break isn't that expensive. And if workers don't want to eat here, we might still get a shot at them in the cafeteria. Just be careful not to overdo it.

Trimming the Google-Plex of Food

. . . .

SOME COMPANIES USE FOOD as a competitive weapon. Take Google. Since opening its binary doors in 1999, it's had the policy of offering bountiful food to all its lucky surfers. When Google decided to make food free, they did it big. First, they installed dozens of free snack rooms they call "micro-kitchens," which are rumored to be within a few dozen steps of most workers. These have all the snacks, cold drinks, coffee, and fruit you can imagine, and you can take it when you want it—before work, during work, and after work (but don't take it home).

Second, they have amazing cafés that serve almost anything you would imagine (sushi, BBQ, curry, burgers, chili, Jell-O, dessert bars) and some foods you wouldn't imagine (kale and pumpkin pizza). Grab a tray and pile it high. Go back for seconds. And again, it's all free, all the time. Management isn't shy about giving the peak performance reasons why:[10]

* **It's a recruiting and retention plus.**
* **It's a culture-creating way to keep supercharged software engineers on-site rather than driving around for an hour looking for the nearest Carl's Jr. or In-N-Out Burger with the shortest line.**
* **It encourages *good* "accidental conversations" with other Googlers (which is what is rumored to have invented Gmail).**
* **It reduces *bad* "accidental conversations"—those involving trade secrets—with pesky neighborhood competitors.**

Unfortunately, there's also the urban legend of the "Google fifteen." It's the fifteen pounds new Googlers—they're called Nooglers—are (wrongly) rumored to gain shortly after joining the tribe. This isn't unique to Google. There are also rumors of the M&M/Mars fifteen and the Nabisco fifteen that happen at other headquarters. In fact, this probably happens at any company where there's lots of tasty food within a few dozen feet of your desk. Like elsewhere in Silicon Valley, food has been a part of the culture from day one, and it's used to help fuel innovation and collaboration. The key is to make sure this is all aligned toward supporting employee well-being. To this end, they did some experiments based on our research.

The first steps to make the micro-kitchens more slim by design were pretty straightforward. Based on the results of our other cafeteria studies and our smarter lunchroom findings (described in the next chapter), the goal was to proactively nudge Googlers to eat a little healthier—to pick up an apple more often than a cookie.[11] We knew the three things that determine what a person eats in a free food environment: what's most convenient, attractive, and normal.[12] So here's what was done:

* **All the healthy snacks—like fruits, baked things, and granola-y things—were put on the top shelves and the less healthy snacks—like Kit Kats and Peanut M&Ms—were reduced to the smaller "Fun Size" and put on the "I-can-barely-see-it-from-here" bottom row.**
* **All the bottled waters and calorie-free flavored waters were put at eye level in the coolers and soft drinks at the bottom—water intake increased by 47 percent, and drink calories dropped by 7 percent.**
* **Fruit bowls are now about the first and last thing you see.**
* **Candy is in opaque bins and not out in plain sight—9 percent less candy was taken in just the first week.[13]**

The challenge with the Google fifteen was to also figure out what to do about the hugely tempting cafés. The first changes were ones we had widely proved to work in other companies—putting the salad at the front of the line and the dessert at the back, offering small plates to diners so they would take less,[14] and downscaling the size of desserts to just three bites.[15] The next changes tackled unseen Googler concerns. In working with Google's Global Food Team,[16] our one-on-one interviews with Googlers pointed to four food concerns: Too much tasty food led them to overeat, to waste food, to feel guilty about its unsustainability, and to gain a Google Gut faster than they could say "The square root of 170 is 13.038."

One approach would be to reduce the variety of food. Sure, if the cafés only served okra and bamboo shoots, people wouldn't overeat . . . at Google. They'd go off-campus to overeat—bad news. A better solution would be to make it less easy—but not impossible—to pile a four-foot stack of food on a tray. Here's what we proposed. First, break down the huge cafeterias into four smaller cafés based on the style of food—Asian, Vegetarian, Italian, and an American Grill. You could still pile on a four-foot stack of food; but you'd have to go in and out of four different doors—probably too much of a hassle for most people most of the time. Analogous to the 100-calorie pack, each time they left one of the four cafés, they'd have to ask themselves if they really wanted to visit the next one. They couldn't blame Google for restricting their choices; they'd just think, *Uhh . . . this is enough.*

And here's what you'd look like 1,500 of these lunches from now.

As for the Googler concerns about waste and sustainability, Google had a stoplight rating system for certain foods. Green was healthy, red was less healthy, and yellow was in between.[17] Some paid attention, but people seemed to ignore it, so here's what we suggested. Since every Googler has an ID card, they could have a debit account linked to it. For every green-dotted food a Googler chooses, it's free. For every yellow-dotted food they choose, their account gets charged 50 cents and Google matches that 50 cents and donates it to charity—such as the probably-not-real "Hungry Kids Without Wi-Fi Foundation." For every red-dotted food they choose, this goes up to a matched $1. Googlers could still have anything they wanted, but they'd have to pause for a second to think about how badly they wanted it. This would be bold but controversial—and it hasn't yet happened.

To tackle the "I gained weight before I knew it" problem, the proposed solution was this. Have you ever seen those phone apps that let you upload a photo of yourself, and it shows you what you would look like if you were twenty or forty pounds skinnier or fatter? This would either motivate or scare the bejesus out of you. Maybe there would be a way to have a "food scanner" set up that could scan someone's tray, and a camera and screen in front of them would take their photo and instantly display what

By combining this with similar efforts we are making in other companies, and even at the Pentagon, the ultimate goal is to develop different templates that could be rolled out at your company.

It's showing how a few small changes in the workplace can change a waistline and might change a culture.

they would look like in five years if they ate this much food every day for lunch. Here's what you look like now, and here's what you'd look like 1,500 of these lunches from now. Not a reality yet, but this would be a big motivator if it ever got scaled up.[18] Again, the bigger goal here isn't just to tinker around in Mountain View and San Francisco but to create a new template for corporate and large-scale feeding that could be rolled out to the sixty thousand meals that Google serves each day around the world. By combining this with similar efforts we are making in other companies, and even at the Pentagon, the ultimate goal is to develop different templates that could be rolled out at your company. It's showing how a few small changes in the workplace can change a waistline and might change a culture. At the end of the day, that would be a lot of pounds. Now let's return to the less-virtual world of cafeteria cuisine and how it can better fit within your wellness program.

←

Cafeteria Cuisine

. . . .

O NE OF THE FIRST THINGS companies try when attempt-
ing a cafeteria makeover is to add a couple of healthier foods—
they throw a new salad on the menu and switch from fried potato
chips to baked ones. They then proudly announce this as evidence of their
commitment to employee wellness. That's like you and me microwaving a
bowl of lima beans, putting them in front of our kids, and announcing it
as our commitment to fight childhood obesity. The cafeteria can offer it,
but we don't have to buy it . . . it's not nutrition until it's eaten.

Few places other than Google offer tastier food at better prices than
the United States Department of Agriculture's cafeteria in Washington,
D.C. The USDA helps set the Dietary Guidelines, and they have nutrition

---

What Your Workplace Cafeteria Can Do to Help You . . .

KEEP YOUR TRAY

Some college cafeterias have been going trayless, thinking it might
help students eat a little less, waste a little less—and cost a little
less. Unfortunately, going trayless also gets them to eat a lot less
salad—and to eat a lot less nutritiously.

If a college student usually goes through a cafeteria line and gets a
salad, an entrée, and a dessert, what do you think they'll leave behind
when they can't carry everything back to their table with just their
two hands? Sixty-two percent left the salad behind but clung to
their dessert.[19] And almost all of the savings in "waste" from going
trayless—which is measured by weight—is from wasted beverages,
not food. Take the tray, or you'll leave the salad.

Instead of dumping trays, downsize them. They might still reduce
waste but not at the expense of salad and nutrition.

---

nailed down: The cafeteria offers great whole-grain bread, huge salad bars, sushi, kimchee, low-fat desserts, and organic, gluten-free, vegetarian specials; they serve 1,400 hungry lunch-goers every day. Yet what would make these lunch specials even more special would be if people actually bought them. Like all cafeterias, the USDA's privately run cafeteria needs to make money, so in addition to the specials, they have tasty bacon cheeseburgers and gourmet pizza to round out your order of curly fries, and they have triple-chunky, full-fat blue cheese dressing and bacon strips to help your side salad provide 100 percent of your daily calorie needs.

But it doesn't matter how healthy the food is; as you well know by now, it's not nutrition until it's eaten. They asked us to help them figure out how they could help guide people to the good stuff.

Here's what happens most weekdays at 12:03: Manager Mike, stressed out and distracted by an urgent deadline, is hurrying down to grab a quick lunch. He charges past the organic, gluten-free, vegetarian special to pick up his favorite default lunch: two slices of the Meat Blaster pizza. As he hurtles past the salad bar, he suddenly sees that the pizza line is too long and course-corrects to the bacon cheeseburger line. He grabs what looks like the biggest burger and curly fries and makes a beeline to the soft drinks and then to the cashier who's closest to the cooler. By the time he arrives with his Coke, there are three people ahead of him. He impatiently shifts from leg to leg, looks around, and grabs a chocolate chunk cookie from the display next to him.

Take the tray, or you'll leave the salad.

Given Mike's mindset, it's going to be hard to convince him to ditch his bacon cheeseburger for a whole-grain turkey sandwich and a banana. That's what most "healthy" cafeterias do wrong. They think they can move Mike to the turkey sandwich by giving him calorie information that compares bananas and bacon. The smarter approach would be to get him to take the turkey sandwich without thinking about it. A senior USDA political adviser asked us to help.

Four of us from the Lab photographed food layouts and signage, mapped out traffic flow paths, and recorded the relevant decision times

QUICK USDA CAFETERIA CHECKLIST

1. Put a menu board of the healthy specials at the cafeteria entrance (but don't call them "healthy") to prime Manager Mike to think about something other than a mindless bacon cheeseburger on his way in.

2. Set up a grab-and-go aisle next to one of the registers with only healthier foods.

3. Place fruit and no-calorie drinks at eye level in bottlenecked areas.

4. Feature the healthier soups in a soup island in the middle of the room; put the pizza station and grill in the very back.

5. Always put the healthy foods in the first place people look, whether it's side dishes or salad toppings.

6. Offer half-size portions, even half a baked potato instead of a whole.

and wait times for the lunch crowd. When we send teams to do corporate cafeteria makeovers, we usually first recommend only the top six changes we think will be the easiest, quickest, and most effective to make. After they make these, we suggest others. The first six we gave the USDA are listed in the box above.[20]

The day after changes such as these are made, it's amusing to watch what people do. People like Manager Mike plow into the cafeteria, jolt to a stop, hold their breath for a second, and look like they've accidentally wandered into an alternate *Twilight Zone* or *Matrix* reality. They then start to tentatively creep around like it's their first day at work. For the first two weeks they usually buy the exact foods they used to buy. It's almost as if being in a strange environment makes them want their favorite foods so they can feel more in control. But after a couple of weeks, people become more familiar with the layout and start acting mindlessly. This time, however, the healthy foods have an edge: Mike's been pre-alerted and primed to them by the "Today's Specials" sign at the entrance, they're the first foods he sees, and they're always the most convenient. Before the cafeteria knows it, they're out of turkey sandwiches because Mike just took the last one.

FRUIT SETS THE TONE

What's the first thing you should put on your tray? If you want to eat healthier, pick up a piece of fruit. When we gave people a free piece of fruit at the beginning of their lunch-line journey, they continued to make healthier lunch choices than those who received nothing. Worst of all, when we instead gave them cookies first, they didn't compensate by getting a salad. They pretty much threw in the towel and headed for the pepperoni-and-sausage pizza.[21]

When we put cut bacon and cheesy eggs as the first thing on a breakfast buffet for corporate wellness trainers, even *they* were three times as likely to take them than if we put them last.[22] When we put cut fruit first, they were twice as likely to take it.

Make fruit the first thing you plop on your tray. It seems to trigger a chain reaction of healthier choices.

CASH FOR COOKIES

A funny thing seems to happen when people pay with cash—they think twice. In our cafeteria studies, people who paid with cash bought more milk, fewer soft drinks, and fewer desserts compared to those who used debit or credit cards.[23]

When people pay with cash:

* They eat slightly better.
* They spend about as much.
* The cafeteria doesn't have to pay the 3 to 5 percent credit-card transaction fee.

So you might be doing both the employees and yourself a favor by offering employees a small discount—maybe 2 or 3 percent—if they use cash instead of credit or debit. They still have the option to do whatever they want, but they're being nudged to be slim by design.

CAFETERIA REDESIGN, D.C.-STYLE

RECOMMENDED USDA CAFETERIA UPDATE

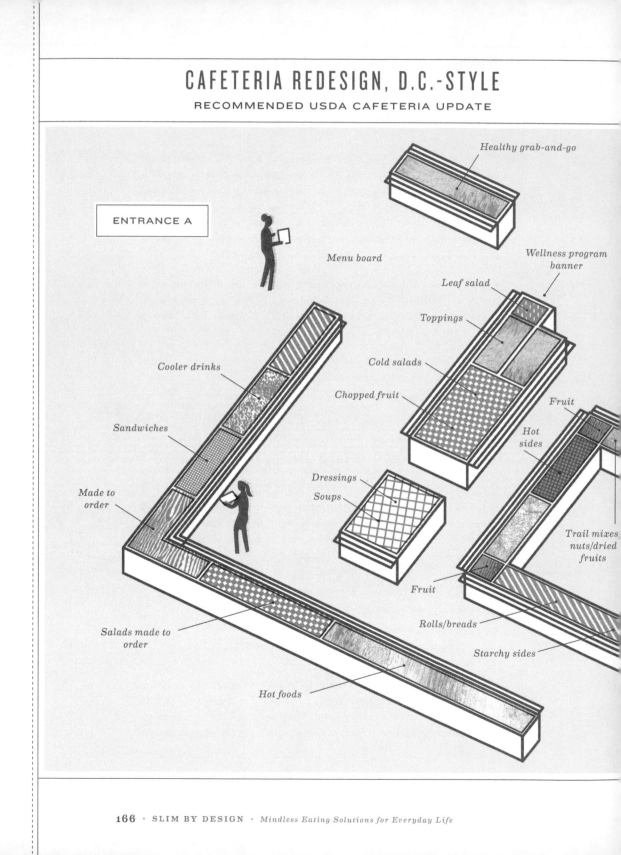

Healthy grab-and-go

ENTRANCE A

Menu board

Wellness program banner

Leaf salad

Toppings

Cold salads

Chopped fruit

Fruit

Cooler drinks

Hot sides

Sandwiches

Dressings

Soups

Made to order

Trail mixes nuts/dried fruits

Fruit

Salads made to order

Rolls/breads

Starchy sides

Hot foods

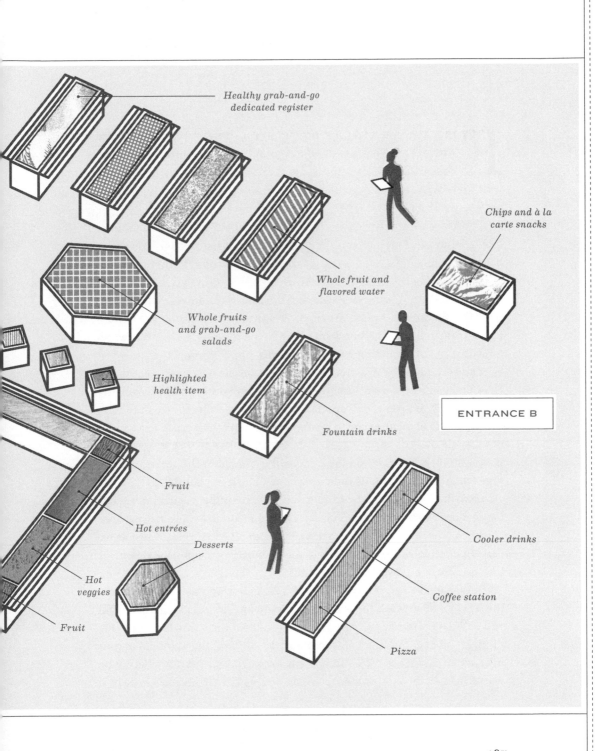

Healthy grab-and-go
dedicated register

Chips and à la
carte snacks

Whole fruit and
flavored water

Whole fruits
and grab-and-go
salads

Highlighted
health item

ENTRANCE B

Fountain drinks

Fruit

Hot entrées

Desserts

Cooler drinks

Hot
veggies

Coffee station

Fruit

Pizza

The Company Health Club

. . . .

FITNESS TRAINERS HAVE A SAYING: "Health clubs are where New Year's resolutions go to die." Companies have high hopes for any new fitness center, workout room, or walking trail they build. But like our New Year's resolutions, they're high hopes with low results.

There are two real problems with health clubs. First, most of us don't like to exercise. Sure, we can get hooked on what it gives us—an energy boost, an endorphin high, or six-pack abs—but we don't inherently like to exercise. It's a means to an end. Even the inspiringly wacky Jack LaLanne—the guy who once swam up the Mississippi River with twelve rowboats chained behind him—said, "I hate to exercise. It's very hard to leave a warm bed and a hot woman for a cold gym." He said that when he was ninety-four (and when his wife was eighty-three).[24]

The second problem is that we use exercise as an excuse to eat more. Ever start a new exercise program and gain weight instead of losing it? Join the club. It's often the case that a new gym membership comes with three pounds of fat attached to it. We work out and then crack open a pint of Häagen-Dazs or eat a bigger dinner because we feel that we earned it. Remember, one hour on the treadmill is erased in the two minutes it takes to get back to inhale the vintage food stash at your desk.

If we don't really like exercising and unknowingly use it as an excuse to eat more, we have three options: (1) We can exercise more and eat less, (2) we can avoid it, or (3) we can do it, but not call it "exercise." Just as we can trick ourselves into mindlessly eating better, we can trick ourselves into mindlessly exercising.

Suppose one day you go on a walk and call it an exercise walk, and the next day you walk the exact same route at the exact same pace, but you call it a scenic walk. Do you think you'll eat the same lunch?

Each spring, my Lab holds Consumer Camp on the Cornell campus in Ithaca, New York. It's a free event for anyone from anywhere who wants to hear about our Lab's news-you-can-use discoveries over the past year.[25] We also use this as an opportunity to involve our guests in different studies. If you'd attended a recent Consumer Camp, Friday would have started with presentations and demonstrations. Then at eleven thirty, just before lunch, one of my researchers would have announced that everyone was going to go on a thirty-minute walk, so we'd have time (wink-wink) to set up for lunch. Half the group would go with Laura Smith and half with Carolina Werle.

Once your group got out of the building, Laura told you that you'd be taking a thirty-minute *scenic* walk that wound around beautiful Beebe Lake (a little over a mile). As you walked briskly, Laura would point out scenic landmarks along with deer, ducks, Bigfoot, and other wildlife. When you returned thirty minutes later, the lunch buffet was ready and you served yourself salad, pasta, and pudding. You finished lunch just in time for the afternoon sessions to start.

What you didn't know was that your best friend—the one who had instead been assigned to Carolina's walking group—had a very different interpretation of what was happening. Although she walked the exact same route at the exact same brisk pace around the exact same lake, Carolina had said they were on an *exercise* walk. Instead of pointing out landmarks and wildlife, she kept pointing out how far they had gone: "Here's the quarter-mile marker," "We're almost halfway there," and so on.

You were told your walk was a scenic walk; your friend was told it was an exercise walk. How do you think you and your friend ate differently? We know because we'd hidden scales under your lunch plates. We knew how much you served yourself, how much you left behind, and therefore how much you ate.

Even though you walked the same distance and route at the same pace, you ate differently. Exercisers rewarded their hard work by taking less salad and by taking more chocolate pudding. After the smoke cleared and they had returned to the afternoon sessions, the people who believed they had exercised had served themselves and eaten 35 percent more chocolate pudding.[26] When we believe we have sacrificed, we compensate by rewarding ourselves later. Oh, yeah, and another group took more than twice as many M&Ms for an afternoon break when we repeated this on a different day.[27]

Suppose your company built a walking trail around its building (or in it). Walking trails are nice, but don't pin high hopes on their wellness

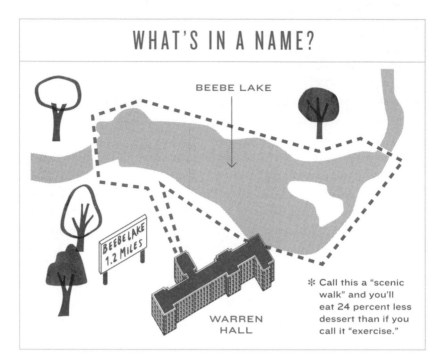

WHAT'S IN A NAME?

BEEBE LAKE

BEEBE LAKE 1.2 MILES

WARREN HALL

✳ Call this a "scenic walk" and you'll eat 24 percent less dessert than if you call it "exercise."

results. Lunchtime is short, and walking trails aren't that alluring—particularly during the winter. In one Snowbelt company we worked with, they even built a walking trail through the factory—using a nice bright yellow line and distance markers—but this didn't move the obesity dial. It got a few more office workers walking, but nothing more. When it comes to working out at work, most of us have (1) no time, or (2) no interest.

Exercise is tough to inspire. Sure, there are a few employees who'll do Pilates and use the Buns-of-Steel-Meister machine in the gym, but they probably would have done it in a different gym anyway. Sure, there will be the Marine Corps Marathon runners and the shirtless Matterhorn climber, but it probably wasn't the company's "Exercise for the Health of It!" flyer that did it. These people were already working out.

But a company can make some changes that make it *necessary* for everyone to move a little more. Changes that make them walk a little farther to the restrooms, or farther from the parking lot. One company moved its walkways from the parking lots so they wrapped three times as far around the scenic back of the building instead of directly into the cold front foyer. Even though some people initially complained when it rained, walking three times as far for a more beautiful view seemed worth it for most. When Steve Jobs was at Pixar, he proposed having only one central bathroom: great for exercise and collaboration, less great for emergencies.[28]

YOU'RE TONING, NOT BURNING

Starting a new weight training or Pilates program? There's nothing like lifting weights and working muscles to make some people want to lift a little extra food.

One way to head this off is to think of strength training as something you do to tone yourself, not to burn calories. Of the fifty gym-goers we worked with, forty-one reported to us that this type of reframing or refocusing made them less likely to reward themselves with extra calories.[29] No proof other than what they told us, but it seems to be a promising mindset to jump-start gym-goers in the right direction.

AVOIDING THE PRESIDENTIAL CHEESEBURGER

When you exercise, you don't always eat less, but you might eat better. If you don't let yourself get carried away, exercise can prime the idea of health, and it might get you to pack your lunch rather than pull into a drive-thru.

I once asked President George Bush (the younger one) how he knew whether he was eating healthy. He said, "I don't know much about nutrition, but my wife jokes that I exercise eight days a week. There's something about running five miles before lunch that makes a cheeseburger and fries seem a lot less tempting." Yet another reason to lace up the Nikes and just do it.

Coaching and Weight-Loss Programs

· · · · · · · · · · · · ·

WEIGHT LOSS IS OFTEN a key corporate wellness goal. But there's no one-size-fits-all solution. People try to do it in all sorts of different ways. As mentioned in chapter 1, some people count calories, some use support groups, some use a fad diet, some skip dessert. People often ask, "What's your best tip?" But the changes or "tips" my family has made to be slim by design might be impractical or ineffective for the family next door or the single woman across the street.

I was recently asked by a large employee union to help develop a program that would help their employees lose weight. Instead of a one-size-fits-all plan, it became a choose-whatever-you-want plan—a wellness buffet. They reimbursed each employee's insurance premium for the year as long as the employee participated in a few activities for just the first six months of the year. After that they could choose to do what they wanted.

As long as your activities added up to 100 points or more, the company paid your premium.

They were then given a list of forty to fifty activities, like go to a gym three times per week, join a worksite TOPS (Take Off Pounds Sensibly) program, take a ballroom dancing class, join a paintball league, sign up for nutrition seminars, take a meditation class, join an online weight-loss program, and so on.[30] Different activities were worth different points, and as long as your activities added up to 100 points or more, the company paid your premium.

Why should your company care whether you bowl, meditate, or rumba? Two reasons: It makes *you* more productive, and it saves *them* money. They save money if you don't need to take as many sick days as you took last year and if you don't have to go to the doctor as often. And

$\longrightarrow$

Why should your company care whether you bowl, meditate, or rumba?

Two reasons: It makes *you* more productive, and it saves *them* money . . . in sick days.

they save a *whole* lot of money if you don't need dozens of prescriptions, undergo heart bypass surgery, or have your stomach stapled.

The program was successful because people could get healthier doing what they wanted to do. Some picked activities that would make them slim by design, and others picked activities that gave them more balance in their lives. But it doesn't really matter—we usually find that both plans intersect. People who lost weight seemed to get more balance in their lives, and vice versa—people who seemed to get more balance in their lives lost weight.[31]

Yet even with these plans, it takes a motivated person to join up and do something they don't have to really do. It relies on you wanting to take the extra effort and time. Sometimes that's asking a lot, especially since it wasn't what you agreed to when you signed on for the job. But what if it *had* been . . .

DO ONLINE WEIGHT-LOSS PROGRAMS WORK?

Online weight-loss programs are sometimes an option with company wellness programs, but do they work? Each one has devotees who say, "That program worked great for me," but those devotees might not be like us. Unfortunately, most of these programs don't give any evidence of how much the *average* person—the person like us—might lose.

One exception was the National Mindless Eating Challenge.[32] My friend Collin Payne and I developed this free-to-the-public online pilot program over a year of nights and weekends by taking 168 research-based tips from the book *Mindless Eating* and giving people three different monthly behavior tips that we had determined were most statistically matched to their lifestyle. People who complied with the tips at least twenty-five days a month lost about 1.9 pounds each month.[33] The results were okay, but no one won the *Biggest Loser* competition. Still, if people are only sixteen pounds from happiness, they'll reach "happy" in less than a year.

When the only published results from an online weight-loss program are only *okay,* what about those programs that don't publish any results? The right online diet program might move your weight in the right direction, but until you have more evidence, it might not be your miracle cure. There's a promising new generation of these programs (see SlimByDesignMethod.com), but always look for the real proof and not just "testimonials."

Would You Sign a Health Conduct Code?

. . . .

IMAGINE IF PART OF YOUR JOB DESCRIPTION was to be healthy. Most companies have a company manual and a conduct code you sign when you start. It tells you generally how to handle company property ("no stealing"), how to deal with coworkers ("no touching"), how to dress ("no Speedos"). We read it, and if we want the job badly enough, we drink the company Kool-Aid, sign it, and we save our Speedos and black mesh T-shirt for the weekend.

What if a new Silicon Valley company—let's call it LeederLab—also had a behavior code related to health? They didn't grade you on your cholesterol or your blood pressure, but you had to agree to exercise at least two days a week, and you had to have an annual physical. Also, if your BMI exceeded 30 at your annual physical, you had to agree to join a weight-loss group—like a company-sponsored TOPS or Weight Watchers program. In all of these cases, the company would pay for the program and give you company time to attend it. Maybe new employees could choose to opt out and not sign the code, but they'd then have to pay for part of their health benefits—or have a higher copay.

> If people are only sixteen pounds from happiness, they'll reach "happy" in less than a year.

If you had already worked for the company, you'd be grandfathered in, but here's what would probably happen. Once exercise and BMI weight-loss programs began to be the norm, the grandfathered employees might also start to "up" their game. If they liked their job, they'd probably—almost subconsciously—gradually step in line. If they weren't that crazy about their job, they'd probably—again almost subconsciously—gradually start looking for a new place to work. Once health started to become the behavioral norm at the company, eating another full box of Samoa Girl Scout cookies at your desk for lunch would become the equivalent of bringing a bong into a board meeting.

This would be a bold and committed company. Some people might decide not to join the company, but those who did would agree to this health code of conduct. This company—LeederLab—doesn't exist yet. But it wouldn't have to be a Silly Valley company that only hires twenty-year-old Stanford computer-science grads. There's no reason it couldn't be a power company in Bozeman or a newspaper company in Baton Rouge.

But would *you* want to work for a company that had a health conduct code?

Eating another full box of Samoa Girl Scout cookies at your desk for lunch would become the equivalent of bringing a bong into a board meeting.

It's surprising how many people would. My colleague Rebecca Robbins and I found that most employees say they'd sign these codes if the requirements were simple—like getting an annual physical or screening exams—and if it came with discounts on insurance, medications, or examinations, or even with a donation to a favorite charity. Most people liked the idea of the health contract. It didn't matter if they were male or female, young or old. What did matter was their weight. People who were just a little overweight loved it and thought it would motivate them. But people who were a *lot* overweight (BMI over 30) were not as giddy.[34]

Your company probably won't introduce a health conduct code on Monday, but it might be coming soon. Meanwhile, there are two changes your CEO could make that would quickly help make your whole company more slim by design. The first would be to seriously explore a health conduct code. The second would be to change the job description of your boss.

JAPAN'S METABO LAW AGAINST FAT

If you're a woman with a waist over 35.4 inches (33.5 for males), you're breaking an insurance company law in Japan. It's their Metabo Law—short for metabolic syndrome.

Since 2008, waist measures are required of all 40- to 75-year-olds during their annual checkups. If you're over, you are referred to counseling, scolded through e-mail and phone correspondence, and given "motivational support."[35] You won't get fined, but if your company doesn't cut down the number of overweight employees, they'll be forced to pay about 10 percent higher health payments.

Companies are offering discounted gym memberships and special diet plans for employees. Since Japan's providing the free health care, they can technically pass whatever requirements they want. But people don't have to follow them. While 13 percent are law-abiding followers of the medical advice, 87 percent break the Metabo Law.[36] That includes Sumo wrestlers. They probably weren't sent the scolding e-mails.

Would *you* want to work for a company that had a health conduct code?

It's surprising how many people would.

Design Your New Boss's Job Description!

· · · · · · · · · · · · ·

SUPPOSE YOUR BOSS'S JOB DESCRIPTION stated that 10 percent of her pay raise depended on what she had done this past year to try to improve your health. Things would quickly change—break rooms, cafeterias, and facility rooms would be improved to nudge you to eat a little better and move a little more. Big transformations don't happen until people are rewarded for wellness.

Who's more productive: the woman who combines thirty-six hours of desk work with four hours of company time at yoga, or the guy who slugs it out for fifty hours every week? Hmmm . . . John Peters, the chief strategy officer of the University of Colorado's Anschutz Health and Wellness Center, asks companies this. At some point, those fourteen extra hours might be resented and not add up—they might actually begin to subtract. Thirty-six hours of energized work might be worth a lot more than fifty hours of stressed-out, perhaps embittered, exhaustion.

Imagine what would happen if your boss—along with other managers in your company—was graded, promoted, and paid partly on how she tried to help make you healthier. Again, healthy employees are good for business—fewer sick days, fewer medications, and fewer heart attacks. Yet if even just 10 percent of your manager's annual salary was based on what she did last year to help improve your health, it would be okay—not weird—for you to sit on a highway-cone-orange exercise-ball chair instead of a black office chair. One-on-one walking meetings would become normal, and desktop lunches might start to look antisocial. You might be thanked when you bring in fruit for your birthday but given the stink eye if you brought two dozen donuts or five pounds of bagels.

This is radical thinking. That's why it's surprising that so many managers are in favor of it. We found that most managers thought that having this health clause in their contracts would clearly incentivize them to make their employees more happy, productive, and cooperative.[37] They liked how most of our recommended changes would be quick and easy to implement—they didn't have to do anything drastic like install a company jai alai court or polo field. We also asked them if they would rather work for Acme Corporation, which did not have 10 percent of their evaluation tied to wellness, or Shangri-La Corporation, which did (okay, those weren't actually the names we used in the study itself). Sixty-four percent wanted to work for Shangri-La. They said they believed it would be a more dynamic, progressive industry leader, with room for more advancement.

Every company talks about health and wellness, but they're either really committed to it or they just aren't. If they're really committed, they need to visualize what this new company looks like—it can't just have a walking trail, a diabetes brochure, or fruit cups in the cafeteria. There's an expression in business that you motivate what you measure. If your boss measures how many insurance policies you sell, how many widgets you make, or how long you spend at your desk, that's what you focus on. If they don't measure it, you don't take it quite as seriously.

What if we measured how hard our company worked to make us healthier? Unless you were sleep-reading through the last three chapters, it's not surprising that a scorecard can be an effec-

Imagine what would happen if your boss was graded, promoted, and paid partly on how she tried to help make you healthier.

tive way to see how they measure up. This Workplace Scorecard is one of the quick initial assessments we use when working with companies to help make their employees healthier. Just like the scorecards for supermarkets and restaurants, it will show your boss or your wellness director how your company stacks up, and what they can specifically do to show leadership in wellness. It will give them some specific changes they can make right away, and it also lets them know someone really cares and might be measuring them. Now, that's motivating.

Think Summer Camp, Not Boot Camp

. . . .

REMEMBER THE FOUR PILLARS of most company wellness efforts and their tenth-grade counterparts? A health education program (health class), company fitness center (gym), new cafeteria foods (boring school lunches), and incentives (grades). It's not surprising that most of these back-to-school-style company efforts don't have widespread or enduring results. Just as when we were fifteen, we resented "the Man" telling us what to do—regardless of how good it is for us.

If company wellness programs are ignored by most workers and used fitfully by others, maybe a better approach would be to change the workplace so that everyone moves in the right direction without resisting. Instead of thinking of wellness programs as boot camp—where everyone's going to get whipped into shape—a better metaphor might be summer camp. Whether it's basketball camp, band camp, church camp, or econometrics camp, summer camps are usually designed so kids can arrange their days to do a lot of what they want.

Companies need to be more like camps. If employees usually grumpily eat lunch hunched over a screen at their desk, the company should give them a reason to move—like a magnetically attractive break room, brown-bag seminar series, or maybe even a fitness room with occasional programs. If employees reach for the cafeteria cheeseburger and fries by default, the company needs to tilt the cafeteria in the direction of the healthier foods so they're the first foods people think about, see, and conveniently grab. If the company is going to give a discount to join health-related activities, they need to give lots of options. That is what a truly great company wellness program would do. It would help us become slim by design—not slim in spite of it.

Slim-by-Design Workplace Self-Assessment Scorecard

. . . .

Is your workplace making you slim by design? To get some early indicators, start by reviewing your workplace against this 100-point scorecard. If management does the majority of these things, you should be in your state fair's six-pack ab competition. If they don't do many, you can let them know what they could do that would help you and others bring home the gold.

INNOVATIVE INCENTIVES

☐ Offers new employees the opportunity to sign an Employee Worksite Wellness Code in exchange for free or discounted health insurance.

☐ Offers health insurance reimbursement or copay if you are involved in physical or stress-reducing activities such as those in an approved menu of options.

☐ At least 10 percent of a manager's (such as your boss's) salary or bonus is based on their efforts to promote workplace wellness among their employees.

☐ An employee survey of workplace wellness preferences has been conducted within the past three years.

☐ Allows flexible work schedules if an employee presents a plan for physical activity.

BREAK-ROOM MAKEOVER

☐ Offers free fruit (such as bananas) in the break room.

☐ Shows the number of calories in items in the vending machine.

☐ Decorates the break room with posters, pictures, and plants; refurnishes the room; repaints the room; chooses soft lighting.

☐ Places a water cooler with cups and free healthy snacks on a table.

☐ Requires that the majority of the items in the vending machines be healthy.

☐ Slightly increases the price of unhealthy snacks and slightly decreases the price of healthy snacks.

☐ Places vending machines in a location that is not easily accessible from the workspaces.

☐ Places healthier snacks at eye level.

☐ Places less healthy snacks at the bottom of the machine.

☐ Has posters of healthy foods near vending machines or in the lunchrooms.

☐ Encourages bringing brown-bag lunches from home.

☐ Promotes a once-a-week snack-free day.

☐ Provides a microwave.

☐ Provides a large refrigerator with an ice maker.

OFFICE ENCOURAGEMENT

- ☐ Hosts a regular lunchtime speakers series on health topics.
- ☐ Encourages employees to keep snacks off their desks.
- ☐ Places water coolers in convenient, easily accessible areas.
- ☐ Promotes a once-a-week vegetarian day (such as Meatless Mondays).
- ☐ Promotes a snack-free day.
- ☐ Offers the option of standard desk chairs or exercise-ball chairs for fitness.
- ☐ Offers at least monthly company-wide health activities, such as a healthy cooking class or wellness seminars.
- ☐ Has a health/fitness discussion thread on the company's Google group or website, or uses other means to encourage group conversations and teamwork on these topics.
- ☐ Holds various workshops on healthy living and eating properly.

ENCOURAGING PHYSICAL ACTIVITY

- ☐ Promotes walking meetings when location or weather permits.
- ☐ Participates in a charity race (such as a 5K).
- ☐ Promotes an online group (using social media such as Facebook, Meetup, or Keas) that is dedicated to healthy lifestyles.
- ☐ Discounts gym membership fees for employees.
- ☐ Sets up an incentivized fitness challenge among employees.
- ☐ Offers cash incentives for employees who participate in various physical activities on a weekly basis.
- ☐ At large worksites (like a campus or a plant), gives free access to bikes to people who need to change buildings.
- ☐ Posts signs by the stairs and the elevator that explain the health benefits of taking the stairs compared to taking the elevator.
- ☐ Stairwell is inviting (is not unattractive) to those who want to walk the stairs.
- ☐ Builds bike racks close to the building entrance.
- ☐ Creates fitness groups (such as walking/jogging).
- ☐ Places water fountains with cups next to vending machines.
- ☐ Provides takeout (not delivery menus) for healthy restaurants.

CAFETERIA AND SNACK KITCHEN MAKEOVERS

- ☐ In dining halls, serves smaller drinks (under 16 ounces) but allows free refills.
- ☐ Allows employees to preorder meals from the cafeteria.

- [ ] Provides a list of nearby healthy fast-food options.
- [ ] Offers a convenience line featuring only healthy prepared foods options.
- [ ] Offers discounts to employees who purchase salads or combos.
- [ ] Places healthier items (such as the salad bar) as the first food visible in the dining hall.
- [ ] Medium-size trays are available upon entering the cafeteria.
- [ ] Displays signs encouraging employees to pay with cash instead of credit.
- [ ] Offers discounts for cash.
- [ ] Creates "diet" tables in the dining halls (tables where dieters can eat, if they wish).

CAFETERIA MENU BOARD REDESIGN

- [ ] At least 3 healthy appetizers are offered.
- [ ] At least 3 healthy entrées are offered.
- [ ] At least 3 healthy desserts are offered.
- [ ] At least 3 healthy beverages (other than water) are offered.
- [ ] Meal combos contain a fruit or healthier salad option.
- [ ] At least 5 healthy items are clustered together in a visible corner of the menu board.
- [ ] Colored or bolded words are used to highlight healthy foods.
- [ ] Logos or icons are used to draw attention to targeted healthy items.
- [ ] Descriptive words are used to describe healthy items.
- [ ] Offers salads as the default while fries may be substituted at an additional cost.
- [ ] In any section, healthier items are listed first on the menu board.
- [ ] A nonstarchy vegetable or fruit is the default side offering.
- [ ] A salad is the default side offering.
- [ ] Calorie levels are provided for selected items.
- [ ] Grab-and-go meals are lower in calories than the dine-in equivalent.
- [ ] Promotes the grab-and-go healthy meals as fresh rather than healthy.

CAFETERIA SPECIALS AND PROMOTIONS

- [ ] At least I appetizer *special* is healthy.
- [ ] At least I entrée *special* is healthy.
- [ ] At least I dessert *special* is healthier.
- [ ] Displays and dramatizes healthy options as first thing seen when entering and as point-of-purchase display, visible and accessible (for example, a salad bar by the counter, apples by the register).
- [ ] A frequent salad-buyer program is available (such as 5 punches = free salad).

PORTION SIZE, PREPARATION, AND SUBSTITUTION OPTIONS

- ☐ Plates are less than 10 inches in diameter.
- ☐ Plates are a darker color than white or beige.
- ☐ Bowls hold 16 ounces or less.
- ☐ Glasses hold 16 ounces or less.
- ☐ Plates have a wide colored rim.
- ☐ Pitchers of water are provided on tables.
- ☐ A double portion of vegetables is available for a side dish substitution.
- ☐ The entrée special is available in a half-size portion.
- ☐ At least 3 entrées are available in half-size portions.
- ☐ The dessert special is available in a half-size portion.
- ☐ At least 3 desserts are available in half-size portions.
- ☐ Vegetable portions are 20 percent larger than in the past.
- ☐ Increase the amount of vegetables on the plate and reduce the other components.
- ☐ When appropriate, offer dressings and sauces on the side.
- ☐ Extra vegetables can be substituted for the starch.
- ☐ Soup can be substituted for the starch.
- ☐ Salad can be substituted for the starch.
- ☐ Offer fruit or a fruit salad instead of traditional desserts.

SCORING BRACKETS

☐ **70–100—Slim-by-Design Workplace—*Gold***

☐ **50–69—Slim-by-Design Workplace—*Silver***

☐ **30–49—Slim-by-Design Workplace—*Bronze***

Chapter Six

SMARTER
LUNCHROOMS

ANYONE WHO'S BEEN A PARENT for more than ten minutes knows that controlling the eating behavior of young kids is tough when they're alone and impossible when they're with their friends. It's like organizing a picnic for squirrels.

Welcome to school lunchtime. If every school lunchroom had a farm-size garden, an extra million-dollar budget, and Chef Boyardee on staff, it still wouldn't really be able to control the way kids eat each week. When it comes to lunch, we can educate, bribe, or restrict what we give kids, but we can't tell them what to eat. And as we know, it's not nutrition until it's eaten.

What we can do, however, is make it more convenient, appealing, or normal to pick up an apple instead of a cookie. This is the smarter lunchroom, the type of lunchroom that can get kids to choose a healthier lunch, to eat it, and to love it—because no one told them what to do.

Whether we live and breathe school lunch or are indifferent to it, we all have an indelible stereotype of school lunch based on when we were in tenth grade. With that in mind, here's a brief history of lunchtime.

It's not nutrition until it's eaten.

School Lunch 101

. . . .

A LOT OF SEEMINGLY UNRELATED THINGS—pajamas, clip-on neckties, Silly Putty, Twinkies, and nylons—were either invented or made popular as a result of World War II.[1] This includes the hot school lunch. Back in the early 1940s, more than a third of the draftees were classified as "4F"—not fit for service—because of malnutrition.[2] They were too skinny, too weak, or had too many nutrition-related health problems.

In 1946, right after the world had again been made free and safe for baseball and apple pie, the federal school-lunch program got started. Its purpose was to help ensure that all schoolchildren had at least one balanced, healthy, hot meal each school day. Since then it's gone through a number of growing pains. Here's one interpretation of how it all went down.

THE MESS HALL ERA (1940S TO 1960S)

The Mess Hall Era had the same take-it-or-leave-it flexibility of Henry Ford's black Model T: You could have anything you wanted as long as it was the one meal on the menu for the day. Monday might be Salisbury steak, tater tots, and carrots, and Tuesday might be chili, corn, and cinnamon rolls. School lunchrooms were a cross between eating on a World War II submarine and the Alcatraz prison chow line. At the time, the food was novel, hot, and got eaten. But whereas all the normal Beaver Cleaver kids ate the school lunch, the cool kids started to bring theirs from home.

THE FOOD COURT ERA (1970S TO 1980S)

To bring more kids and more dollars back into the cashier line, innovative lunchrooms started offering more hot-lunch options—two or three entrées or side dishes—and they began trucking in the tasty stuff:

cheeseburgers, pizza, French fries, chocolate shakes, tacos, and brownies. The progressive schools even had actual express carts and kiosks from the big chains like Pizza Hut and Subway. At this point it seemed that most people ate at school, including the cool kids—who bought[3] the tasty stuff but not the fish sticks and lima beans.

THE NUTRI-LUNCH ERA (1990S TO TODAY)

Food pyramids, dietary guidelines, and helicopter parenting all converged to focus on filling kids up with the right foods. As some of the indulgences left the cafeteria, some kids found less reason to eat there, and the lunch lines started thinning out. The cool kids started leaving campus for lunch, bringing in a Mountain Dew and Funyuns, or having Domino's pizza delivered to a side door.[4]

Most of the big reports, guidelines, and dietary standards that are set for schools are pretty much "nutrition by committee."[5] They're good in theory, but they wrongly focus on what kids *ought to do* and ignore what kids *will do*.[6] They can make schools serve tofu and kale, but they can't make kids eat it. Kids will eat what they want. Kids can leave campus, bring Cheetos, skip lunch, or order pizza—but they don't have to eat tofu and kale if they don't want to.

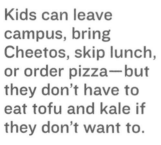

Kids can leave campus, bring Cheetos, skip lunch, or order pizza—but they don't have to eat tofu and kale if they don't want to.

It's temptingly hopeful to think that the best way to get kids to eat healthier is to make sure the only school foods they can buy aren't full of salt, sugar, and fat. But kids learn from their role models—us. *We* like variety and indulgence—salt, sugar, and fat—and so do they. Take that away, and they'll look for lunch elsewhere. We'd do the same if our boss did that where *we* work.

Take chocolate milk. It's a battle zone. Some critics hate it for what it *is*—it's milk with added sugar and flavoring. Some supporters love it for what it's *not*—a soft drink, an expensive vitamin water, a high-calorie sports drink, or an overpriced water in an environmentally unfriendly bottle. Some say it's less perfect than white milk; others say at least it's more nutritious than just about everything else. Both are right.

When Chocolate Milk Attacks

. . . .

A FEW WEEKS AFTER WE STARTED the Smarter Lunchroom Movement in February 2009, we were asked to visit a school that had proudly hired a new food-service director (a.k.a. head lunch lady) with a dreamy combination of two skills. She was a registered dietitian who had also graduated from a culinary school. What could be more perfect? But by the time we arrived, three weeks later, it was clear she wasn't the model of success the school had expected.

THINGS BANNED FROM SCHOOL LUNCHROOMS

POKEMON CARDS *(promotes occultism)*	THE FLAG *(incites emotions)*	POGS *(too violent)*
RED-INK PENS *(for teachers only)*	HUGS *(too distracting)*	THE HOKEY POKEY *(too provocative)*
DICTIONARY *(inappropriate words)*	CHOCOLATE MILK *(high sugar content)*	BAGGY PANTS *(high underwear content)*

Grace Green, "The 17 Weirdest Things Schools Have Banned," Huffington Post, September 8, 2010

Everybody's first week on the job is crazy. It doesn't matter whether you're in a tollbooth, a warehouse, or the White House; you feel pretty much in the dark. But if you're standing in the dark and lighting a match to get your bearings, it's good to let your eyes adjust before charging full speed in the direction you think is right. When we arrived, the new food-service director looked as if she hadn't slept three hours in the three weeks since she'd started. Here's what had happened.

We never tell them they can't have chocolate milk—that backfires. We just make them think twice about whether they really want it bad enough to wait twenty extra seconds.

She spent her first week boldly eliminating chocolate milk from her lunchroom because of its sugar content. She spent her second week besieged by irate students, teachers, and parents who wanted it back. All sales went down, and many kids stopped eating school lunch altogether—they either skipped it or brought a sad-sack lunch from home. To stop the milk hemorrhage, she brought chocolate milk back on two days a week. The complaints continued. The town newspaper even wrote a front-page feature on her. Not the nice kind.

Kids love chocolate milk. If you tell them, "No chocolate milk," many will become indignant. You're the evil adult— the Man—telling them what they can and cannot do. So one key is to *not* take chocolate milk away, but give them a choice—make them decide just *how badly they want it*. For example, kids might like chocolate milk, but they also like hanging out with their friends more than waiting in line.

Here's what we suggested: Offer them chocolate milk every day, but put it in an inconvenient cooler behind the white milk. If they want chocolate milk they can get out of the main lunch line, walk around back, wait in a twenty-second bottleneck, and finally get their chocolate milk. We never tell them they can't have it—that backfires. We just make them think twice about whether they really want it bad enough to wait twenty extra seconds.

In our experience with other schools, some kids will wait, but a lot won't—most would rather hang out with their friends than hang out in line. But here's what's important: *Nobody* complains, because they know

CHOCOLATE MILK REDESIGN

DON'T BAN IT—MAKE IT LESS CONVENIENT!

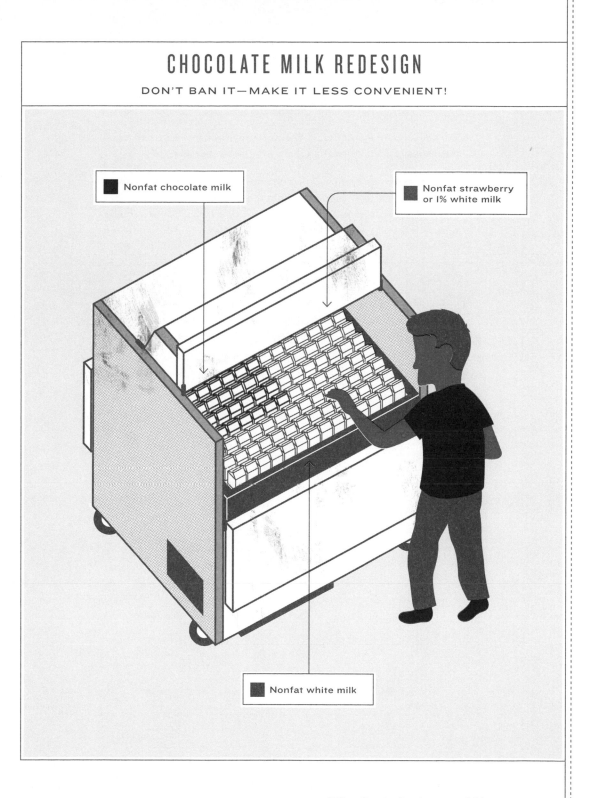

Nonfat chocolate milk

Nonfat strawberry or 1% white milk

Nonfat white milk

CHOCOLATE MILK CONSEQUENCES?

The consequences of serving chocolate milk are that kids consume more sugar and calories than if they drank white milk.

The consequences of *not* serving chocolate milk are that many don't drink milk at all. We discovered that when eleven Oregon schools banned chocolate milk, 10 percent fewer kids drank milk, 29 percent more of the white milk taken was thrown away, and 7 percent fewer kids ate school lunches.[7]

they can still have chocolate milk if they want it bad enough. There's no one to blame; it was their choice. When we make chocolate milk less convenient, even simply putting white milk in the front of the cooler and chocolate in back, white milk sales increase by 30 to 40 percent.[8] No complaints. No front-page stories creating movie-ready bad guys out of well-meaning local dietitians.

More Fruit by Design

· · · · · · · · · · · ·

I N T H E S P R I N G O F 2 0 0 9 we got a call from the New York State Department of Health with a "quick question." They were giving $3,000 pilot grants to some schools near Lake Placid, New York—near the heart of the Adirondack Mountains—to see if they could increase the amount of fruit kids ate by 5 percent. Their question: "How much do these schools need to drop the price of fifty-cent apples and pears in order to sell five percent more of them?"

Our guess was that price had nothing to do with it. You could double the price or halve the price, and sales wouldn't change. Kids who want an apple will take one, and kids who don't . . . won't. Thinking there's probably a better solution than blindly changing the price, we loaded up two Jeeps and made a late-night six-hour drive to the Adirondacks to see what was *really* going wrong in the fruit world. After a short night of sleep in a log cabin inn, we divided into two teams and began doing recon in the different lunchrooms in the school district.

First, we saw that cutting the price of fruit wouldn't do jack—no kid knew the price of anything on the lunch line, and they weren't paying for it anyway. Kids pay for lunches with debit cards, PIN numbers, finger-print scans, or eyeball scans that subtract the price of their lunch from a magical debit account that their parents charge up with money every month or so. Nobody was counting out nickels to pay for an apple or pear. It was paid with these magical, invisible funds.[9]

Then we looked at the fruit itself. Imagine all the different ways you could display fruit to kids. Now think of the worst way you could do it. In school after school, anemic-looking fruit had been tossed into those big steamer pans (appetizingly called "chaffers") and pushed under acrylic "sneeze shields." You pretty much had to contort like a Cirque du Soleil performer to retrieve your apple from something that looked like a family-size hospital bedpan. Given how inconvenient and unappetizing the fruit looked, taking 20 cents off the price would have been a joke. The cafeteria would simply have made less money and sold no more fruit.

When we met the next day with five of these food-service directors, we said, "Don't lower the price. Just make two changes. Put the fruit in a nice bowl and set it out on a well-lit part of the line." We said it didn't matter what the bowl looked like. It could be from Target, TJ Maxx, Goodwill, or a lunch lady's basement. It just couldn't look like a family-size hospital bedpan behind a sneeze shield.

This seemed pretty simple. Three of the schools jumped on board, and they pledged to make this change and track their fruit sales. Three months later, they reported that sales hadn't increased by only 5 percent. Instead sales had popped up *103* percent and stayed there for the entire semester.

These were pretty simple directions: *Put the fruit in a nice bowl and set it out on a well-lit part of the line.* Yet when we checked in with the fourth school, they told us they had bought a nice bowl, but then got a little bit mixed up. Instead of putting the bowl of fruit in a well-lit part of the line, they had instead taken an old desk light and simply put it up on the lunch line and shined it on the fruit—an apple-pear spotlight dance. Sales shot up by 186 percent.[10]

The last school never made the changes, and they had what they thought were good excuses: It wouldn't work, they were too busy, they weren't certain what type of bowl to buy, they didn't have the spare cash or slush fund to buy a bowl, they couldn't bring one from home, they weren't sure whether the bowl met health standards, they wanted to make sure the shape of the bowl didn't offend anyone's religion, and so on. They had lots of reasons why they couldn't "put the fruit in a nice bowl and set it out on a well-lit part of the line." And they didn't sell any more fruit.

Telling a food-service director not to serve cookies is one way to change the lunchroom—but it has its problems. The food-service directors are the queens or kings of their domain. They often have twenty years of expertise in designing menus, finding the perfect suppliers, tweaking recipes, predicting sales volume, managing leftovers, and keeping food safe. They're often resistant to changing the food they serve, but they'll often change their lunchroom to help kids pick up an apple instead of a cookie— especially if it's a change that can be done quickly and inexpensively.[11]

Put it in a nice bowl and set it out on a well-lit part of the line? It works. If the food was attractively presented, it looked yummier. Moreover, if it was in their faces, it was on their plates. Nowhere is this more vividly illustrated than with a salad bar.

The Salad Bar Solution

. . . .

VEGETABLES ARE A BATTLEGROUND where the will of a child fights the will of a parent. A similar battle is waged in American lunchrooms, where 32 million kids eat school lunches every day. But here it's a battle between pizza-loving kids and salad-serving lunch ladies. At most schools it's a losing battle for the salad bar. The USDA even called us and asked if we had any insights on how to get high school kids to pile it on their plate. How could we turn this around?

We *typically* think that if we want kids to eat salad, we either have to educate them or entice them. When education doesn't work, we try to entice them by cutting the price or adding those miniature corn-on-the-cobs that look like something Malibu Barbie would eat. The problem with these approaches is that "educating" students requires a plan, a time slot, and a teacher; moreover, "enticing" them costs money to subsidize or to buy the extra Malibu Barbie corn.

If we were to ask kids why they didn't eat salads, their knee-jerk answers would be predictable—too icky or boring compared to pizza. That's what they'd say—but they'd be wrong. Here's the real answer: The big reason they don't buy salad is simply that they don't think about it. Just like us, they have their lunchtime habits—and they don't include picking away at a salad bar. But if something made them think about salad—even for a second—it might lead a high schooler to pick up the tongs.

Within a month of making our pilgrimage to Lake Placid to help schools increase fruit sales, we stumbled across the chance we needed to follow up on the USDA question about salad bars. We got a call from an award-winning food-service director who asked what would be the best way to increase salad-bar sales in all of her lunchrooms. Because of the bigger-picture USDA synergy, we hustled out to her district to see what was going on. Our first stop was a middle-school lunchroom.

SALAD BAR REDESIGN

INCREASE SALAD SALES 200 TO 300 PERCENT WITHIN TWO WEEKS!

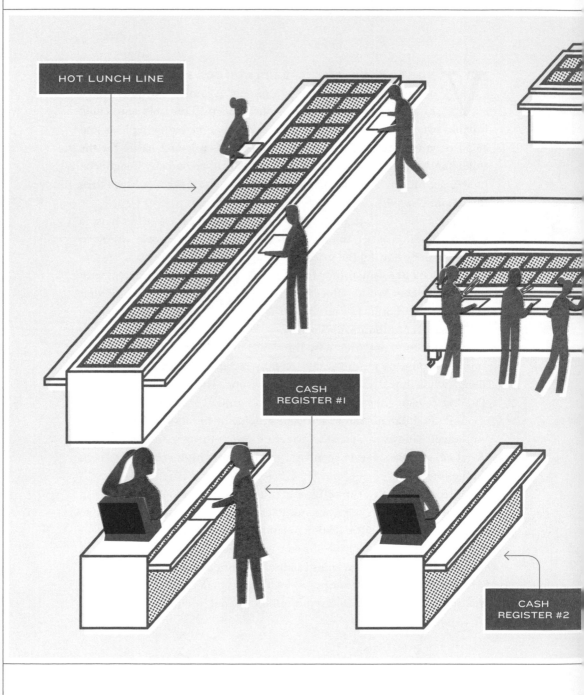

HOT LUNCH LINE

CASH REGISTER #1

CASH REGISTER #2

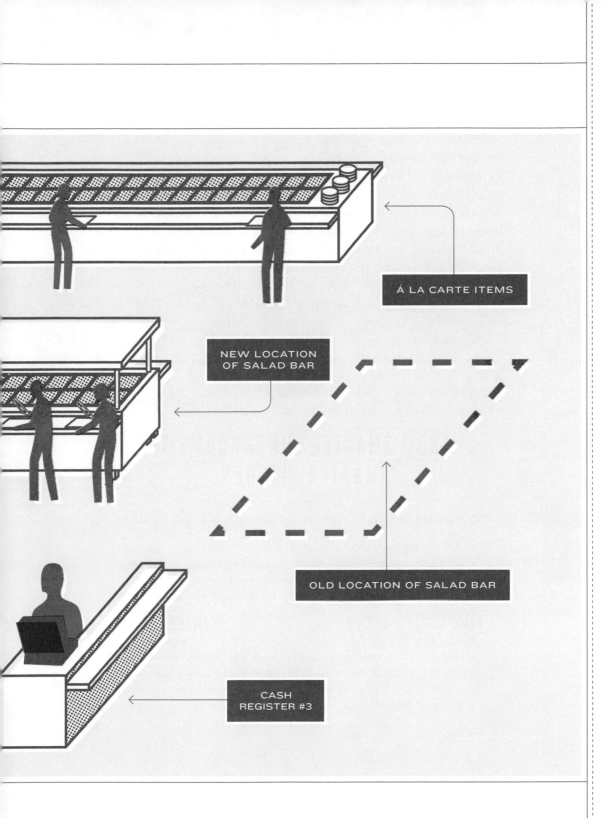

Á LA CARTE ITEMS

NEW LOCATION OF SALAD BAR

OLD LOCATION OF SALAD BAR

CASH REGISTER #3

See the layout of the lunchroom on pages 196–97. The salad bar is pushed against one wall and virtually ignored. It's as easy to walk by and ignore as a wall flyer for last Tuesday's blood drive. Here's what's instructive. The sixty-second solution was to wheel the salad bar ten feet out from the wall and turn it sideways. This way kids couldn't walk by it; they had to walk *around* it to get to the cash registers. For the first couple of weeks kids would pick up their standard lunch, bump into the salad bar, pause, walk around it, and pay for their food. After a while, however, these pauses got a little bit longer. Eventually, some students broke from their remote-control lunch pattern to try the salad. It didn't happen every day, but it was frequent enough that within a couple of weeks the salad bar sales increased 200 to 300 percent.[12]

When the salad was in their face, it was on their mind. They might say *no* nine days in a row, but every once in a while a *yes* would squeak by. No price cuts, no expensive Malibu Barbie corn additions, no complaints, and no salad leftovers to throw into the mulch pile.

What You Can Do . . .

FROM SMARTER LUNCHROOMS TO SMARTER KITCHENS

Every home has its own food-service director. It's probably you.

The first thing you can do is dust off a fruit bowl and place it within a two-foot reach of where everyone walks when they go through the kitchen. In one of our studies, the average time fruit lasted in a fruit bowl was eight days. The average time it lasted in the refrigerator? Seventeen days.

If you want to keep fruit in the fridge, put it on the middle shelf whole, or cut it up and put it in plastic bags. Elementary-school kids are 35 percent more likely to take fruit that's been cut up compared to whole fruit.[13] One solution for people with more cash than time is to buy a fruit sectionizer for the counter. One push = six pieces.

Lunch-Line Redesign, MTV-Style

. . . .

WE'VE DISCOVERED MORE THAN one hundred changes that lunchrooms can make to nudge students to eat better. For instance, if you show a kid three consecutive pans of vegetables—green beans, corn, and carrots—they'll take 11 percent more of whatever vegetable is in the first pan. It doesn't matter what it is. They're hungry, and what's first looks best. To help schools visualize how they could go through their lunchrooms and make a bunch of low-cost/no-cost changes, my friend and colleague David Just and I wrote an infographic editorial for the *New York Times* that inspired the one on the next page.[14] One teacher said she even printed this out for her students and had them color it in class. High school math class just isn't what it used to be.

> The sixty-second solution was to wheel the salad bar ten feet from the wall and turn it sideways.

Shortly after the op-ed was published, a television producer wanted to film us doing a before-and-after smarter-lunchroom makeover of a middle school. Why a middle school? Apparently elementary students act too randomly in front of TV cameras (remember that picnic for squirrels?), and most high schoolers aren't photogenic enough for television—too many strange clothes, weird hair colors, piercings, or "bit**y resting faces." The TV people wanted us to find a middle school that would do a total lunchroom makeover for less than fifty dollars—and film it all MTV-style.[15]

After finding the perfect middle school and watching students eat lunches for a week, we isolated ten changes we could easily make for less than fifty dollars total that would probably help them eat better without realizing it—things like changing the location of the fruit, giving fun names to healthy foods, moving the cookies behind the counter, putting

LUNCH-LINE REDESIGN

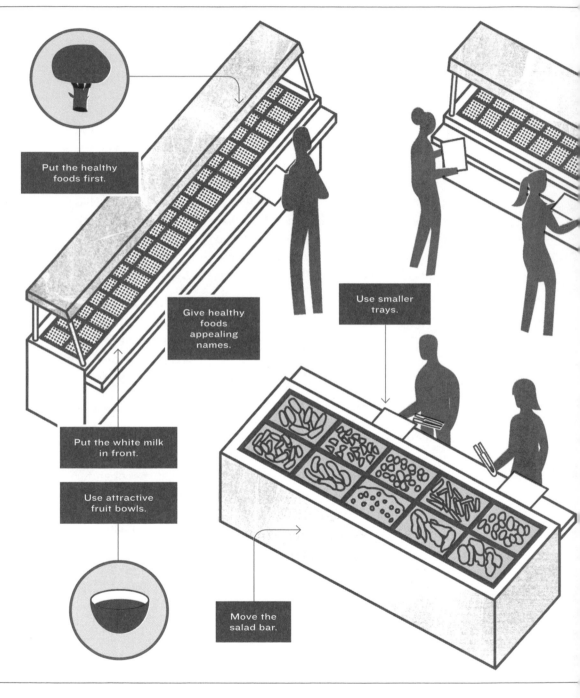

Put the healthy foods first.

Give healthy foods appealing names.

Use smaller trays.

Put the white milk in front.

Use attractive fruit bowls.

Move the salad bar.

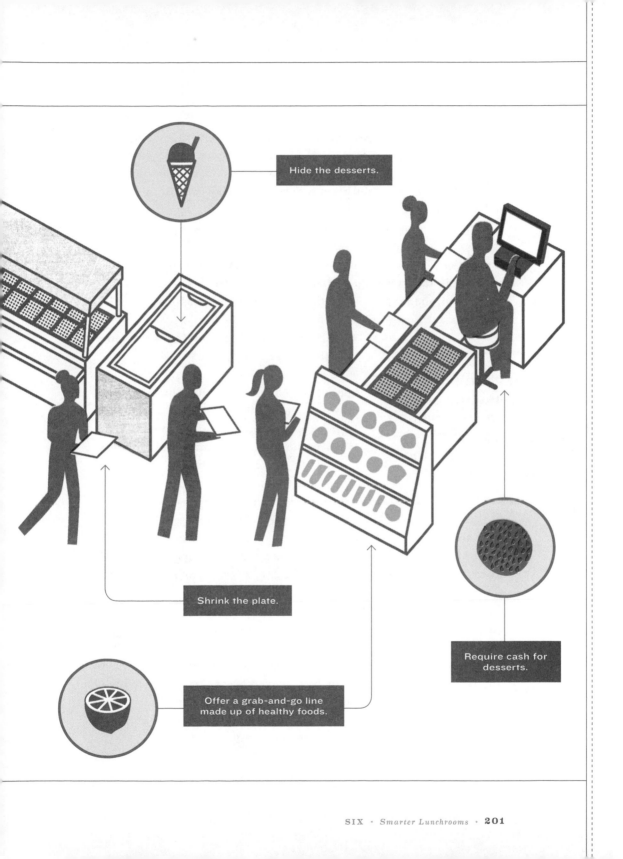

Hide the desserts.

Shrink the plate.

Offer a grab-and-go line made up of healthy foods.

Require cash for desserts.

the vegetables first, and so on. The food-service director and producer were cool with the changes, so we got to work.[16] Twenty-five kids were handpicked to be secretly filmed by three hidden cameras. We hid cameras in a ceiling tile, a hat, and even in our fake water bottle. Everything was set—and then came the catch. Unexpectedly, we were asked, with the cameras rolling, to predict *exactly* how much the sales of each item would change after we did our makeover. That's not something you like to be forced to commit to on national TV.

After lunch was over, the smoke cleared, and the dishes were washed, we were able to calculate just what had happened. The makeover was a nutritional victory—kids took a lot more salads, fruit sales doubled, white milk sales went up 38 percent, sugary drinks sales dropped by 17 percent, and they ran out of the healthy bean burritos—renamed Big Bad Bean Burritos—for the first time ever. These kids ate an average of 18 percent fewer calories, and they ate better than they typically did.[17]

> They ran out of the healthy bean burritos—renamed Big Bad Bean Burritos—for the first time ever.

What didn't work was putting the cookies behind the counter. We thought this would decrease sales by 30 percent, but it did nothing. Even worse, we predicted that moving vegetables to the front of the line would increase sales by 11 percent, but it instead dropped by 30 percent.[18] What happened?

A little bit of sleuthing showed that cookies were the cafeteria's big "destination food." They were five inches of hot, freshly baked gooey goodness—the main reason some kids ate school lunch. Wild horses couldn't have pulled these kids away from the cookies without pulling them away from eating lunch there altogether.

The vegetables were a different story. As I mentioned, our lab studies showed that lunchgoers were 11 percent more likely to take whatever vegetable they saw first compared to whatever they saw third. Well, that's true when three vegetables are in the *middle* of the serving line, but here we put them in the *front* of the line. Nobody scoops up a plate of green beans and then looks for the entrée that goes with it. People pick out the entrée and *then* the vegetable. They didn't want to take a veggie until they knew what they were having for a main course.

When the interview got to this point, the producer asked, "You've been doing eating research for twenty-five years. Sales didn't increase by 11 percent, they dropped by 30. Why were you so far off?" I said, "Well, if we always knew exactly what would happen, we wouldn't call it research." (He seemed amused enough by this answer to downplay these missed predictions in his story.)

Still, nailing five out of seven predictions was pretty decent. Our prediction report card wasn't straight A's, but it was better than the report cards I got in high school. Most important, we were able to show in real-TV-time how only thirty-eight dollars and two hours of tweaking made a bigger difference than hefty expert commission reports.

OUR LUNCHROOM MAKEOVER REPORT CARD FOR THAT DAY

	OUR BEST GUESS	ACTUAL CHANGE	
Put fruit bowl out.	+100%	+102%	A
Put white milk in front.	+40%	+34%	A-
Rename the bean burrito to Big Bad Bean Burrito.	+30%	+40%	A
Say "Do you want salad with that?"	+40%	+48%	A
Put smaller spoon in potato salad.	-15%	-12%	A
Put cookies in back of the line.	-30%	-1%	D
Put vegetables at the front of the line.	+11 %	-38%	F

Where should a school start? Start with the Smarter Lunchroom Starter List below and choose three easy changes to get the ball rolling. When we were first beginning to launch our Smarter Lunchroom Movement back in 2009, we would work with schools individually by sitting down with the food-service directors and managers and specifically telling them what they were doing exceptionally well. We'd then mention some other ideas they could consider, and we'd ask them to pick no more than three. Some schools wanted to try the whole list, but while ambition may soar in the heat of the moment, when it comes to implementation, making more than three initial changes can seem so overwhelming that often nothing gets changed. Focus on three and save the rest for later.

The Smarter Lunchroom Starter List

When we do smarter-lunchroom makeovers, it's easy to find ten or more simple changes a lunchroom can make overnight or over a weekend for less than fifty dollars. Yet for most, even making a couple of small changes can have a dramatic impact. Here are easy changes we've designed to get you started:

TO INCREASE FRUIT SALES . . .

- ☐ Display fruit in two locations, one near the register.
- ☐ Display whole fruits in a nice bowl or basket.
- ☐ Employ signs and suggestive selling to draw attention to the fruit.

TO INCREASE VEGETABLE SALES . . .

- ☐ Give vegetable dishes creative/descriptive names.[19]
- ☐ Display the names on menu boards and at the point-of-purchase.

TO INCREASE WHITE MILK SALES . . .

- ☐ Place white milk in the front of the cooler.
- ☐ Place white milk in *every* cooler.
- ☐ Make sure fat-free (skim) white milk accounts for at least one-third of all milk displayed.

TO INCREASE HEALTHY ENTRÉE SALES . . .

- ☐ Make the healthy entrée the first or most prominent item in the lunch line.

☐ Give the targeted entrée a creative or descriptive name.

☐ Feature it on a menu board outside the cafeteria.

TO INCREASE THE NUMBER OF COMPLETE HEALTHY MEALS SOLD . . .

☐ Place key meal items at the snack window.

☐ Move chips and cookies behind the serving counter and offer them by request only.

☐ Create a healthy-items-only grab-and-go "convenience line.[20]

It's easy to find ten or more simple changes a lunchroom can make overnight or over a weekend for less than fifty dollars.

Yet for most, even making a couple of small changes can have a dramatic impact.

What's Your Lunchroom Score?

· · · · · · · · · · · · · ·

SOME PEOPLE HAVE A HARD TIME believing that simply moving a fruit bowl or the white milk can change overnight what kids eat. But when they do it and see that it works, they become huge converts and want to know what to do next. It's good to get advice, but once we get rolling, most food-service directors pretty much know what will work best for them and what won't.

To help schools figure out whether they have a smart lunchroom and what they can do next, we've designed a do-it-yourself scorecard that lunch managers, parents, or students can use. All it takes is the Smarter Lunchroom Scorecard on page 219, a pencil, and a lunchroom—you can even skip the pencil and download our free app. Each lunchroom can get as many as 100 points, because there are 100 tasks or changes that help kids choose better and eat better. The more changes your school makes, the higher the score. Most schools first score around 20 to 30, but they can quickly move up to 50 within a couple of weeks if they focus.

How smart is your school's lunchroom?

These are all research-based changes that we have found help kids make smarter choices.

We're still discovering new changes, so every school year there are a few new ones we rotate in and a few less effective ones we rotate out, but a school that got a 75 last year will probably get about a 75 this year if they haven't made any changes or if they haven't backslid.

School lunch directors like this because the most innovative ones are naturally competitive and because it strokes them for what they've done right, and this scorecard specifically gives them a list of the other things they could do to offer an even smarter lunchroom. There are already twenty thousand schools using at least part of the program, and our "70/70 by 2020" goal is to get at least 70 percent of all American schools to have a score of 70 or higher by the year 2020.

These changes are the common ones that will benefit all schools. Since 2009, we've worked directly or indirectly with more than twenty thousand schools, and every time we go into a new school, we find unique changes that will have a huge impact in that school but won't be broadly applicable. The 100 most common changes can all be found in the scorecard, but some of the others are more unique to your school.

So how do you discover those mysterious, subtle changes that may perfectly fit the needs of your school? After you make some of the more basic changes and feel good about how things are going and are ready for the next challenge, go stand with the kids in the front of the lunch line and ask yourself, "WWMcD?"

SMARTER LUNCHROOM SCORECARD—70/70 BY 2020

How smart is your school's lunchroom? There's a 100-point scorecard that quickly shows how it measures up with thousands of schools across the country.

By 2020, our goal is that 70 percent of all U.S. schools will have a 70 percent score or higher. Anyone can copy the scorecard at the end of the chapter, download it, or review it online (SmarterLunchrooms.org) or with the app (Smarter Lunchroom Score). It shows what's going well and how to easily improve. Spread the low-cost/no-cost good news.

WWMcD—WHAT WOULD McDONALD'S DO?

You can love Big Macs or hate them . . . but it's hard to argue that McDonald's isn't great at serving lunch.[21] They make Happy Meals and happy diners. But what do they know that a school lunch director doesn't? Oh, sure, they're backed up by $750 million in advertising, lots of spare cash, a mom-friendly drive-thru, and laser-precision quality control. But how well would these smarty-pants managers do if they were thrown into a school lunchroom and given only fifty dollars to improve it? WWMcD?

I wanted to find out, so I enlisted a handful of former fast-food managers and employees to join me for lunch at three different schools. I wanted their impression of what they would do if I were to put *them* in charge of these forlorn lunchrooms and give them only fifty dollars—not millions—to play with. What would they do to get more kids to eat lunch and to enjoy it more?

After less than five minutes of watching kids order and eat, they started firing off ideas. What's important is that *nobody* said a word about changing the food. One said he would put one of those Italian-style menu boards outside the cafeteria and write down the names of the three or four healthier items with Day-Glo marker colors. This way kids could make precommitted decisions and the non-lunch-goers could see what they were missing. Another said she would close the main door to the lunchroom and funnel everyone (even those with sack lunches) through the serving area so they would at least see what was offered. Another said she would make the serving area more attractive by playing low-level popular music and putting some backlighting on the wall. A fourth person said he would move the fruit by the cashier and have her ask, "Do you want an orange or do you want an apple with that?" The last said he would move the condiments line to outside the main serving area so this main serving area didn't look so congested and unappealing.

These were their very first comments at the very first school. Again, *nobody* said they needed a $750 million advertising budget or a bigger food budget. Nobody said it was a lost cause, threw up their hands, or pouted. They all had a low-cost or no-cost solution.

A LUNCHROOM MAKEOVER—
McDONALD'S STYLE

Take a visit to a high school cafeteria and then to the nearest McDonald's. After taking former fast-food managers into three schools, we asked them what they did differently. Most changes could be made over the weekend for little or no cost.

	HIGH SCHOOL CAFETERIA	THE NEAREST McDONALD'S
YOU FIRST SEE . . .	Blank walls, except for a fire drill instruction sign	Posters of new foods and daily specials
ONCE INSIDE, YOU'RE GREETED BY . . .	A gray, 32-gallon garbage pail at the head of the food line	A brightly lit menu board and ordering station
ORDERING A FULL MEAL CONSISTS OF . . .	Separately ordering 3 to 5 foods from the different USDA food groups	Saying something like "I'll have the #2 combo"
IF YOU ORDER ONLY ONE ITEM . . .	No suggestive selling. No cashier asked, "Do you want fruit or a salad with that?"	The cashier asks, "Do you want fries with that?"

Looking at a school lunchroom and asking, "What would McDonald's do?" may seem too crass or too contrary to how we believe our kids should eat. But who knows better how to give people what they want? We need to have a new model to think of how things *could* be. Nobody makes more out-of-home diners happy each day than McDonald's. It's not about what they serve. It's about how they serve it.

SMARTER SOUP KITCHENS AND FOOD PANTRIES

Each blizzardy February I ask my Lab researchers to volunteer three days in a local soup kitchen or food pantry. Some embrace it, but others are really uncomfortable. Nothing makes your day-to-day problems look more anemic than comparing them with those of a soft-eyed, homeless mother of a coughing three-year-old.

People in soup kitchens eat surprisingly like high schoolers: They gravitate to the starch—potatoes, pasta, and bread—and away from the vegetables. They take too much of the processed food and not enough of the healthy foods.

But we've found that the same slim-by-design techniques that work in school lunchrooms also work for soup kitchens, and the ones that work for grocery stores also work for food pantries. If you're a food-pantry supervisor, volunteer, or donor, you can learn how to help make your local soup kitchen and food pantry smarter at SlimByDesign.org.[22] And don't forget to serve a day or two every so often—especially if your day-to-day problems are feeling extra burdensome.

The Lunchtime Report Card

· · · · · · · · · · · · ·

THE ONLY WORSE SCHOOL DAY than Vaccination Day is Report Card Day. It's the day to face the music. While Tiger Moms are obsessed with this day, some other parents don't care as much, and kids mostly care in relation to their parents. Report cards are a way of checking in and reminding both kids and parents how the year is going—the good, the bad, and the ugly.

What if there were lunchtime report cards?[23] What if every Friday, parents got an e-mail telling them what their little angels bought for lunch that week? It would tell which of their kids bought cookies and Gatorade and which ones bought apples and white milk. As with real report cards, you can imagine that some parents couldn't care less, and others would lose sleep over it. Some parents might care more about what the kids are eating, and others might care more about how much they're spending. But would it change what kids order?

> All you need to do is ask, "*Sooooo* . . . what did you have for lunch today?"

Each Friday for a month, we sent parents the list of all the foods their kids (K–12) bought for school lunch. What happens when families get these report cards is kind of funny. The bottom line is that little Valerie and little Teddy mysteriously start buying cookies one-third less often and start taking twice as much fruit.

You might think kids changed what they bought because their parents had heart-to-heart nutrition talks with them, but that's not always the case. It seems that simply knowing someone is *aware* of what they're doing—and maybe cares—gradually bumps these kids back into line. After all, Big Mother is watching.[24]

While you can ask your children's school to start a Lunchtime Report Card program, you don't have to wait. All you need to do is ask, "*Sooooo* . . . what did you have for lunch today?"

TALKING TATER TOTS WITH TEENS

If you don't want to wait for your school to adopt Lunchtime Report Cards, here's what you can do yourself.

* **Find out if your school tracks—at least in a rough form— what each child purchases each day.** Some schools can automatically e-mail[25] the weekly records of what your kids order. If they can't do this, enough requests like yours might move them in that direction.

* **Ask your kids what they had for lunch and snacks that day.** Although they might fudge a little on what they remember to report, it might prompt them to eat better the next day, knowing they might be asked.

They were interested in knowing if there was such a thing as "healthier cafeteria trays."

The ideal tray would magically make the entrée, the starch, and the dessert look *huge* and satisfying (even if they were smaller); it would make the vegetable and fruit look enticing.

Designing a Smarter Lunchroom Tray

. . . .

L ATE ONE WINTER AFTERNOON, we had a mysterious four-thirty conference call with the Robert Wood Johnson Foundation. They had been collaborating with an innovative food-service director who was preparing to buy new trays for her school district in St. Paul, Minnesota, and they were interested in knowing if there was such a thing as "healthy cafeteria trays." That was the purpose of this call. After twenty minutes of preamble, their question to us was "Can you develop a Mindless Eating lunchroom tray that could help kids eat better?" They were familiar with the book *Mindless Eating* and wondered if the principles could be used to get kids to mindlessly eat better.

Coincidentally, we had started down this road a year earlier, but the unfortunate reality of lunch trays is that they've been dying off and replaced with disposable trays. There are two reasons: First, some school lunchrooms can't wash trays because they have "heat and serve" kitchens. Second, some disposable tray (paper) companies are really, really good at persuading schools to buy disposable trays. But the right reusable tray— one that caused kids to eat better—might tip the balance back and lead some schools to return to real trays rather than disposables. This call was the excuse we needed to get back on task.

When we ask kids what they want from school lunches, they say (1) bigger portions of foods they like, (2) foods that are fun or "cool," and (3) foods that taste good. So the ideal tray would magically make the entrée, the starch, and the dessert look *huge* and satisfying (even if they were smaller); it would make the vegetable and fruit look enticing; it would keep the vegetable hot and the fruit cold; and it would make everything look like it was going to taste better.

What's important is that these perceptions are subjective. How much you eat, how full you feel, and how much you like it are partly psychological.

Similarly, eating the same amount of food on a smaller plate makes us think we're more full than when we eat it on a larger plate—it's psychological.[26] Foods that are more easily seen and closer to us look more normal and natural to eat.[27,28,29]

> **As we know from Happy Meals and Chuck E. Cheese, nothing makes food taste better than when it's surrounded by fun.**

So we created a new tray that (1) makes the entrée and starch look larger (and more satisfying) while it makes the vegetables and fruit appear smaller (and less intimidating); (2) allows a full cup of vegetables to be served and stay hot; (3) makes milk, fruit, and vegetables seem like a normal thing everyone eats; and (4) reduces the energy cost of cleaning.[30]

If a small plate makes food look bigger, why not make shallower and smaller compartments for the main courses and the starches to make them look huge? Because kids like what's cool, textured icons of a fruit or vegetable could be printed in the fruit and vegetable compartment.[31] It's like the divided grocery cart that made people think it was normal to take more fruits and vegetables. Next, build the tray in a way that it would look normal to have *both* a fruit and vegetable—they wouldn't have to take both, but the tray would be a daily reminder of the norm they're deviating from.[32] These two compartments could also be moved to the front edge of the tray, flanking the entrée. This makes them look central to the meal and a normal thing to eat that shouldn't be overlooked.

To make milk seem like the norm, it's easy to restyle the beverage compartment so that it holds only milk cartons. If a school district used milk cartons, the tray would have a square cutout so that the square milk carton would fit nicely in this space, but the rounded bottles of other beverages would fit awkwardly or fall through.

Research about how color influences how much you like food isn't clearcut, but people intuitively believe that yellow, gold, and red can stimulate appetite and may complement the look of some foods.[33] If nothing else, offering the trays in bright school colors might at least make lunch seem more fun. As we know from eating Happy Meals, Chuck E. Cheese pizza, or hot dogs at a ball game, nothing makes food taste better than when it's surrounded by fun.

Last, most standard reusable lunch trays fit singly through the automated dishwashers. By reshaping these new trays to be longer and skinnier than the conventional trays, two of them can be vertically stacked side by side and washed in one slot of the dishwasher instead of two. This would save energy and washing costs to the ballpark tune of 15 to 30 percent, which could be enough of a reason to bring some schools back around to reusable trays.

Helping Your School Become Slim by Design

· · · · · · · · · · · · ·

THERE'S A STORY OF A MOTHER who's trying to get a whiny, belligerent son off to high school in the morning, but the son kicks and screams that he doesn't want to go because all the kids hate him and make fun of him, and all the teachers nag him and think he's dumb. When his mother pleads, "But you have to go to school," he says, "Give me one good reason." Mom replies, "Because you're the principal."

Aside from the principal, no school employee gets beaten up more than the school lunch lady. She's gone from being the punch line of hairnet jokes to being played by a dirty-dancing, karaoke-singing Chris Farley on *Saturday Night Live*. Now she even has her own $10.95 action figure.[34] The Lunch Lady Action Figure wears heavy black-rimmed glasses and a blue, 1950s Chris Farley–size dress. She has the forearms and calves of a Nebraska linebacker and is armed with her secret weapon: a serving spoon shaped like an ice-cream scoop.

This is a terrible stereotype, and most of us realize that. But what we don't often appreciate is that this woman is the true Iron Chef. Each week she orchestrates five breakfasts and five lunches, delivers them to 500-plus impatient diners, has two to four consecutive seatings, takes complaints in stride, and inspires twelve staffers who work four hours every school day for minimum wage. She does all this and feeds our kids for less than $1.36 per meal. Let's see Chef Morimoto do that.

Here's what else you wouldn't realize. After analyzing thousands of Smarter Lunchroom schools results across the country, we've found that the biggest determinant of whether a student eats a school lunch is how much he likes the lunch lady. The more he likes the lunch lady, the more often he eats lunch.[35] Or maybe it's the more often he eats lunch there, the more he likes the lunch lady. It doesn't matter. Either way, it's touching: After 175 meals a year, they can still make it personal.

→

HELPING SCHOOLS BECOME SLIM BY DESIGN

On the battleground of school lunches, the lunch lady reports to the school lunchroom manager, who reports to the food-service director for the whole school district. Unfortunately, the closer a person is to serving the food, the less power they have to make changes, and neither the manager nor the director has the dollars, time, or patience to listen to another helicopter parent or food extremist tell her what to do. They might, however, have time for someone who wants to help.[36] Here's what they say works:

* **Thank them for all they do.** They do a big job on a small budget, and they usually just hear from the complainers.

* **Complete the Smarter Lunchroom Self-Assessment Scorecard.** Besides showing how well your school is doing on a 100-point scale, it shows exactly what small, easy changes can be made to improve that score.

* **Tell them you learned about how there are low-cost/no-cost changes that can help kids eat better.**[37] **Some are as simple as giving kids the healthy foods first; making them tasty by giving them a cool name; or making it less convenient to eat the indulgent foods.** Maybe even print out some ideas to save them that step.

* **Ask how you can help.** Maybe there's an informal advisory board or a "Kitchen Cabinet" group you could join or start. The purpose would not be to critique but to help provide a solution. Enlist other parents from the PTA, and aways think WWMcD— what would McDonald's do?

* **Offer to put together a SNAC.** Offer to assemble a SNAC (Student Nutrition Action Committee).[38] You can run a discussion group about what easy nonfood changes the kids think could help them eat better. This can be an advisory committee, but it should also be the group that gets the work done and sees themselves as advocates for school lunch.

* **Enlist the Health and Wellness Committee.** Every school district has this committee, and your food-service director is on it. Ask her how you can get involved in sharing these same low-cost/no-cost changes.

A SLIM-BY-DESIGN LUNCH TRAY

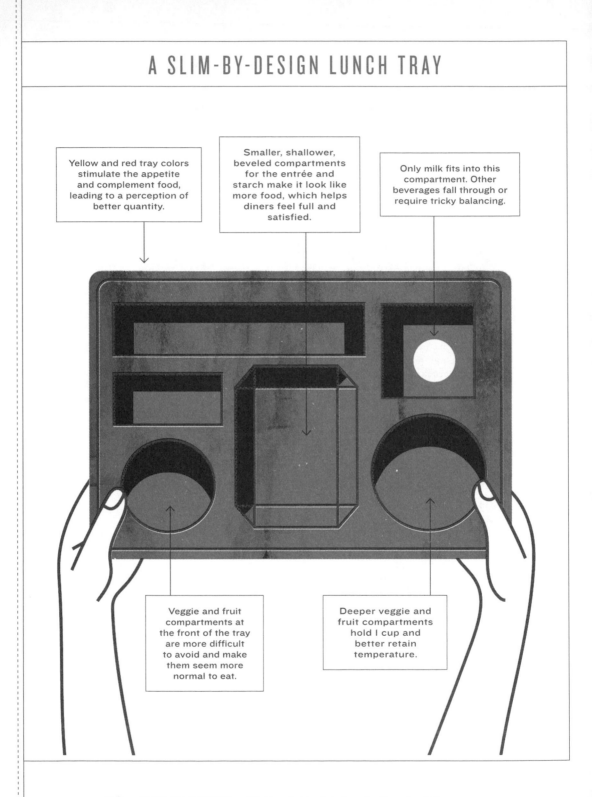

Yellow and red tray colors stimulate the appetite and complement food, leading to a perception of better quantity.

Smaller, shallower, beveled compartments for the entrée and starch make it look like more food, which helps diners feel full and satisfied.

Only milk fits into this compartment. Other beverages fall through or require tricky balancing.

Veggie and fruit compartments at the front of the tray are more difficult to avoid and make them seem more normal to eat.

Deeper veggie and fruit compartments hold I cup and better retain temperature.

The Smarter Lunchroom
Self-Assessment Scorecard

. . . .

Read each of the statements below as you walk through the lunchroom. For each true statement, check the box in front of it. After you have completed the checklist, count up all of the boxes with checkmarks and write this number at the end. This number represents your lunchroom's score. A perfect score of 100 is pretty much impossible, and most schools score between 20 and 30 the first time they complete the scorecard. The good news? Most schools can bump this up to 50 within two weeks if they really want to—one or two weekends of work. And it doesn't need to cost even a dollar. There's a new app available (SlimByDesign .org) that you can use to grade the lunchroom regardless of whether you manage it, are a concerned student who eats there, or are a helicopter parent with a little time and a lot of dedication.

FOCUSING ON FRUIT

☐ At least two types of fruit are available daily.

☐ Sliced or cut fruit is available daily.

☐ Daily fruit options are given creative, age-appropriate names.

☐ Fruit is available at all points of sale, such as the deli line, snack windows, à la carte lines, and so on.

☐ Daily fruit options are available in at least two different locations on each service line.

☐ At least one daily fruit option is available near all registers (if there are concerns regarding edible peels, fruit can be bagged or wrapped).

☐ Whole fruit options are displayed in attractive bowls or baskets (instead of chafing/hotel pans).

☐ A mixed variety of whole fruits are displayed together.

☐ Fruit options are not browning, bruised, or otherwise damaged.

☐ Daily fruit options are easily seen by students of average height for your school.

☐ Daily fruit options are bundled into all grab-and-go meals available to students.

☐ Daily fruit options are written legibly on menu boards in all service and dining areas.

PROMOTING VEGETABLES AND SALAD

- ☐ At least two types of vegetables are available daily.
- ☐ Vegetables are not wilted, browning, or otherwise damaged.
- ☐ At least one vegetable option is available in all food-service areas.
- ☐ Individual salads or a salad bar is available to all students.
- ☐ The salad bar is highly visible and located in a high-traffic area.
- ☐ Self-serve salad-bar utensils are at the appropriate portion size or larger.
- ☐ Self-serve salad-bar utensils are smaller for croutons, dressing, and other nonproduce items.
- ☐ Daily vegetable options are available in at least two different locations on each service line.
- ☐ Daily vegetable options are easily seen by students of average height for your school.
- ☐ A daily vegetable option is bundled into grab-and-go meals available to students.
- ☐ A default vegetable choice is established by pre-plating a vegetable on some of the trays.
- ☐ Available vegetable options have been given creative or descriptive names.
- ☐ All vegetable names are printed/written on name cards or product IDs and displayed next to each vegetable option daily.
- ☐ All vegetable names are written and legible on menu boards.
- ☐ All vegetable names are included on the published monthly school lunch menu.

MOVING MORE WHITE MILK

- ☐ All beverage coolers have white milk available.
- ☐ White milk is placed in front of other beverages in all coolers.
- ☐ White milk crates are placed so that they are the first beverage option seen in all designated milk coolers.
- ☐ White milk is available at all points of sale (deli line, snack windows, à la carte lines, and so on).
- ☐ White milk represents at least one-third of all visible milk in the lunchroom.
- ☐ White milk is easily seen by students of average height for your school.
- ☐ White milk is bundled as the default beverage into all grab-and-go meals available to students.
- ☐ White milk is promoted on menu boards legibly.
- ☐ White milk is replenished so all displays appear "full" continually throughout meal service and after each lunch period.

ENTRÉE OF THE DAY

- [ ] A daily entrée option has been identified to promote as a "targeted entrée" in each service area and for each designated line (deli line, snack windows, à la carte lines, and so on).
- [ ] Daily targeted entrée options are highlighted on posters or signs.
- [ ] Daily targeted entrées are easily seen by students of average height for your school.
- [ ] Daily targeted entrées have been provided creative or descriptive names.
- [ ] All targeted entrée names are printed/written on name cards or product IDs and displayed next to each respective entrée daily.
- [ ] All targeted entrée names are written and legible on menu boards.
- [ ] All targeted entrée names are included on the published monthly school-lunch menu.
- [ ] All targeted entrées are replenished so as to appear "full" throughout meal service.

INCREASING SALES OF REIMBURSABLE MEALS

- [ ] A reimbursable meal can be created in any service area available to students (salad bars, snack windows, speed lines, speed windows, dedicated service lines, and so on).
- [ ] Reimbursable "combo meal" pairings are available and promoted daily.
- [ ] A reimbursable meal has been bundled into a grab-and-go meal available to students.
- [ ] Grab-and-go reimbursable meals are available at a convenience line/speed window.
- [ ] The convenience line offers only reimbursable grab-and-go meals with low-fat, nonflavored milk, fruit, and/or vegetable.
- [ ] Grab-and-go reimbursable meals are easily seen by students of average height for your school.
- [ ] The school offers universal free lunch.
- [ ] A reimbursable combo-meal pairing is available daily using alternative entrées (salad bar, fruit and yogurt parfait, and so on).
- [ ] Reimbursable combo-meal pairings have been provided creative or descriptive age-appropriate names (for example, Hungry Kid Meal, Athlete's Meal, Bobcat Meal, and so on).
- [ ] Reimbursable combo-meal pairing names are written/printed on name cards, labels, or product IDs and displayed next to each respective meal daily.
- [ ] All reimbursable combo-meal names are written and legible on menu boards.
- [ ] All reimbursable combo-meal names are included on the published monthly school-lunch menu.
- [ ] Reimbursable combo-meal pairings are promoted on signs or posters.
- [ ] The named reimbursable combo meal is promoted

during the school's morning announcements.

☐ Students have the option to preorder their lunch in the morning or earlier.

☐ The cafeteria accepts cash as a form of payment.

SIGNAGE AND PRIMING

☐ Posters displaying healthful foods are visible and readable within all service and dining areas.

☐ Signage/posters/floor decals are available to direct students toward all service areas.

☐ Signs promoting the lunchroom and featured menu items are placed in other areas of the school, such as the main office, library, or gymnasium.

☐ Menu boards featuring today's meal components are visible and readable within all service and dining areas.

☐ A dedicated space/menu board is visible and readable from five feet away within the service or dining area where students can see tomorrow's menu items.

☐ Dining space is branded to reflect student body or school (for example, school lunchroom is named for school mascot or local hero/celebrity).

☐ All promotional signs and posters are rotated, updated, or changed at least quarterly.

☐ All creative and descriptive names are rotated, updated, or changed at least quarterly.

☐ A monthly menu is available and provided to all student families, teachers, and administrators.

☐ A monthly menu is visible and readable within the school building.

☐ A weekly "Nutritional Report Card" is provided to parents detailing what their student has purchased during the previous week.

LUNCHROOM ATMOSPHERE

☐ Trash on floors, in, or near garbage cans is removed between each lunch period.

☐ Cleaning supplies and utensils are returned to a cleaning closet or are not visible during service and dining.

☐ Compost/recycling/tray return and garbage cans are tidied between lunch periods.

☐ Compost/recycling/tray return and garbage cans are at least five feet away from dining students.

☐ Dining and service areas are clear of any nonfunctional equipment or tables during service.

☐ Sneeze guards in all service areas are clean.

☐ Obstacles and barriers to enter service and dining areas have been removed (garbage cans, mop buckets, cones, lost and found, and so on).

☐ Clutter is removed from service and dining areas promptly (empty boxes, supply shipments, empty crates, pans, lost and found, and so on).

☐ Students' artwork is displayed in the service and/or dining areas.

☐ All lights in the dining and service areas are currently functional and on.

☐ Trays and cutlery are within arm's reach to the students of average height for your school.

☐ Lunchroom equipment is decorated with decals, magnets, signage, and so on wherever possible.

☐ Teachers and administrators dine in the lunchroom with students.

☐ Cafeteria monitors have good rapport with students and lunchroom staff.

☐ The dining space is used for other learning activities beyond meal service (home economics, culinary nutrition education activities, school activities, and so on).

☐ Staff is encouraged to model healthful eating behaviors to students (dining in the lunchroom with students, encouraging students to try new foods, and so on).

☐ Staff smiles and greets students upon entering the service line continually throughout meal service.

☐ Students who do not have a full reimbursable meal are politely prompted by staff to select and consume a fruit or vegetable option.

STUDENT INVOLVEMENT

☐ Student groups are involved in the development of creative and descriptive names for menu items.

☐ Student groups are involved in creation of artwork promoting menu items.

☐ Student groups are involved in modeling healthful eating behaviors to others (mentors, high school students eating in the middle school lunchroom occasionally, and so on).

☐ Student surveys are used to inform menu development, dining-space décor, and promotional ideas.

☐ Students, teachers, and/or administrators announce daily meal deals or targeted items in daily announcements.

RECOGNITION AND SUPPORT OF SCHOOL FOOD

☐ The school participates in other food-program promotions such as: Farm to School, Chefs Move to Schools, Fuel Up to Play 60, Share Our Strength, and so on).

☐ A local celebrity (mayor, sports hero, media personality) is invited to share lunch with students three or four times a year.

☐ The school has applied or been selected for the Healthier U.S. School Challenge.

Á LA CARTE SALES

☐ Students must ask to purchase à la carte items from staff members.

☐ Students must use cash to purchase à la carte items that are not reimbursable.

☐ Half portions are available for at least two dessert options.

SCORING BRACKETS

☐ **70–100—Slim-by-Design Lunchrooms—**_Gold_

☐ **50–69—Slim-by-Design Lunchrooms—**_Silver_

☐ **30–49—Slim-by-Design Lunchrooms—**_Bronze_

Chapter Seven

SLIM BY DESIGN FOR LIFE

S UPPOSE TOMORROW YOU BANNED ice cream from your home, McDonald's stopped selling French fries, and your local school eliminated chocolate milk. How long would it take before we were all *Mad Men* thin? Fifty years of psychology research would predict . . . never. Removing temptation only works when we're really, really serious. But when it comes to food, we don't *seriously* want to give up ice cream and French fries, and our kids don't seriously want to give up chocolate milk, so bans quickly backfire. We might not eat ice cream today, but tomorrow then becomes our personal All You Can Eat Ice Cream Thanksgiving Day. We may not eat any French fries today at McDonald's—but tomorrow we're first in line for Burger King's Satisfries. Our child might not drink chocolate milk tomorrow, but they'll start drinking Mountain Dew the day after.

In late 2012, we received a call from a guy whose voice sounded like Alec Baldwin's. He said he was with the Department of Defense and that he and two others wanted to meet with me and my Lab's deputy director, Adam Brumberg, the next day about "a matter of national security." We shuffled things around for an eight-thirty meeting in the Lab. "A matter of national security" . . . I'm picturing Adam and I debonairly saving the world from some *Hunt for Red October*-style nuclear incident or a *World War Z*-type zombie apocalypse.

After their arrival the next day and a few minutes of debriefing, I learned that the phrase "a matter of national security" is thrown around *waaay* too loosely. Just as I'm planning how to respond to a request to zombie-proof the Pentagon cafeteria, I hear the actual request: They wanted us to make their military bases slim by design and thwart an obesity overrun. This included their mess halls, the fast-food restaurants on base, canteens, snack bars, and grocery stores (PXs). You don't see a lot of fat eighteen-year-old marines, and the idea was to keep it that way. This was called the Healthy Base Initiative. Even though my Walter Mitty dreams of an action movie had just been crushed, I snapped back to reality and said, "Absolutely. When do we start?"

In the meetings that followed over the next months, they kept saying, "We can do anything on these bases that you advise. We can get rid of any food—like desserts, mayonnaise, or French fries. We can close restaurants early, or we can cut portion sizes in half."[1] They assumed that if you wanted soldiers to lose weight, it made sense to serve them only healthy foods and in smaller portions. Just like we can tell ourselves, "No ice cream in the house," and our kids "No chocolate milk in the lunchroom," they expected that we'd want them to tell soldiers, "No fast food after nine P.M., and no French fries at all."

There's a better answer. Again, bad things happen when we tell people—even ourselves—that they can't have something they really want. They devise clever solutions that often have worse consequences than the original. If soldiers can't buy French fries on base, they might leave the base to get them, possibly resulting in more car accidents, more drinking, more DUIs, more smuggled "black market" food—more of everything except healthy eating. People always have options, so telling soldiers what they "can't" do won't lead them to eat better—only to eat elsewhere.

Hearing "can't" dares a person to find a workaround. It's a basic psychological theory called reactance—telling someone "no" just makes them want it more. If you tell your daughter she can't date Spike anymore, the next time she calls will be from a Las Vegas wedding chapel.

CHANGING "SMALL-P" POLICIES

When we think of "policy" we often think of Congress and laws—
that's policy with a capital "P." But every person and household has
policies, their habits and daily patterns, like the policy to hang up
your keys when you get home or to take off your shoes. It might be
a policy to eat breakfast every day or to not keep a candy dish on
your desk or cookie jar in the kitchen.

Just as we have personal policies, restaurants, schools, grocers, and
workplaces also have policies. Some are written down, and some are
simply rules of thumb, like the customer is always right, or always
put a bread basket on the table. These policies are all flexible. If a
company's policy caused it to lose money or customers, it could be
changed overnight. This is where we come in. We can help encourage these places to make profitable changes to their policies that
make it even easier for us to be slim by design. The best policies
are the ones that are win-win. They're the ones that let restaurants,
companies, grocery stores, and schools benefit—and us as well.[2]

Hearing "can't" dares a person to find a workaround.

If you tell your daughter she can't date Spike anymore, the next time
she calls will be from a Las Vegas wedding chapel.

From Can't to CAN

. . . .

INSTEAD OF TELLING SOLDIERS what they *can't* eat, we told our Department of Defense friends that we would help guide or nudge their soldiers to what they *can* eat by making the healthier foods the most convenient, attractive, and normal foods to choose. Many of the same changes that you've read about throughout this book were the ones we've recommended and are helping implement for the Healthy Base Initiative.

Many of these are changes that simply make healthier food more convenient, attractive, or normal to snack on, order off the menu, or throw in the shopping cart.[3] When we put the fruit in a nice well-lit bowl next to a cash register, we make it more convenient, attractive, and normal to grab a banana than the chocolate-chip-cookie-dough ice cream in the far back of the freezer. When restaurants give the high-profit shrimp-salad appetizer an enticing name, highlight it on the menu, and have the waitress point it out as a special, it becomes more convenient, attractive, and normal to order that than the deep-fried onion rings on the back of the menu.

Instead of banning chocolate milk, we make white milk more *convenient* (put it in the front of the cooler), more *attractive* (sell it in a shapely bottle), or more *normal* (give it half of the cooler space instead of a small corner of the cooler) to choose. Instead of promoting the Doritos, a grocery store could make a healthier, high-margin food more convenient (place it in the first aisles of the store), more attractive (use spotlighting, better displays, or wider aisles), and normal (use a half-cart divider). If the store still wants to put a slot-allowance-paying Doritos display on an end aisle, they can at least co-promote it with a fresh, healthy salsa.

> Simply make healthier food more convenient, attractive, or normal to snack on, order off the menu, or throw in the shopping cart.

FROM CAN'T TO CAN: CONVENIENT, ATTRACTIVE, AND NORMAL

	1. MAKE IT MORE CONVENIENT	2. MAKE IT MORE ATTRACTIVE	3. MAKE IT MORE NORMAL
A mother who wants her kids to eat better at home . . .	Puts precut vegetables on the middle shelf of the fridge and the cookies out of sight	Buys more tempting salad dressings with cool names and less tempting bread	Sets salad bowls on the dinner table every day
A restaurant owner who wants to sell high-margin shrimp salads . . .	Makes it easy to find on the menu by putting it on the first page and in a bold font	Gives it a catchier or more appealing name	Describes it as a special or a manager's favorite
A grocery store manager who wants to sell more fish at full price . . .	Places fish in a center cooler at the end of the vegetable section	Offers easy fish-recipe ideas on note cards next to the fish	Puts floor decals near it or a green dashed line pointing toward the fish
An office manager who wants her workers to leave their desk and eat in the new healthy cafeteria . . .	Asks the cafeteria to add a $5 grab-and-go line filled with healthier foods, and maybe an honor system cash box	Helps design a more attractive cafeteria or break room, or an appealing brown-bag series	Posts notices and news on bulletin boards in the cafeteria, break room, or fitness room, and not in the work area
A school-lunch manager who wants to get more kids to take and eat fruit . . .	Puts it within easy reach in two different parts of the line—the beginning and end	Puts it in a colorful bowl and gives it a colorful sign	Puts it in front of the cash register with a sign saying, "Take an extra one for a snack"

From Me to We

· · · · · · · · · · · ·

A BRITISH ROCK BAND called Ten Years After had a catchy 1971 hit that was inspirationally titled "I'd Love to Change the World." It's YouTube-able, and the cigarette-lighter-waving chorus goes, "I'd love to change the world, but I don't know what to do . . . so I'll leave it up to you." In our enthusiasm to make the world a healthier place, it's easy to point a finger at what restaurants, schools, governments, or the food industry should do to solve the problem, but that's being an inactive activist. Besides, anybody who's ever been eight years old has been told "Any time you point a finger at someone else, three fingers point back at you." Instead of just pointing at what we think is wrong and discussing it, we can instead help change it.

Changing the whole world is overwhelming, but changing *our* personal food radius is very doable. We start with our own home and move outward to where we dine, shop, work, and go to school. This second step involves asking your neighborhood grocery store, restaurants, workplace, and school to help in a way that also benefits them—a win-win approach. Let's say you believe it would be easier for you and your family to eat healthier if your favorite restaurant offered half-size portions of food. You could demand they do it (which probably wouldn't work), you could support a city law that forced them to do it (which would take forever and probably backfire), or you could show them how they'd make more money *if* they did it (which *would* work). It's all in the approach you take.

> Changing the whole world is overwhelming, but changing *our* personal food radius is very doable.

ACTIVISM AND CLICK-TIVISM

Some people are activists and other people are more comfortable being click-tivists. We might not want to ask to speak to a restaurant manager, but we will click on a "Like" button, or forward a tweet, or send a Web-page link to an activist friend.

Even these little actions can create big movements. As they gain traction, restaurants, grocery stores, companies, and even schools cannot ignore becoming slim by design without losing customers, employees, or students. Clicking, liking, texting, tweeting, e-mailing, and forwarding are all places the click-tivist can start.

Suppose your neighbors are having a loud, late-night party that's keeping you far from your well-deserved dreamland. There are at least three approaches you can take to try to solve the problem. You could take the antagonistic approach—you could stomp over and demand they shut off the music or you'll call the police. They might turn the music down, but what happens next month when you want them to sign your neighborhood petition, buy your daughter's Girl Scout cookies, or hire your son for a summer lawn-mowing job? You've broken the relationship.

You could try the legal approach—you could encourage city council members to write a stricter noise ordinance against loud late-night parties in your neighborhood. This would take time, hassles, and headaches, and even if the law passed, you still might not get much sleep when they threw their next party—they might choose to ignore the law, crank up the stereo, and wait for the police to call it a problem.

Your third alternative would be the win-win approach. You'd explain to them that you're having problems sleeping because of the noise, and let them know what you've been doing to try to sleep—you closed your doors and windows, put the pillow over your ears, and so on. You'd then ask if they could help you with this problem. Maybe they could move the party inside, turn down the music, move the stereo speakers, or ask the loudest partiers to call it a night. What they probably won't do is blow you off. Helping you is in their best neighborly interest. No ill will, no visits from the police, and you've given them the chance to be heroically good and to build some neighborly loyalty and goodwill.

HOW MANY DOES IT TAKE?

A short while ago I was at a reception at the George Washington estate in Mount Vernon, Virginia, with some congressional staffers. I asked them how many letters, e-mails, or phone calls they needed to receive about a new issue before their bosses—our congressional representatives—sat up and took note. The number was around ten. If a congressperson gets only ten calls, e-mails, or letters on an issue—whether it's about calorie labeling, foie gras, or National Donut Day—it gets their attention. If that number reaches 100, he or she usually takes a position on it, talks about it, and eventually votes on it. They don't wait for a majority. If they hear from a few people, they assume it's the tip of a very big iceberg.

Same is true with restaurants and supermarkets. These managers are smart, and even if only a few customers start asking for half-size servings or a candy-free checkout aisle, they'll do something about it rather than risk losing you. The leaders at your company and your child's school need to get only a few requests about flexible fitness hours or smarter lunchrooms before they realize they too need to act or else be left behind—by you.[4]

Asking your loud neighbor to help you sleep better is like asking the neighbors in your food radius—your favorite restaurant, local grocery store, workplace, and schools—to help you eat better. You can demand they do it, but that creates resistance and enemies. You can try to get your city council to regulate them, but that takes time and the faith that it won't backfire. Or you can tell them what you're doing to try to eat better, and suggest what they could profitably do to help.[5] If they don't, your *new* favorite restaurant or grocery store might be the one that does. It isn't coercive or threatening—it's a free-market approach to getting what will make you healthier and happier. You're asking them to change in a way that keeps you as a customer and helps them make more money.

THE FOUR STEPS TO BECOMING SLIM BY DESIGN

We can start becoming slim by design by walking the talk. We first make easy changes to our food radius, and *then* we enlist the places around us to help. Let's start here and benefit today while the others get on board:

STEP 1. **Focus on your food radius.** Let's start with your home, your two most frequented restaurants, your favorite grocery store, your workplace, your children's school.

STEP 2. **Change what you can for yourself.** Start small with one change in each of the five places or zones in your food radius.

STEP 3. **Ask your favorite food places to help.** You'll have your own style, but let the Action Plan starting on page 254 guide you. It contains e-mails and tweets you can send, letters you can give, and a place to post your ideas so others can benefit from them.

STEP 4. **Share your success.** Blog, tweet, Facebook, or talk up your successes so that others can start changing their food radius and help make themselves slim by design. There's an online community that can help: SlimByDesign.org.

We can start becoming slim by design by walking the talk.

We first make easy changes to our food radius, and *then* we enlist the places around us to help.

Getting Started

. . . .

YOUR HOME AND HABITS are as unique as your finger-
prints. There are lots of personal ways you can start to become
slim by design, but they all start with your home. After that,
where you'll want to go depends on your lifestyle. Of these five common
lifestyles, which one or two look most familiar?

* The HOMEBODY **spends the majority of their time
  working or relaxing around their home or apartment. It's
  where he or she grazes and dines.**
* The WORKING SINGLE **works outside the home and
  spends more time out and about—eating at restaurants
  and socializing—than he or she spends at home.**
* The ENTERTAINER **can take any shape—married or
  single, younger or older—but they all make fun food and
  fun times.**
* The WORKAHOLIC **has a life that revolves around the
  office, and so does the way he or she eats.**
* The OVERSTRESSED PARENT **could work either at
  home or away—and has the added burden of keeping little
  ones happy and well fed.**

Most people have lifestyles that can fit roughly into one or two of
these categories. For instance, double-income couples with no children
would look more like a Working Single person's profile, a retired empty-
nester would look more like a Homebody, and a workaholic father might
look more like an Overstressed Parent even if it isn't parenthood that's
causing him stress.

To figure out your own slim-by-design action plan, first look at the
profile you identify with the most. Your lifestyle will help you prioritize
the changes that will help you the most.

←

THE HOMEBODY

Whether working at home, from home, or retired, this person spends most of his or her time in or around the home or apartment, whether socializing or relaxing. I'm a Homebody. When not teaching, traveling, speaking, or conducting crazy eating experiments, I'm in my basement man cave working in caveman solitude. Lots of us are homebodies, but whether we're work-at-home spouses, telecommuters, or happy retirees, we all face the same problem. After ninety minutes of focusing on our work, chores, or hobby, we need a break—often something as simple as a trip to the kitchen for whatever looks good to eat. My award-winning research colleague and good buddy Pierre Chandon once told me he could be even more productive if he worked at home instead of at his office—uninterrupted by calls, students, e-mails, and colleagues—but that he'd also weigh fifty pounds more because he'd constantly be grazing through the kitchen. It's one of the perils of being a Homebody.

Audrey (not her real name) is a homebody telecommuter who wears jeans at her home office job that's half interesting and half a grind. Keeping on schedule is a challenge—especially having to respond instantly to e-mails. While she can stay on task for ninety minutes or so, after that she needs to get up for a break to look out the window, grab a cup of coffee or glass of water, or lurk through the kitchen for a goodie as a reward for her ninety minutes of diligent sacrifice.

Her first two weeks of becoming slim by design looked like this:

Audrey's Action Plan for a Homebody

- ☐ Fills out Home Scorecard.
- ☐ Moves all food off counter.
- ☐ Adds a fruit bowl next to the door.
- ☐ Pre-plates off stove and counter.
- ☐ Uses the Half-Plate Rule.
- ☐ When at her desk, she only eats out of small bowls.

A SLIM-BY-DESIGN HOME ACTION PLAN

Slim-by-design homes really start first with the grocery store, because what you buy determines what you eat at home. We'll soon get to your grocery store, but let's first set up your home so it's ready.

1. **Fill out the In-Home Slim-by-Design Self-Assessment Scorecard on page 60.**

2. **Move the comfy chairs and the television out of the kitchen to make it less convenient to snack and graze.** This is doubly true with the big destination kitchens that we see in newer houses. "I can hang out in my kitchen and not snack," said no one ever.

3. **Do a fifteen-minute kitchen makeover.** Make the healthy foods really convenient and the junk foods really hard to find.

    * Clear the counters of any food other than a fruit bowl.
    * Put the healthiest foods out front and center in your cupboards and pantry.
    * Put cut fruit and vegetables in plastic bags on the eye-level shelf of your fridge.
    * Wrap indulgent leftovers in aluminum foil or put in opaque containers.
    * Have a separate, hard-to-reach snack cupboard and consider a child's lock for it, just as a reminder.
    * Make it easier and more convenient for you to cook healthy food, with a clear counter, handy cutting board, a well-stocked basic pantry, and a range of fresh ingredients available.

4. **Fat-proof your dinner table.**

    * Use dinner plates that are 9 to 10 inches in diameter.
    * Pre-plate your food from the stove or counter.
    * Use either tall or small glasses for anything that isn't water.
    * Use smaller serving bowls and teaspoons as serving spoons.
    * Use the Half-Plate Rule.

5. **Make sure if there's any food in the TV room that it's in a bowl—a small one.**

THE WORKING SINGLE

Working singles can be younger or older, quiet or crazy, living downtown with a roommate or in the suburbs alone, but their days are fairly structured and social. One person's day looks like this: get up ten minutes late, grab something to eat on the way to work, eat lunch with a coworker, meet up with a friend after work for dinner or drinks, go home, and repeat. While it's important for the working single to first fill out their Home Scorecard and make the changes they can there, the next priority is to focus on the restaurants they go to most frequently. This starts with their making some easy changes to eat a little better or a little less, and then involves their asking their favorite restaurants for a little help.

Lieve is a working single. After having "done time" in graduate school, she's now successful, single, social, and living near the downtown buzz. Although a decent cook and an intermittent vegetarian, she'd rather eat out than eat in. She figures once she marries and moves to the burbs she'll quickly get her fill of her own food. Now's the time to live it up and let someone else do the dishes. Her action plan started with taking ten minutes to fill out her Home Scorecard. She made a couple of changes there, and she then moved on to her favorite restaurants.

Lieve's Action Plan for a Working Single

HOME

- ☐ Fills out Home Scorecard.
- ☐ Buys a dozen low-fat yogurts, string cheese, and bananas.
- ☐ Buys some multivitamins and puts the bottle next to her toothbrush.

RESTAURANT 1: THAI-TANIC

- ☐ Asks to sit as near to the front window as possible.
- ☐ Asks for a half-size portion of a favorite entrée. Is told "No."
- ☐ Tells the manager they should offer half-size options.

A SLIM-BY-DESIGN RESTAURANT ACTION PLAN

1.   Sit where the slim people sit . . .

     * **Well-lit areas or next to windows.**
     * **Far from televisions and noise.**
     * **At high-top tables.**
     * **Away from the kitchen and bar.**

2.   Ask the server to bring the water and not the bread.

3.   Find the hidden treasures on the menu.

     * **Ask the server, "What are your two or three lighter entrées that get the most compliments?" or "What's the best thing on the menu if I want a light dinner?"**
     * **Look again for buried gems, and think twice if something has an overly seductive description.**

4.   Ask for a half-size portion or commit to taking half the meal home in a to-go bag.

5.   Talk to, text, or e-mail the restaurant's manager about how they can help you eat better (see page 255 for wording suggestions). For instance . . .

     * **Ask them to offer half-size portions.**
     * **Suggest they come up with two new lighter meals or side dishes.**
     * **Ask them to offer a salad/vegetable substitution option for the starch.**
     * **Suggest they create a fruit-only dessert option, such as a bowl of berries or a melon plate.**
     * **See if they can offer a tasting size or a tasting platter for desserts.**

6.   Tweet your friends about what you like about the restaurant and what you'd like them to improve. Mention the restaurant's name with a reply sign (@) or hashtag (#) so that the restaurant will be notified of your tweet (see page 254).

- ☐ Asks for a to-go box.
- ☐ Tweets "Ever hungry for only a half portion? The #Thai-tanic would rock if they had half portions, but they don't. Text if you want them.

RESTAURANT 2: SCENES FROM . . . AN ITALIAN RESTAURANT

- ☐ Asks the waiter to keep the bread and bring the water.
- ☐ Asks waiter, "What's new that's light but really filling?"
- ☐ Orders the Berries & Sherbet for dessert.
- ☐ Thanks manager, encourages more, clicks "Like" on Facebook, and makes a comment about what they do well and what else they could do.

THE ENTERTAINER

Entertainers can take any form—a homebody, working single, workaholic, or stressed parent. Their fortunate friends love that they create fun times and serve great food. Our study of 453 of these entertainers found that most of them are good cooks, with one of five cooking styles:[6]

* **GIVING COOKS (22 percent). Friendly, well-liked, enthusiastic cooks who specialize in comfort foods for family gatherings and large parties. They use the same standard recipes over and over.**
* **HEALTHY COOKS (20 percent). Optimistic, book-loving nature enthusiasts who are most likely to experiment with fish and with fresh ingredients, including herbs.**
* **INNOVATIVE COOKS (19 percent). The most creative and trendsetting of all cooks. They seldom use recipes— they often look at food photos for inspiration—and they experiment with ingredients, cuisine styles, and cooking methods.**
* **METHODICAL COOKS (18 percent). Often weekend hobbyists who are talented but who rely heavily on recipes. Although somewhat inefficient in the kitchen, their creations always look fairly close to the picture in the cookbook.**
* **COMPETITIVE COOKS (13 percent). The Iron Chefs of the neighborhood. Competitive cooks are dominant personalities who cook in order to impress others.**

Where things backfire in the food life of entertainers is when they go grocery shopping. They'll make whatever ingredients they come home with. Yet if some mysterious force leads them to pick up Chinese long beans instead of croissants, everyone benefits.

Take Randy, a teacher who's an innovative cook and who does most of the cooking for his wife and daughter—at least on the weekends. Today's Saturday, and he's going to do his weekly shopping trip for his family as well as for four friends who are coming over at seven tonight. He's decided on pork loin but hasn't thought through the rest of the meal. Whatever he buys that isn't served tonight will be prepared and eaten during the week. But here's the problem: If he happens to grab his cart when he's hungry, he'll definitely buy less healthy food—more processed food, frozen food, cookies, crackers, and cereal. That won't only taint tonight's meal, but it will curse his family's meals for the rest of the week. Here's the plan he decided on.

Randy's Action Plan for an Entertainer

HOME

- ☐ Fills out Home Scorecard.
- ☐ Rearranges cupboards and fridge.
- ☐ Buys two dozen 9-inch china plates from an antique store.

GROCERY STORE

- ☐ Shops after lunch and pops a piece of gum when he arrives.
- ☐ Divides his cart in half with his jacket—fruit and vegetables up front.
- ☐ Shops healthy aisles first.
- ☐ Asks to see the store manager, and tells him he'd make a higher profit margin if he put all the healthy foods in the first three aisles.
- ☐ Recommends that the manager check out SlimByDesign.org for ways to make more money by helping people shop healthy.

A SLIM-BY-DESIGN GROCERY STORE PLAN

1. Have a healthy snack before shopping. It won't make you buy less, but it will make you buy better.

2. Grab some gum. It keeps you from imagining how great those potato chips will taste. Mint and sugarless gum seem to work best.

3. Divide your cart and reserve the front half for fruits and vegetables. Use anything you have as a divider—coat, purse, briefcase, or sleeping child.

4. Keep the Half-Plate Rule in mind when you shop—half of your plate should be fruits, vegetables, or salad. But in order for that to happen, you have to be well stocked with these foods.

5. Shop the healthy aisles first: produce, lean meat, lean dairy, and the whole grain aisle.

6. Rely on your intuition first and the label last. We generally know that plain oatmeal is better for us than a box of Super Sugar Crisp-rageous, so you can skip the label. Use the nutrition label if you want to break a tie between Count Chocula and Boo Berry.

7. Talk to or e-mail the store's manager about how they can help you shop better (see page 259). For instance . . .

   * **Ask if he can offer a candy-free checkout line.**
   * **Suggest he consider providing divided half carts that encourage people to put their fruits and vegetables in front.** The dividers can be paint, duct tape, mats, whatever is easiest.
   * **Ask if his store would promote the Half-Plate Rule in the produce aisle.**
   * **See if he could combine the regular promotion with a healthy food complement on the end-of-aisle displays.**

8. Tweet your friends about what you like about the store and what you'd like them to improve. Mention the store's name with a reply sign (@) or hashtag (#) so that the word gets around (page 258).

THE WORKAHOLIC

Unlike working singles, workaholics often aren't single—and they have an unbalanced work life versus social life. Male or female, their obsessive focus might also be possible because they have a supportive spouse who shoulders the home duties. In order for work-away workaholics to become slim by design, their company's going to have to help. And the company will help—the workaholic is probably one of their most dedicated, productive, valued—and profitable—employees. To not help them is like giving the Golden Goose high blood pressure and a heart attack.

Meet Alex. He once famously introduced himself at a new employee orientation by saying, "Hi, my name's Alex, and I'm a workaholic." This was famously funny because Alex isn't—he's famously serious. Though he's spent nearly twenty years at the same Chicago company, only a few colleagues know he's married (to his second wife) and no one's really sure if he has children at home—or ever did. He's a rate-busting peak performer. He's in the office before anyone else, leaves around 6:30 P.M., sends e-mails throughout the night, and only really talks about work or work-related gossip—never about family, vacations, or free time. A couple of years ago, he still had some boyish good looks and wasn't any more overweight than the average forty-six-year-old non-exercising man. In the last two years, however, his face has aged ten-plus years and he's gained ten-plus pounds. Here's his plan to turn things around.

Alex's Action Plan for a Workaholic

HOME

- ☐ Asks wife (!) to fill out the Home Scorecard.
- ☐ Starts eating instant oatmeal every weekday.

WORKPLACE

- ☐ Has a fruit bowl on an end table in his office; refills it on Mondays.
- ☐ Stands or walks when on the phone.
- ☐ Plans on having lunchtime walking meetings from April to October.

☐ Copied the 100-point Slim-by-Design Company Scorecard and gave it to his boss, his boss's boss, and the human resources director.

A SLIM-BY-DESIGN WORKPLACE PLAN

1. Pack a lunch. We're feeling a lot less indulgent when we're packing a lunch at home than when we're smelling burgers and fries in the company cafeteria at noon.

2. Eat with a friend, and not at your desk. Try the break room, cafeteria, conference room, or the outdoors.

3. Whenever you eat in the cafeteria, pick up a piece of fruit first.

4. If you must have a candy dish, move it at least six feet from your desk.

5. Using the company fitness room? Think of it as "toning" and not as burning calories. You'll eat a lot less later on.

6. Print out, drop off, or e-mail the Slim-by-Design Workplace Self-Assessment Scorecard on page 181 to your manager, human resources director, or the company wellness director.

THE OVERSTRESSED PARENT

Overstressed parents come in different flavors—Tiger Mothers, Helicopter Dads, Two-Job Working Moms, and so forth. When their kid gets an "above average" checkmark on their report card, they either think Carnegie Hall, Nobel Prize, or U.S. senator. Part is projection, part is expectation, and all is ambition. If their kid's doing fine in class, it's time to start obsessing about their soccer practice, swim lessons, dance lessons, piano lessons . . . and their school lunch.

Valerie's the mother of three elementary-school-age boys and the wife of a dentist. While she's slim, she's afraid her two oldest sons are a little bit overweight, like her husband. With her youngest now in first grade, she's returned to work as an office manager for a physical therapy practice. She sits front-row at all of the parent-teacher organization meetings and fund-raisers, and is now adding the school lunchroom to her Tiger Mom action plan of making her family slim by design. Here's the plan.

Valerie's Action Plan for an Overstressed Parent

HOME

- ☐ Fills out the Home Scorecard.
- ☐ Puts cut fruit in front of refrigerator.
- ☐ Serves salad and vegetables first at dinner.

RESTAURANT: HINDEN-BURGER

- ☐ Allows her boys to order only milk or seltzer water with their meal.
- ☐ Shares one order of fries with everyone at the table.
- ☐ Sits in the darkest, quietest part of this fast-food restaurant.

GROCERY STORE

- ☐ Chews mint gum.
- ☐ Creates a shopping list that's half fruits and vegetables.
- ☐ Shops the cereal aisle—only when not with her boys.

A SLIM-BY-DESIGN LUNCHROOM PLAN

1. Think twice before packing a lunch for your child. Three out of four home-packed lunches are less nutritious than the average school lunch. A meat-blaster sub, bacon-flavored chips, Juicy Juice, and a double-stuffed Oreo is not the best way to show your third grader you love them.

2. Thank the school lunch manager for all they do, and give them a copy of the 100-point scorecard on page 219. Tell them you learned about low-cost/no-cost changes that can help kids eat better. Print out the Lunchroom Scorecard to save them that step (page 219). They can help kids make the right choice by making little changes like . . .

   * Display fruit in two or more locations, 1 near the register.
   * Display whole fruits in a nice bowl or basket.
   * Give foods creative/descriptive names.[6]
   * Place white milk first in the cooler.
   * Make sure white milk accounts for at least one-third of all milk displayed.
   * Make the healthiest entrée the first or most prominent in the lunch line.
   * Move chips and cookies behind the serving counter and make them by request only.
   * Create a healthy-items-only grab-and-go convenience line.[7]

3. Ask how you can help. Maybe there's an informal advisory board or a "Kitchen Cabinet" group you could join or start.

4. Suggest easy changes you can help her make, or ask if there are other slim-by-design changes you could help them with to make their job easier. Enlist other parents from the PTA. And think WWMcD—what would McDonald's do?

5. Share the same low-cost/no-cost changes with your district's health and wellness committee. Your food-service director is on it—ask her how you can get involved.

6. Download new ideas from SmarterLunchroom.org.

SCHOOL

- ☐ Thanks the school lunch manager for all she does.
- ☐ Gives her a copy of the Smarter Lunchroom Self-Assessment Scorecard (www.SlimByDesign.org) and gives two examples.
- ☐ Asks how she and other parents can help.
- ☐ Fills out a second scorecard herself when visiting her sons for lunch.
- ☐ Presents the scorecard to the next PTA-PTO meeting and asks for volunteers to help.

A ONE-MONTH PLAN

All that's important is that you start. You can start tonight in your own home, but what happens after that? You're only a month away from having the slim-by-design ball rolling for your whole neighborhood. Here's what it might look like.

Next Week (Week 1)

When you drop off your child at school, leave a note in the front office telling them how their lunchroom can help kids become slim by design (see the template on page 263) and drop off a Lunchroom Scorecard. If you want to take a stronger step, tell the principal, lunchroom manager, or food-service director that you'd be willing to help. Send the same letter to the chair of your school district's health and wellness committee. Their names and addresses are on the school website, and somewhere on the school secretary's desk.

Week 2

When you're at work—just before noon—make two copies of the "Office Space and Workplace" chapter starting on page 148 and of the Workplace Scorecard on page 181. Instead of eating lunch at your desk, drop one copy off at your boss's desk with a note telling her that if there's anything you can do to help with this, you'd appreciate the opportunity to discuss it further. Drop the second copy off with your human resources or corporate wellness manager.

Week 3

When you pick out a shopping cart at the local grocery store, divide it in half with your jacket or purse and place fruits and vegetables in front and everything else in back. After you've finished your grocery shopping, ask to see the manager. Tell him what you like most about his store and why you're a regular customer. Ask him if he ever considered having at least one candy-free checkout aisle. If the conversation goes well, mention the divided cart and tell him that you read about some easy ways other grocery stores are making healthy win-win changes. Offer to share the information. Before you leave, thank him again for the specific things he does with his store that you appreciate the most.

Week 4

You're a few minutes late when you arrive at one of your favorite restaurants. Although you requested a well-lit table, it's too crowded, so the hostess seats you in a dark corner booth and gives you a menu. Instead of letting your eye get caught by the specialties on the menu or the foods that are boxed or located in the corners, you ask the waiter for the chef's suggestion for something on the healthier side and have them pack half to go when it arrives. Toward the end of the dinner, when the manager (or waiter or hostess) asks how your meal was, tell them that you love the restaurant and would come even more often if they also served some of their most popular entrées in half-size versions. If your conversation at the restaurant goes well, share some other win-win ideas. If they show interest, tell them where they can learn more and get the Restaurant Scorecard. If they don't show interest, try again later, or check out a new restaurant. Checking out a new restaurant will definitely get their attention.

YOUR SLIM-BY-DESIGN
ACTION PLAN KIT

Whatever your lifestyle, this is easier than you think, because there are tools that can help. You can start to become a Slim-by-Design promoter without even leaving your house. The Action Plan Kit is downloadable (SlimByDesign.org) and has ready-to-send letters for you to mail or hand-deliver to whatever restaurant, school, grocer, or boss you want, and it has tips for you as a shopper, diner, cook, or parent. Here's what you'll get:

✳   **One-page overview.** Download, print, and share (pdf format).

✳   **More Slim-by-Design tips.** For shoppers, diners, cooks, and parents.

✳   **Samples.** Letters, e-mails, tweets, and Facebook posts to send to your favorite restaurants, grocery store, workplace, and school.

✳   **Slim-by-Design makeover tip sheets.** For managers of restaurants, grocery stores, workplaces, and schools.

✳   **Slim-by-Design podcast series.** Separate short, tailored podcasts and videos for the people and places mentioned above.

✳   **Slim-by-Design book club materials.** Includes a Facilitator's Guide.

✳   **Slim-by-Design personal scorecard.** Tailor this to your own needs.

If you don't have Internet access or a printer, we can mail you a free trimmed-down version of the kit along with a reminder magnet. Just send a letter-size self-addressed stamped envelope along with your e-mail address to:

Professor Brian Wansink
Cornell Food and Brand Lab—SBD Action Plan Kit
Dyson School—110 Warren Hall—Cornell University
Ithaca, NY 14853 USA

Design Trumps Discussion

. . . .

I N 2 0 0 7 , M Y F A M I L Y A N D I moved to Washington, D.C., for two years because the White House had appointed me to be in charge of the USDA's 2010 Dietary Guidelines. During this time, reporters and audience members at speeches would often ask, "What needs to be done to solve the obesity crisis?" Since I was a political appointee, most expected me to suggest a magical law or a silver-bullet policy solution. Instead, I'd say, "If you're really serious about making a change, the quickest *guaranteed* success will be in your own home. We control about 72 percent of what our family eats, for better or worse.[7] It's for the better if we have a fruit bowl in the kitchen instead of a cookie jar. It's for the better if we give our kids a snack pack of cut vegetables in a Baggie instead of two dollars to buy whatever snack they want. It's for the better if we go to a restaurant with them and order the Cajun Chicken Salad instead of the Bloomin' Onion. Changing what you do at home is the easiest *guaranteed* first step."

They'd rather discuss the problem than fill up the fruit bowl.

This was seldom what they wanted to hear, because it wasn't the magical silver-bullet policy solution that someone else would implement for them. They'd rather discuss the problem than fill up the fruit bowl.

But the changes laid out in this book are easy, and they're only the beginning of a long list of win-win solutions that can help make us all slim by design. Yet what they need is action. In the same time it would take for us to complain to our dinner partner about the restaurant's ginormous portions, we could have told the manager that we'd eat there more often if he offered a half-size version. It would have taken the same time, but it would have been a lot more constructive.

Small actions spark movements. Becoming slim by design can start immediately. It doesn't take a committee, city, consultant, or deep-pocketed health-care provider.[8] It all starts as soon as you change your home and start asking the places around you to help make it easier for you to eat and live the way you want.

Action makes the difference. That's why this book is called *Slim by Design* and not *Slim by Discussion*. Slim by Design works because it's tangible, win-win, mindless, and scorecard-specific.

It's easier to change your eating environment than to change your mind.

HOW DO I START?

You can start tonight. The ideas in these chapters are win-win ways to design your food radius so that it works for you and your family. Here's yet another way to take a first step:

TODAY	NEXT WEEK	WEEK 2	WEEK 3	WEEK 4
After finishing dishes tonight, fill out the Slim-by-Design Home Scorecard. Make any changes you easily can, and plan to change a couple more in each of the next weeks.	Print out and drop off that Slim-by-Design cafeteria note for your daughter's principal.	Download and drop off a copy of the Office Space and Workplace Scorecard with your boss and your company wellness manager	After grocery shopping, ask to talk with the manager. Compliment him and ask about possibly implementing candy-free aisles.	Dinner at the Heights Café. If the owner's in, suggest a half-serving size for some popular entrées.

Sample Scripts

· · · · · · · · · · · ·

AGAIN, WHATEVER YOUR LIFESTYLE, this is easier than you think, because there are tools that can help. You can download whatever tailored parts of an Action Plan you wish at SlimByDesign.org. Here are some sample scripts for contacting the manager of your favorite restaurant, the food-service director of your child's school, the manager of your go-to grocery store, and your company's wellness manager. You can also visit SlimByDesign.org for more ideas, as well as sample tweets and Facebook messages that you can forward to like-minded friends.[9]

HOW TO REACH OUT TO YOUR FAVORITE RESTAURANT VIA TWITTER

I.   Reply to or mention their name with "@."
2.   Mention their name with a hashtag "#."
3.   Link these suggestions to Slim by Design: #slimbydesign.

Some Sample Tweets:

@dennysdiner: Did you know that if you cut your meal portions in half, you'll sell more food? I'd buy more. #slimbydesign.

I wish *@olivegarden* had a "fruit-only" dessert option. Then I'd buy a dessert. #slimbydesign.

Check out the list on page 265, or go to SlimByDesign.org/Restaurants for a list of the Twitter handles for the top restaurant chains.

HOW TO CONTACT YOUR FAVORITE RESTAURANT VIA SNAIL MAIL

Some restaurants can make some changes at their individual locations, but others are made at the corporate level. Find these addresses starting on page 265 or at SlimByDesign.org/Restaurants for a list of the company addresses for the top restaurant chains.

Sample letter to your favorite local restaurant

Dear Manager,

For some time, your restaurant has been one of my favorites. I dine here fairly regularly with my family, friends, or visitors at work because I like the variety, the energy in the atmosphere, the engaging waitstaff, and your food. Thank you for all that you do to make it a special experience.

Recently, my family and I have been trying to eat both healthier and less than we have in the past. At home, for instance, we've moved all the snack food off the counter and rearranged the cupboards. We're also using smaller-size plates and pre-plating our food off the counter.

The reason I mention this is that there might be some easy ways your restaurant could also profitably help people like us eat a little better and a little less—so we could come in more often. For instance, we're often looking to eat smaller portions. There are a couple of ways your restaurant could help. For one, you could offer half-size portions of some of the menu items. Although you might be afraid you'll lose sales, the book *Slim by Design* shows that the opposite usually happens. Restaurants end up selling more—more sides and more drinks—and they attract some new customers. Having half-size portions would make us even happier with our visits. To help people eat less, you could also train servers to encourage customers to take home "to-go" boxes by specifically having them mention this before people order.

Your customers would also appreciate some little additions to the menu that would make it easier to eat healthier—a couple of healthy new entrées or side dishes, a double vegetable option instead of the starch, a fruit-only dessert, or a dessert tasting menu. When it comes time for a menu redesign, the menu can be designed in a way that can better lead people to buy these healthier foods. There are a lot of other easy changes that you can find at SlimByDesign.org to help you profitably help your loyal customers and new customers to eat better.

Thanks for taking the time to consider how you can help make us healthier and happier. I look forward to visiting you again soon and finding it easier to eat a little bit healthier and a little bit less. Let me know if you would like to discuss this further, and let me know how I can help you.

Sincerely,

Sample letter to your favorite fast-food chain

Dear Public Affairs Director,

For some time, your chain has been one of my family's favorites. Specifically, the location where we eat the most often is at [address] in [your city, state]. Thank you for what your company does to offer convenient and tasty food for reasonable prices.

Recently, my family and I have been trying to eat both healthier and less than we have. At home, for instance, we've moved all the snack food off the counter and rearranged the cupboards. We're also using smaller-size plates and are pre-plating our food off the counter.

The reason I mention this is there might be some easy ways your chain could also profitably help people like us eat a little better and a little less. For instance, I'd be more likely to eat healthier if there were low-fat options for your meals. It would be easier for me to help my kids eat better if there were posters encouraging the kids to take the milk instead of soft drinks and to choose the healthy side dishes—such as apple slices, yogurt, and side salads—instead of the fries. It would be great if your company offered a five-cent discount if you buy a diet soft drink (instead of a regular one), or a loyalty club card for people who order healthy meal combos.

There are a lot more ideas in the book *Slim by Design* and a lot of compelling best practices that other fast-food restaurants have been implementing at SlimByDesign.org/FastfoodBestPractices. Check it out—it will help you profitably encourage your loyal customers, and draw in newer health-conscious customers as well.

Thanks for taking the time to consider how you can help make us healthier and happier. I look forward to visiting you again soon and finding it easier to eat a little bit healthier and a little bit less. Let me know if you would like to discuss this further, and let me know how I can help you.

Sincerely,

Sample letter to your favorite casual dining chain

Dear Public Affairs Director,

For some time, your chain has been one of my family's favorites. Specifically, the location where we eat the most often is at [address] in [city and state]. I really enjoy the variety of your menu, the energy in the atmosphere, the engaging waitstaff, and the consistent quality of the food at a reasonable price. Thank you for all that you do to make it a special experience.

Recently, my family and I have been trying to eat both healthier and less than we have in the past. At home, for instance, we've moved all the snack food off the counter and rearranged the cupboards. We're also using smaller-size plates and pre-plating our food off the counter.

The reason I mention this is that there may be some easy ways your chain could also profitably help people like us eat a little better and a little less. For instance, we're often looking to eat smaller portions. There are a couple of ways your restaurant could help. For one, you could offer half-size portions of some of the more popular entrées and charge 50 to 60 percent of the price of a full portion. Although you might be afraid you'll lose sales, the book *Slim by Design* shows that the opposite usually happens—restaurants end up selling more sides and more drinks and they attract some new customers. Having half-size portions would make us even happier with our visits. To help people eat less, you could also train servers to encourage people to take home "to-go" boxes by specifically having them mention this before people order.

You could make some little additions that would make it easier to eat healthier, such as a couple of new healthy entrées or side dishes, a double vegetable option instead of the starch, a fruit-only dessert, or a dessert tasting menu. When it comes time for a menu redesign, the menu can be designed in a way that can better lead people to buy these healthier foods. You can find a lot of other easy changes at SlimByDesign.org. Check it out—it will help you profitably encourage your loyal customers, and draw in newer health-conscious customers as well.

Thanks for taking the time to consider how you can help make us healthier and happier. I look forward to visiting you again soon and finding it easier to eat a little bit healthier and a little bit less. Let me know if you would like to discuss this further, and let me know how I can help you.

Sincerely,

HOW TO REACH OUT TO YOUR GROCERY STORE VIA TWITTER

1. Reply to or mention their name with "@."
2. Mention their name with a hashtag "#."
3. Link these suggestions to Slim by Design: #slimbydesign.

Go to SlimBydesign.org/GroceryChains for a list of the Twitter handles for the top sixty-five grocery chains, or see the list at the end of this book.

HOW TO CONTACT YOUR FAVORITE GROCERY STORE VIA SNAIL MAIL

Grocers can make some changes at their individual stores, but others are made at the corporate level. The addresses for the top sixty-five of these major grocery chains can be found at the end of this chapter or at SlimByDesign.org/GroceryChains.

Sample letter to your favorite grocery store

Dear Manager,

For some time, your grocery store has been my go-to store for all my family's groceries. I really enjoy your responsive employees, your wide selection, and the cleanliness of the store. Thank you for all that you do to make shopping a special experience.

Recently, my family and I have been trying to buy healthier food—more fruits, vegetables, and lean meat—and less of the highly processed foods. For instance, we've been doing things like dividing our cart in half with a coat or purse and filling the front half with these healthier foods. We've also been walking through the healthier aisles first so that we fill our cart with healthier food.

The reason I mention this is there might be some easy ways your grocery store could profitably help make it easier for people like us to shop for healthier food. For instance, having a candy-free checkout aisle would help cut down candy impulse purchases, and you could replace the candy with other high-margin impulse purchase items such as batteries, desk accessories, and so forth. Parents with small children might even choose your store because you give them an option that keeps kids from having a candy meltdown at the checkout line, which nobody enjoys.

The book *Slim by Design* offers many other ways you could profitably make it easier for your customers to shop healthier—ideas that have worked at other stores, such as angling the produce displays at 30 and 45 degrees, using floor decals, putting your healthiest food in Aisles 1, 2, and 3, and using healthy co-promotions on end-aisle displays. You can also find a lot of these at the website SlimByDesign.org.

Thanks for taking the time to consider how you can help make us healthier and happier. I look forward to visiting you again soon and finding it easier to shop a little bit healthier so we will eat a little bit healthier. Let me know if you would like to discuss this further, and let me know how I can help you.

Sincerely,

Sample letter to a grocery store's CEO

Dear [name],

For some time, your grocery store in [city, state] has been my go-to store for all my family's groceries. Your manager there works to make shopping a special experience, and I really enjoy his responsive employees, wide selection, and the cleanliness of the store.

Recently, my family and I have been trying to buy healthier food—more fruits, vegetables, and lean meat—and less of the highly processed foods. For instance, we've been doing things like dividing our cart in half with a coat or purse and filling the front half with these healthier foods. We've also been walking through the healthier aisles first so we fill our cart with healthier food.

The reason I mention this is there might be some easy ways in which you as the CEO could profitably help make it easier for people like us to shop for healthier food in your stores. For instance, having a candy-free checkout aisle would help cut down candy impulse purchases, and you could replace the candy with other high-margin impulse purchase items such as batteries, desk accessories, and so forth. Parents with small children might even choose your store because you give them an option that keeps kids from having a candy meltdown at the checkout line, which nobody enjoys.

The book *Slim by Design* offers many other ways you could profitably make it easier for your customers to shop healthier—ideas that have worked at other stores, such as angling the produce displays at 30 and 45 degrees, using floor decals, putting your healthiest food in Aisles 1, 2, and 3, and using healthy co-promotions on end-aisle displays. You can also find a lot of these at the website SlimByDesign.org.

Thanks for taking the time to consider how you could make small changes to your stores to help make us healthier and happier. I look forward to visiting you again soon and finding it easier to shop a little bit healthier so we'll eat a little bit healthier. Let me know if you would like to discuss this further, and let me know how I can help you.

Sincerely,

Sample letter to your company's health and wellness director

Dear [name],

I appreciate what you and your staff have been doing to try to make all of us employees think twice about our health and wellness and to begin moving in a healthy direction. It not only helps make us happier and healthier, but it's also good for retention.

One habit that a number of my coworkers and I have is that we tend to eat at our desks. Although I'd like to think it's because we're super hard, dedicated workers, it probably has something to do with the lack of more attractive options, such as brown-bag lunch presentations, outings, or team lunches, and that the break room could use a serious makeover for those of us who bring our lunches. Also, the cafeteria could make a lot of changes—rearranging the placement of foods, promoting healthy convenience combo-lunches, and so forth—that could make it more money and would make us healthier.

The reason I mention this is there are a lot of easy changes that you, as our company's health and wellness director, might do to make it easier for us to start improving our health—beginning here at work. Ideas such as a multi-activity wellness plan or a Health Conduct Code would be great ways to start. The book *Slim by Design* offers many other ways you could profitably make it easier for the company to help us become healthier. You can also find a lot of these at the website SlimByDesign.org.

Thanks for taking the time to consider how you could make small changes to help make us healthier and happier. I look forward to visiting you again soon. Let me know if you would like to discuss this further, and let me know how I can help you.

Sincerely,

Sample letter to your boss or your company's CEO

Dear [name],

I appreciate what you and the wellness director have been doing to try to make all of us employees think twice about our health and wellness and to begin moving in a healthy direction. It not only helps make us happier and healthier, but it's also good for retention.

One habit that a number of my coworkers and I have is that we tend to eat at our desks. Although I'd like to think it's because we're super hard, dedicated workers, it probably also has something to do with the lack of more attractive options, such as brown-bag lunch presentations, outings, or team lunches, and that the break room could use a serious makeover for those of us who bring our lunches. Also, the cafeteria could make a lot of changes—rearranging foods and promoting healthy convenience combo-lunches, and so forth—that could make it more money and would make us healthier.

The reason I mention this is there are a lot of easy changes that you and the company's health and wellness director might do to make it easier for us to start improving our health—beginning here at work. Ideas such as a multi-activity wellness plan or a Health Conduct Code would be great ways to start. The book *Slim by Design* offers many other ways you could profitably make it easier for the company to help us become healthier. You can also find a lot of these ideas at the website SlimByDesign.org.

Thanks for taking the time to consider how you could make small changes to help make us healthier and happier. I look forward to visiting you again soon. Let me know if you would like to discuss this further, and let me know how I can help you.

Sincerely,

Sample letter to your child's school-lunchroom manager

Dear [name],

My name's [____] and I'm [your child's name]'s parent. Thank you for all that you do to help the children at [_____] School to eat better. That's a huge job on a tight budget, and our family appreciates all you do.

I've recently been hearing about something called the Smarter Lunchroom Movement. It's a low-cost—and usually no-cost—way to guide kids to select the healthiest foods in the lunchroom without making any changes to what's being offered. The idea is that by making small changes to the layout or signage in a lunchroom, you can guide kids to the apple instead of the cookie. By doing simple things like putting fruit in a nice fruit bowl next to the cash register, giving vegetable dishes a name, or making white milk the most convenient beverage in the cooler, kids will be more likely to take them and not waste them.

These principles are already being used in more than twenty thousand schools. The book *Slim by Design* offers many other ways you could profitably make it easier for your lunchroom to help kids eat healthier and also to increase participation in the lunch program. I've enclosed a one-page printout of the program and the self-assessment scorecard. You can also find a lot more information at the website SlimByDesign.org or at SmarterLunchrooms.org.

Thanks for taking the time to consider how you could make small changes to help make our kids healthier and happier. I look forward to visiting you again soon. Let me know if you would like to discuss this further, and let me know how I can help you.

Sincerely,

Sample letter to the health and wellness committee for your child's school district

Dear [name],

My name's [____] and I'm the parent of [your child's name] in [their school]. Thank you for all that you do to volunteer to help our children be healthier and happier. My family appreciates what you do.

I've recently been hearing about something called the Smarter Lunchroom Movement. It's a low-cost—and usually no-cost—way to guide kids to select the healthiest foods in the lunchroom without making any changes to what's being offering. The idea is that by making small changes to the layout or signage in a lunchroom, you can guide kids to the apple instead of the cookie. By doing simple things like putting fruit in a nice fruit bowl next to the cash register, giving vegetable dishes a name, or making white milk the most convenient beverage in the cooler, kids will be more likely to take them and not waste them.

These principles are already being used in more than twenty thousand schools. The book *Slim by Design* offers many other ways you could profitably make it easier for your lunchroom to help kids eat healthier and also to increase participation in the lunch program. I've enclosed a one-page printout of the program and the self-assessment scorecard, and I've also shared this with the lunchroom manager at the school. You can also find a lot of these at the website SlimByDesign.org or at SmarterLunchrooms.org.

Thanks for taking the time to consider how you could make small changes to help make our kids healthier and happier. I look forward to visiting you again soon. Let me know if you would like to discuss this further, and let me know how I can help you.

Sincerely,

Make It Happen

· · · · · · · · · · · ·

HERE'S HOW TO REACH your favorite fast-food and casual eating restaurants and grocery stores. Their current e-mail addresses are available at SlimByDesign.org.

FAST FOOD

Arby's
@arbys
#Arbys, #arbysbrisket,
#LeagueOfBrisket, #Curly-
Fryday, #Saucepocalypse
Arby's Restaurant Group,
Inc.
1155 Perimeter Center
West, 12th Floor
Atlanta, GA 30338
678-514-4100

Burger King
@BurgerKing
#BurgerKing, #Whopper,
#whopperjr
Burger King Worldwide
5505 Blue Lagoon Dr.
Miami, FL 33126
305-378-3000
866-394-2493

Chick-fil-A
@ChickfilA
#chickfila, #chickenfor-
breakfast, #Deliciously-
Witty, #EatMorChikin,
#GuessThatMoovie,
#CowAppreciationDay
Chick-fil-A, Inc.
5200 Buffington Rd.
Atlanta, GA 30349-2998
866-232-2040

Chipotle Mexican Grill
@ChipotleTweets, @
ChipotleMedia
#chipotle, #ChipotleGang,
#chipotleworld
Chipotle Corporate Office
Headquarters

1543 Wazee St., Suite 200
Denver, CO 80202
303-595-4000

Dairy Queen
@DairyQueen
#DQ, #BLIZZARDTreats,
#PumpkinPieBlizzard,
#DQGRILLBURGER,
#TreatTrader
American Dairy Queen
Corporation
7505 Metro Blvd.
Minneapolis, MN
55439-0286
952-830-0200

Domino's Pizza
@dominos
#ThePizzaIsGone,
#dominos, #LavaCakes,
#PIZZAPICS
Domino's Pizza LLC
30 Frank Lloyd Wright Dr.
Ann Arbor, MI 48106
734-930-3030

Dunkin' Donuts
@DunkinDonuts
#DunkinDonuts, #dunkin,
#weekenDD, #dresseDD,
#dunkinreplay, #mydunkin
Dunkin' Brands
130 Royall St.
Canton, MA 02021
781-737-3000

Five Guys Burgers and
Fries
@Five_Guys
#FiveGuys,

#FiveGuysFanatic,
#FiveGuysBurgers
Five Guys Enterprises, LLC
10440 Furnace Rd., Suite
205
Lorton, VA 22079
866-345-4897

In-N-Out Burger
@innoutburger
#innoutburger
In-N-Out Burgers Corpo-
rate Office
4199 Campus Dr., 9th Floor
Irvine, CA 92612
800-786-1000

Jimmy John's
@jimmyjohns
#jimmyjohns, #freakyfast
2212 Fox Dr.
Champaign, IL 61820

KFC
@kfc
#SecretRecipe, #kfc,
#GoCup
Community Relations
1900 Colonel Sanders Ln.
Louisville, KY 40213

Krispy Kreme
@krispykreme
#KrispyKreme, #Krispy,
#Krispyskremes
Krispy Kreme Doughnut
Corporation
P.O. Box 83
Winston-Salem, NC 27102
800-457-4779

McDonald's
@McDonalds, @
Reachout_McD
#mcdonalds, #bigmac,
#MomentsOfWonder
McDonald's Corporation
2111 McDonald's Dr.
Oak Brook, IL 60523
800-244-6227

Moe's Southwest Grill
@Moes_HQ
#moes, #moeschimi, #WelcomeToMoes, #moescaters
Moe's Southwest Grill
200 Glenridge Point Pky.,
Suite 200
Atlanta, GA 30342
Attn: Moe
877-663-7411

Panera Bread
@panerabread
#Panera, #panerabread,
#cinnamoncrunch
Panera Bread
3630 S. Geyer Rd., Suite
100
St. Louis, MO 63127
855-372-6372

Papa John's
@PapaJohns
#betteringredients, #better-pizza, #papajohns,
Papa John's International,
Inc.
P.O. Box 99900
Louisville, KY 40269-9990
877-547-7272

Pizza Hut
@pizzahut

#3CheeseStuffed,
#pizzaconfessions,
#MakeItGreat
Pizza Hut, Inc.
7100 Corporate Dr.
Plano, TX 75024
800-948-8488

Popeyes Louisiana
Chicken
@PopeyesChicken
#popeyes,
#lovethatchicken,
#WaffleTenders
AFC Enterprises, Inc.
400 Perimeter Center Ter.,
Suite 1000
Atlanta, GA 30346
877-767-3937

Sonic Drive-In
@sonicdrive_in
#ultimatedrinkstop
SONIC Corporate
Headquarters
300 Johnny Bench Dr.
Oklahoma City, OK 73104
405-225-5000

Starbucks
@Starbucks
#payitforward, #coffee,
#psl, #starbucks, #venti,
#trenti
Starbucks Customer
Relations
P.O. Box 3717
Seattle, WA 98124-3717
800-782-7282

Subway
@SUBWAY

#SUBWAYVictoryChallenge, #eatfresh, #StuffSubsSay, #SUBWAYsays
800-888-4848

Taco Bell
@TacoBell, @TacoBellTeam, @TacoBellTruck
#tacobell, #tacobelltruck,
#DoritosLocosTacos,
#FieryDLT, #livemas
1 Glen Bell Way
Irvine, CA 92618
800-822-6235

Tim Hortons
@TimHortons, @
TimHortonsUS
#timhortons, #timbits,
#TimsCoffeeArt, #TimbitsHockey, #SmileCookie
874 Sinclair Rd.
Oakville, ON L6K 2Y1
888-601-1616

Wendy's
@Wendys, @IAmBaconator
#PretzelLoveStories,
#Wendys, #6secondsflat,
#baconator
The Wendy's Company
One Dave Thomas Blvd.
Dublin, OH 43017
888-624-8140

Whataburger
@whataburger
#Whataburger,
#ProudToServeYou
Home Office
300 Concord Plaza Dr.
San Antonio, TX 78216
210-476-6000

CASUAL EATING

Applebee's
@Applebees
#Applebees, #Fanapple,
#BeesFanZone
Applebee's Services, Inc.
8140 Ward Pky.
Kansas City, MO 64114
888-592-7753

Baja Fresh
@boldbajafresh
#BajaFresh
Baja Fresh® Home Office

320 Commerce, Suite 100
Irvine, CA 92602
877-225-2373

Benihana
@Benihana
#BenihanaSushi,
#SakeTriviaSaturday
8750 NW 36th St., Suite
300
Doral, FL 33178

Boston Market
@bostonmarket
Boston Market Corporation
Attn: Guest Contact Center
14103 Denver West Pky.
Golden, CO 80401
800-365-7000

Buffalo Wild Wings
@BWWings
#bwwings, #WingWager

Carrabba's Italian Grill
@Carrabbas
#Carrabbas, #FirstTastes
2202 N. West Shore Blvd.,
5th Floor
Tampa, FL 33607

Chili's
@Chilis
#chilis

Cracker Barrel Old Country Store
@CrackerBarrel
Cracker Barrel Old Country Store
P.O. Box 787
Lebanon, TN 37088-0787
800-333-9566

Denny's
@DennysDiner
#dennys,
#MiddleEarthsDiner
Denny's Call Center
203 East Main St. P-8-6
Spartanburg, SC 29319
800-733-6697

Golden Corral
@goldencorral
#GoldenCorral
Golden Corral Corporation
5151 Glenwood Ave.
Raleigh, NC 27612
800-284-5673

IHOP
@IHOP
#ihop,
#DoItForThePancakes
450 North Brand Blvd.
Glendale, CA 91203
866-444-5144

Olive Garden
@olivegarden
#NeverEndingPasta
Olive Garden

P.O. Box 695017
Orlando, FL 32869

Outback Steakhouse
@Outback
#BloominMonday

P. F. Chang's
@PFChangs
#PFChangs
7676 E. Pinnacle Peak Rd.
Scottsdale, AZ 85255
866-732-4264

Perkins Restaurant and Bakery
@EatAtPerkins
6075 Poplar Ave., Suite 800
Memphis, TN 38119
901-766-6400

Red Lobster
@redlobster
#CrabFest,
#CheddarBayBiscuit
Red Lobster Guest Relations
P.O. Box 695017
Orlando, FL 32869
800-562-7837

Red Robin
@redrobinburgers
#MillionReasons
6312 S Fiddlers Green Cir.,
#200N
Greenwood Village, CO 80111
303-846-6000

Round Table Pizza
@RoundTablePizza
#PZAday
Round Table Pizza
1320 Willow Pass Rd., Suite 600
Concord, CA 94520
925-969-3900

Ruby Tuesday
@rubytuesday

#RubyTuesday
Ruby Tuesday Restaurant Support Center
150 West Church Ave.
Maryville, TN 37801

Steak 'n Shake
@SteaknShake
#steaknshake,
#steakburger
36 S. Pennsylvania St.,
Suite 500
Indianapolis IN 46204
317-633-4100

T.G.I. Friday's
@TGIFridays
#TGIFStackedBurgers

Texas Roadhouse
@texasroadhouse
#texasroadhouse
6040 Dutchmans Ln., Suite 200
Louisville, KY 40205
502-426-9984

The Cheesecake Factory
@Cheesecake
#cheesecake,
#CheesecakeFactory
26950 Agoura Rd.
Agoura Hills, CA 91301
818-871-3000

Waffle House
@WaffleHouse
#wafflehouse
Waffle House Inc.
5986 Financial Dr.
Norcross, GA 30071
770-729-5700

Zaxby's
@Zaxbys
Zaxby's Franchising, Inc.
1040 Founders Blvd.
Athens, GA 30606
866-892-9297

GROCERY STORES

A&P
@AandPStores

Acme Fresh Market
@acmefreshmarket

#acmemarkets
Acme Fresh Markets
Consumer Marketing
P.O. Box 1910

Akron, OH 44309
330-733-2263

Albertszs
@Albertsons, @
AlbertsonsHelpr
#albertsons
877-932-7948

Andronico's
@Andronicos1
#Andronicos

Associated Supermarkets
@myassociated
#AssociatedSupermarket
1800 Rockaway Ave., Suite
200
Hewlett, NY 11557
516-256-3100

Baker's Grocery
@BakersGrocery
The Kroger Co.
1014 Vine St.
Cincinnati, OH 45202-1100
800-576-4377

Bashas' Supermarkets
@BashasMarkets
#bashas, #BashasMarkets
Bashas' Corporate Offices
22402 S. Basha Rd.
Chandler, AZ 85248
800-755-7292

Big Y Markets
@BigYFoods
#BigYFoods
800-828-2688

Bi-Lo
@BILOSuperSaver
#bilo
BI-LO, LLC
Attn: Customer Support
Center
P.O. Box 99
Mauldin, SC 29662
800-768-4438

BJ's Wholesale
@BJsWholesale
#bjswholesale

Brookshire Brothers
@BrookshireBros
#BrookshireBros
Brookshire Brothers
Attn: Customer Relations
1201 Ellen Trout Dr.
Lufkin, TX 75904
936-634-8155

Brookshire's
@Brookshires_
#Brookshire
888-937-3776

Buehler's Fresh Food
@BuehlersGrocery
#buehlers
Consumer Affairs
Buehler's Fresh Foods
P.O. Box 196
Wooster, OH 44691
888-283-4537

City Market
@MyCityMarket
The Kroger Co.
1014 Vine St.
Cincinnati, OH 45202-1100
800-576-4377

Costco
@CostcoTweets
#costco

C-Town Supermarkets
@CtownMarkets
Alpha I Marketing Corp.
65 West Red Oak Ln.
White Plains, NY 10604
Attn: Alpha I Marketing
Operations
914-697-5300

Defense Commissary
Agency
@YourCommissary
#Commissary, #milfam,
#milspouse, #milso

Dillons
@DillonsGrocery
The Kroger Co.
1014 Vine St.
Cincinnati, OH 45202-1100
800-576-4377

Dominick's
@Dominicks
#Dominicks
Customer Service Center
Safeway Inc. M/S 10501
P.O. Box 29093
Phoenix, AZ 85038-9093
877-723-3929

Family Fare
@shopfamilyfare
800-451-8500
Fareway Food Stores

@Fareway_Stores
#fareway

Fiesta Mart
@FiestaMart
#FiestaMart

Food 4 Less
@Food4Less
#Food4Less
The Kroger Co.
1014 Vine St.
Cincinnati, OH 45202-1100
800-576-4377

Food City
@FoodCity
#FoodCity

Food Lion
@FoodLion
#foodlion
Food Lion
Attn: Customer Relations
P.O. Box 1330
Salisbury, NC 28145-1330
800-210-9569

Fred Meyer
@Fred_Meyer
#fredmeyer
866-518-2686

Fry's Food Stores
@FrysFoodStores
#frysfood
The Kroger Co.
1014 Vine St.
Cincinnati, OH 45202-1100
800-576-4377

Giant Eagle
@GiantEagle
#gianteagle
800-553-2324

Giant Food Stores
@GiantFoodStores
888-814-4268

Giant of Maryland
@GiantFoodSC
8301 Professional Pl., Suite
115
Landover, MD 20785
301-341-4100
888-469-4426

Grocery Outlet
@GroceryOutlet
#groceryoutlet,
#BargainMarket

2000 Fifth St.
Berkeley, CA 94710
510-845-1999

Hannaford
@Hannaford
#hannaford,
#HannafordHelpsSchools
Hannaford Supermarkets
145 Pleasant Hill Rd.
Scarborough, ME 04074
800-213-9040

Harris Teeter
@HarrisTeeter
#HarrisTeeter
Harris Teeter Inc.
Attn: Customer Relations
P.O. Box 10100
Matthews, NC 28106-0100
800-432-6111

H-E-B
@HEB
#primopicks, #HEB
H-E-B
Attention: Customer Relations Department
P.O. Box 839999
San Antonio, TX
78283-3999
800-432-3113

Hy-Vee
@HyVee
#hyvee
Hy-Vee, Inc.
5820 Westown Pky.
West Des Moines, IA
50266-8223
800-772-4098

Jewel-Osco
@jewelosco
#jewelosco
Attn: Customer Service
157 S. Howard St.
Spokane, WA 99201
877-932-7948

Kroger
@kroger
#kroger
The Kroger Co.
1014 Vine St.
Cincinnati, OH 45202-1100
800-576-4377

Lowes Foods
@LowesFoods
#SmartShopper,

#SuperDoubles, #lowesfood
Lowes Foods
ATTN: Merchandising
P.O. Box 24908
Winston-Salem, NC
27114-4908
888-537-8646

Market Basket
@mydemoulas
#marketbasket,
#mydemoulas

Market Street
@MarketStreet_TX
#marketstreet
Store Support Center
United Supermarkets, LLC
7830 Orlando Ave.
Lubbock, TX 79423
877-848-6483

Marsh Supermarkets
@MarshGrocery
#marshsupermarkets
800-382-8798

Meijer
@meijer
#Meijer, #MeijerGame-
Face, #meijerstyle
Meijer
2929 Walker Ave. NW
Grand Rapids, MI
49544-9424
877-363-4537

Pathmark
@Pathmark
#pathmark

Pick 'n Save
@PicknSaveStores
#MyPicknSave,
#PickNSave
866-279-6269

Price Chopper
@PriceChopper
#pricechopper,
#choppinprices
Price Chopper
Supermarkets
461 Nott St.
Schenectady, NY 12308
Attn: Consumer Services
800-666-7667

Publix
@Publix, @PublixHelps
#Publix
Publix Super Markets

Corporate Office
ATTN: Customer Care
P.O. Box 407
Lakeland, FL 33802-0407
800-242-1227

Raley's Supermarkets
@raleysstores
#raleys, #5DollarMonday
Raley's Service Center
500 West Capitol Ave.
West Sacramento, CA
95605
800-925-9989

Ralphs
@RalphsGrocery
The Kroger Co.
1014 Vine St.
Cincinnati, OH 45202-1100
800-576-4377

Randalls
@Randalls_Stores
#Randalls
Customer Service Center
Safeway Inc. M/S 10501
P.O. Box 29093
Phoenix, AZ 85038-9093
877-723-3929

Safeway
@Safeway
Customer Service Center
Safeway Inc. M/S 10501
P.O. Box 29093
Phoenix, AZ 85038-9093
877-723-3929

Save Mart
@SaveMart
#FreshComesFirst, #Make-
MealsPeppy, #Savemart
Save Mart Supermarkets
Attn: Consumer Relations
P.O. Box 4278
Modesto, CA 95352
800-692-5710

Save-A-Lot
@savealot

Schnucks
@SchnuckMarkets
#schnucks

Sedano's Supermarkets
@Sedanos
#Sedanos
3140 West 76 St.
Hialeah, FL 33018
305-824-1034

ShopRite
@ShopRiteStores
#shoprite
ShopRite Customer Care
P.O. Box 7812
Edison, NJ 08818
800-746-7748

Smart & Final
@smartfinal
#ChooseSmart,
#SmartFinal
600 Citadel Dr.
Commerce, CA 90040
323-869-7500

Sprouts Farmers Market
@sproutsfm
#sproutsfm,
#sproutsfarmersmarket
Sprouts Farmers Market
Corporate Office
11811 N. Tatum Blvd., Suite
2400
Phoenix, AZ 85028
888-577-7688

Stater Bros. Market
@Stater_Brothers
#StaterBros,
#StaterBrosCustomers
Stater Bros. Corporate
Office
301 S. Tippecanoe Ave.
San Bernardino, CA 92408
888-992-9977

Strack & Van Til
@StrackAndVanTil
#StrackAndVanTil

Straub's Markets
@StraubsMarkets
#straubs
8282 Forsyth Blvd.
Saint Louis, MO 63105
314-725-2121

Target
@target
800-591-3869
No Target Grocery social
media presence

The Fresh Market
@TheFreshMarket
#thefreshmarket
Attn: Customer Loyalty
628 Green Valley Rd., Suite
500

Greensboro, NC 27408-7041
866-817-4367

The Ingles Advantage
@InglesAdvantage
#InglesAdvantage
P.O. Box 6676
Asheville, NC 28816
828-669-2941

Tops Friendly Markets
@TopsPRODUCE
TOPS Markets
Attn: Customer Service
P.O. Box 1027
Buffalo, NY 14240-1027
800-522-2522

United Supermarkets
@UnitedWestTexas
#UnitedSupermarkets
Store Support Center
United Supermarkets, LLC
7830 Orlando Ave.
Lubbock, TX 79423
877-848-6483

Vons
@Vons_Pavilions
#vons
Customer Service Center
Safeway Inc. M/S 10501
P.O. Box 29093
Phoenix, AZ 85038-9093
877-723-3929

Waldbaum's
@waldbaums
#waldbaums

Walmart
@Walmart, @
WalmartHealthy
#GreatForYou
No all-around Walmart
Grocery social media
presence

Wegmans
@Wegmans
#Wegmans
Wegmans Food Markets
1500 Brooks Ave.
P.O. Box 30844
Rochester, NY 14603-0844
800-933-6267

Weis Markets
@WeisMarkets
#WeisRD
1000 South Second St.
P.O. Box 471

Sunbury, PA 17801
866-999-9347

Whole Foods
@WholeFoods
#WFMdish,
Whole Foods Market, Inc.
550 Bowie St.
Austin, TX 78703-4644
512-477-4455

WinCo Foods
@WinCoFoods
#WinCo
P.O. Box 5756
Boise, ID 83705-5756
208-377-0110

Winn-Dixie
@WinnDixie
#AskWinnDixie, #ImBeef-
People, #winndixie
P.O. Box B
Jacksonville, FL
32203-0297
866-946-6349

Woodman's Food Market
@WoodmansFood22, @
WoodmansFood14, @Wood-
mansFood33, @Woodmans-
Food29, @WoodmansFood1,
@WoodmansFood27, @
WoodmansFood16, @
WoodmansFood20, @
WoodmansFood39, @
WoodmansFood35, @
WoodmansFood37, @
WoodmansFood24, @
WoodmansFood30, @
WoodmansFood31, @
WoodmansFood40
#woodmans,
#WoodmansFoodMarket
922 Milton Ave.
Woodman's Corporate
Offices
2631 Liberty Ln.
Janesville, WI 53545
608-754-8382
608-754-8317

Acknowledgments

. . . .

I RECENTLY READ A BOOK dedication that read, "This book is dedicated to my family, without whom it would have been finished three years ago." Being less terse, here's four groups of superstars that need my thanks.

My Family. For Jennifer, Audrey, Valerie, and Lieve, who put up with no real family vacations for the past four years and who were content to feed me by sliding a plate under my office door. For my parents, John and Naomi Wansink, and my brother, Craig, and his kids, Katrina and Teddy, for putting up with my being at the library whenever we were together.

My Fun, Funny, Tireless Friends, Coauthors, and Team Members. No one has been blessed with more brilliant, funny, and genuine co-authors than I have been. Many of these people were mentioned in the acknowledgments of my book *Mindless Eating,* but the ones who are prominent in this book are Pierre Chandon, Koert van Ittersum, Collin Payne, David Just, Bill Schulze, Aner Tal, Kevin Kniffin, and Drew Hanks. And thanks to the amazing people in the Food and Brand Lab: Sandra Cueller, Laura Smith, Adam Brumberg, Kathryn Hoy, Julia Hastings Black, Pam Staub, Gretchen Gilbert, Nicole Albright, and many others.

Our Generous Sponsors. Most notably the USDA and people like JoAnn Guthrie, Kevin Concannon, Cindy Long, Jackie Haven, and Jerold Mande.

The Slim-by-Design Shapers. These include the two people who had the greatest impact on my writing style: Dr. Robert Ridings and the inimitable Toni Burbank, my editor on *Mindless Eating.* To the amazing Star Li, a former Lab alumna who built the initial websites, and whose humor and edits helped make the book hopefully a bit more hip. To my literary agent, Suzanne Gluck, for her wisdom and energy, and to the Eric Lupfer, for his insight and timely solutions. And finally to my editor, Cassie Jones, who has always seen my vision for the impact I have wanted this book to have on the way we eat. Her ability to quickly see what will work best and how to make it have a visual and conceptual punch is stunning.

←————

Notes

. . . .

INTRODUCTION

1. While we didn't do packaging size studies with competitive eaters, we have done other studies with them, and they won't be much different than the rest of the world when it comes to overeating during a nonwork day. Brian Wansink, "Can Package Size Accelerate Usage Volume?," *Journal of Marketing* 60, no. 3 (July 1996): 1–14.

2. This same theater was also one we used a couple of years later when I showed that people would eat 34 percent more popcorn from large buckets even if it was five days old and tasted like rancid Styrofoam.

3. In reality, the large size we gave them was closer to 437 calories and the smaller ones were 109 calories. I called these "mini-size packaging" during the presentations, but the executives shortened these to 100-calorie packages in our discussions. We published a similar study for validation: Brian Wansink, Collin R. Payne, and Mitsuru Shimizu, "The 100-Calorie Semi-Solution: Sub-Packaging Most Reduces Intake Among the Heaviest," *Obesity* 19, no. 5 (Spring 2011): 1098–100.

4. This same study was replicated in a lab study at Wharton with similar results. While lab studies are a lot more boring than studies in bargain movie theaters, they're tighter. Nobody comes in late, asks for different snacks, or makes out in the back row.

5. This varies depending on the type of snack and type of person, which is why, thankfully, no company has tried to use this as a claim. Our studies usually show that about 70 percent of the people given these smaller packages eat less during that occasion. For the other 30 percent, some eat about the same and others eat slightly more. If they want about 270 calories of a snack, two packages give them too little and three give them a bit too much, but they choose them anyway. Thankfully, the people who seem to benefit most from 100-calorie packages are those who need it most—overweight people and dieters. The 30 percent who don't eat less (and some eat more) have been studied by others: Maura L. Scott, Stephen M. Nowlis, Naomi Mandel, and Andrea C. Morales, "The effects of reduced food size and package size on the consumption behavior of restrained and unrestrained eaters," *Journal of Consumer Research* 35, no. 3 (2008): 391–405.

6. More ideas at Brian Wansink and Mike Huckabee, "De-Marketing Obesity," *California Management Review,* 47, no. 4 (Summer 2005): 6–18; also Brian Wansink, "Can Package Size Accelerate Usage Volume?," *Journal of Marketing* 60, no. 3 (July 1996): 1–14.

7. See more at Brian Wansink and Jeffrey Sobal, "Mindless Eating: The 200 Daily Food Decisions We Overlook," *Environment and Behavior* 39, no. 1 (January 2007): 106–23.

8. Interestingly, the people who make the most decisions about food every day are the people on the extremes. Slim people make about 225 and heavy people make about 250. The difference is that the answers are different. Slim people might be more likely to say, "No," and heavy people, "Yes." This is nicely covered in the article by Sobal and me cited in the previous note.

9. These articles have been published in some of the best medical, psychology, nutrition, obesity, consumer behavior, marketing, and economic journals. Most of these won't show up in a PubMed search because they aren't indexed there. Check out Web of Science and other resources for lots of other great things scholars have done in this area.

10. They weigh seven pounds more when there is food like cereal that is visible in the kitchen. Brian Wansink, Andrew S. Hanks, and Kirsikka Kaipainen, "Kitchen Counter Correlates of Obesity: An Observational Study," forthcoming.

11. Once we know these, we can work to change them ourselves, and we know how the places around us can help us eat better.

CHAPTER ONE: MINDLESS EATING SOLUTIONS

1. Because I used to write a bimonthly column in *AARP* magazine called "Chew on This," I got a close look at the interviews for the magazine. The "Yeast and Potting Soil Diet" was mentioned in a funny interview by the witty NBC News anchor Brian Williams. It's equally effective and ill-advised as the "cardboard only" diet.

2. There's a saying among psychology and consumer behavior researchers that "Research is me-search."

3. More at Kathryn Hoy and B. Wansink, "Our Food Radius: Americans Purchase or Eat 75% of Their Food within Three Miles of Home," *Journal of Nutrition Education and Behavior* 45, no. 4S (2013): 47.

4. They all move us in the direction of becoming more slim by design. A lot of enlightened companies want to do what's right and they want to do it profitably. My government service, as executive director of the USDA's agency in charge of the Dietary Guidelines, made me realize that there are many win-win ways to do this if we think win-win instead of the more common win-lose or us-them mentality.

5. From my working paper, Brian Wansink, "The Food Radius of an American," under review.

6. *Bob's Burgers* is a *Family Guy*–like animated series whose title character is voiced by H. Jon Benjamin (the voice of Archer). If you don't mind snorting milk out of your nose as you watch it, it's a must-see for anyone who loves fast food and the animated spy series *Archer*.

7. More on this can be found in chapter 9, "Fast Food Fever," of Brian Wansink, *Mindless Eating: Why We Eat More than We Think* (New York: Bantam-Dell, 2006).

8. This line is compliments of the late, great Minneapolis comedian Mitch Hedberg, who also made the comment that if you're a fish and want to be a fish stick, you have to have really good posture, otherwise you'd be a fish clump, and nobody will take you to parties.

9. Incidentally, all of these studies are preapproved. Today, each study planned by university researchers must be submitted to that university's Institutional Review Board to ensure it will not harm the participants. Why would someone participate? If they are college students, they usually get extra credit. If they are "real people," they are usually paid $10–$30, or given free food, movie tickets, and so on. Their identity is always protected, whatever they say and do is anonymous, and any record of their participation is eliminated once we analyze the data. Until a few years ago, most research in business schools, and often that related to sensory studies and food intake, was given a general class of approval or exemption. This was given as long as the research did not threaten the participants, and as long as they gave their consent and could quit the study at any time. Because of litigation related to medical-school research, such exemptions are no longer possible. Everything from a laddering interview to an observation study at a restaurant now needs detailed prior approval by the Institutional Review Board at most schools.

10. This is a standard way of assessing the extent to which a person is overweight. Following the guidelines of the World Health Organization, people are classified as overweight if their body mass index (BMI) is greater than 25 and obese if their BMI is greater than 30. Body mass index is computed as the ratio of weight, measured in kilograms, to squared height, measured in meters. Those with a BMI over 30 are considered obese, between 25 and 30 is considered overweight, and under 25 is considered normal. Since the word "normal" is a little bit off-putting to some, I'm using the word "slim" as a shortcut, although "slimmer" would be geekily accurate.

11. The Acme Corporation name in these *Road Runner* cartoons is especially ironic, since the Greek word *akme* meant peak or prime, and Acme's products are total generic pieces of garbage.

12. Many of the details of this can be found at Brian Wansink and Collin R. Payne, "Eating Behavior and Obesity at Chinese Buffets," *Obesity* 16, no. 8 (August 2008): 1957–60. To better nail down the distance slim versus heavy diners sit from the buffet, the sixteen-foot distance was determined in a separate study of two buffets (one in Washington, D.C., and one in Cortland, New York) that allowed diners to seat themselves.

13. It wasn't just how they served themselves and where they sat; the thinner people were three times as likely to use chopsticks (23.5 versus 7 percent) and nine times as likely to use a small plate (13.7 versus 1.4 percent), and they even chewed their food 24 percent more. Thinner people chewed their average mouthful of food 14.8 times, compared to 11.9 times for the heavier people.

14. Buffet connoisseurs might also find two of our other buffet studies of interest: Brian Wansink and Mitsuru Shimizu, "Eating Behaviors Predict the Number of Buffet Trips: An Observational Study at All-You-Can-Eat Chinese Restaurants," *American Journal of Preventive Medicine* 44, no. 4 (April 2013): e49–e50; David R. Just and Brian Wansink, "The Flat-rate Pricing Paradox: Conflicting Effects of 'All-You-Can-Eat' Buffet Pricing," *Review of Economics and Statistics* 93, no. 1 (February 2011): 193–200; and Brian Wansink and Andrew S. Hanks, "Slim by Design: Serving Healthy Foods First in Buffet Lines Improves Overall Meal Selection," *PLoS One* 8, no. 10 (2013): e77055.

15. A person eating an $8.00 buffet might eat $2.50–$3.00 worth of food. If they waste even one-tenth of what they take (25¢–30¢ worth of food), and if there are 100 total people who eat there for lunch and for dinner, that's a conservative $25/day.

16. Except at the real extremes, how heavy we are doesn't have to do with how often we eat fast food or drink soft drinks: David R. Just and Brian Wansink, "Why Isn't Fast Food Intake Frequency Related to BMI Except at the Extremes?," under review.

17. One of the more notable of these studies traced people in the National Mindless Eating Challenge. Keeping consistent—regardless of the advice one's been given—was a huge predictor in weight loss. See Kirsikka Kaipanen, Collin R. Payne, and Brian Wansink, "The Mindless Eating Challenge: Retention, Weight Outcomes, and Barriers for Changes in a Public Web-based Healthy Eating and Weight Loss Program," *Journal of Medical Internet Research* 14, no. 6 (2012): e168.

18. Brian Wansink, Aner Tal, and Mitsuru Shimizu, "The Wichita 'One-Ton' Weight Loss Program: Community Weight Loss and the National Mindless Eating Challenge," *FASEB Journal* 25 (2011): 974.2.

19. Special thanks for Dr. Bill Dietz, formally of the Centers for Disease Control, for this joke.

20. Lots of great examples of this can be found in Lisa R. Young's book *The Portion Teller* (New York: Morgan Road Books, 2005). Also see Lisa R. Young and Marion Nestle, "The Contribution of Expanding Portion Sizes to the US Obesity Epidemic," *American Journal of Public Health* 92 (2002): 246–49.

21. This is slightly more for women than for men. Brian Wansink and Simone Dohle, "'Little to Lose:' Surprising Weight Loss Aspirations of American Women," under review; and Brian Wansink, Simone Dohle, and Katherine I. Hoy, "Fifteen Pounds to Happiness: The Personal Obesity Crisis and Weight Loss Ideals of American Women," *Journal of Nutrition Education and Behavior* 45 (2013): 4S, 41.

22. I used to say that counting calories doesn't work for 90 percent of the population, but 90 percent is probably low. It only includes the people who have tried to diet. There's a sizable population who have never needed to, tried to, or cared to.

23. I am also a big believer in the research and clinical work done around mindful eating by wonderful people such as Drs. Susan Albers, Jean Krisilis, and Jan Chozen Bays, and I've been honored to write introductions for their books and blurbs for their covers. It's worked well for many people, and there are great

insights for anyone willing to take a little bit of effort and discipline to do it as it should be done. It's also one of the best and easiest ways to both appreciate the food and enjoy its taste.

24. Some studies suggest that 50 percent of our food is eaten away from home. What that doesn't account for is how much of that came from the home in the form of a packed lunch, snack, or granola bar that was grabbed on our way out the door. Even much of the food purchased outside the home—such as carry-out or home delivery—is eaten in the home.

25. More details of this can be found in chapter 7, but the whole article is Brian Wansink, Andrew S. Hanks, and Kirsikka Kaipainen, "Kitchen Correlates of Obesity," under review.

26. Seeing a food is one of the biggest triggers of eating bouts. The first study of mine to attract popular attention: Brian Wansink, "Antecedents and Mediators of Eating Bouts," *Family and Consumer Sciences Research Journal* 23, no. 2 (December 1994): 166–82.

27. Actually eye contact, even with these freakish little two-dimensional characters, makes you feel more connected with the brand and prefer it more. In a recent study, we showed that 51 of 57 cartoon characters end up—at least incidentally—making eye contact as you and your children walk down the cereal aisle. They might be looking more at the cereal than you, but the damage is done. It's a fun study and one that has key lessons for how cereal companies can sell the healthier stuff, too. More at Aviva Musicus, Aner Tal, and Brian Wansink, "Eyes in the Aisles: Why Is Cap'n Crunch Looking Down at My Child?," *Environment & Behavior*, 0013916514528793, first published on April 2, 2014.

CHAPTER TWO: YOUR SLIM-FOR-LIFE HOME

1. The whole key is to have high contrast between the color of the food you serve and the color of the plate you use. Since we're most in danger of overserving starches, and since most starches are white—pasta, rice, potatoes—it's easy to just have a set of darker plates for those foods. We used red plates in the study, which took place at a Cornell Alumni Reunion. "Look . . . a free pasta lunch!" More at Koert van Ittersum and Brian Wansink, "Plate Size and Color Suggestibility: The Delboeuf Illusion's Bias on Serving and Eating Behavior," *Journal of Consumer Research* 39 (August 2012): 215–28.

2. More at Brian Wansink, "Slim By Design: Kitchen Layouts of the Thin or Famous," *Journal of Nutrition Education and Behavior* 44, no. 4 (July–August 2012): S21.

3. People who have succeeded in being slim all their life end up learning some amazing secrets. Often each person only has one or two rules of thumb that pretty much keep them on track. If you're one of these people, consider joining the Slim-by-Design Registry. You can keep yourself on track and help others also. Sign up at SlimByDesignRegistry.org.

4. This coverage of my kitchen makeovers was nicely reported by Sarah Wildman, "One-Bite-at-a-Time Diet Makeover," *O, The Oprah Magazine*, October 2008.

5. Secrets for this person and people like her who have been able to stay slim for their entire life are shared at SlimByDesignRegistry.org.

6. Yes, yes, yes, they would have had to leave both their Iron Man costume and their giant blue Avatar prosthesis head with the studio wardrobe. But imagine if they *were* to wear them home. Better yet, imagine them on the drive home. They'd always have the right of way.

7. To give you some idea of how this works, let's take a look at a series of makeovers I did for *O* (October 2008) and *Grazia*—a hip British woman's magazine (November 2009, 111–12). The results show how this works. Fat-proofing your house is not only meant to get rid of food booby traps, but to also set it up so it's easier to eat the right thing and not too much of the bad.

8. But not knowing anything at all about a person, there are still obvious places to start. Of the five places the book *Mindless Eating* identified as being where most people overeat—(1) meal stuffing, (2) snack grazing, (3) party bingeing, (4) desktop/dashboard dining, and (5) restaurant indulging—the first two are what happens at home. Some of the more basic ideas on how to tackle these are detailed in chapter 10 of *Mindless Eating*.

9. A number of the studies in these first chapters are correlational; they are not causational. They are more like epidemiology and less like carefully controlled (but often artificial) lab research. Now, most people don't care—because it makes sense that there's causality. But you probably wouldn't be reading this endnote unless you were really interested in research. As we underscore in all of these journal articles, this suggests a relationship, but not the direction of the relationship. The articles will give you more detail, and you can get them online or e-mail me and we'll get you copies.

10. At 121 inches per year, it is the highest snowfall of any large United States city. While the city's 145,000, the metro area is closer to 660,000.

11. In fairness to the rest of the team, I was the geeky one and they were the cool ones: They included Laura Smith, Cassie Miller, Margaret Sullivan, Will Wiese, Julia Hastings Black, Rich Patterson, Norman Porticella, David Sharp, and others.

12. This was one small piece of a large, six-month study that was funded by the NIH White House Challenge Grants. People were recruited in a variety of ways, and when agreeing to be in the study, they were aware that we would be photographing and weighing them. There was no indication that the study would be about weight loss.

13. The Withings scale, made by a French company, cost $180 when we conducted the study and is now $150.

14. All of these differences, except for fruit, are significant at the $p < .05$ level. More detail can be found in the working paper, Brian Wansink and Drew Hanks, "How Visible Food in Kitchens Relates to Weight," under review.

15. This is an observational study—not unlike the Chinese buffet study in chapter 1. Although not causal, these exploratory findings raise some interesting questions, such as why people with diet soft drinks on the counter seem as similar to those with regular soft drinks. Also, these results are different for men, presumably because they spend less time at home and less time tempted by the goodies in the kitchen. More at Brian Wansink, Andrew S. Hanks, and Kirsikka Kaipainen, "Kitchen Counter Correlates of Obesity: Observational Study," working paper.

16. In recent years, architects and kitchen remodeling couples have asked us how to design a kitchen that can help them lose weight and be slim by design. This is a reversal from the 1940s, when homemakers were less concerned about their weight than how they were going to make three meals from scratch. They wanted efficiency.

17. Efficiency researchers proved that the most efficient kitchen is the one that minimizes movement between the refrigerator, stove, and sink. They reasoned that if you took a top-down blueprint of the kitchen and drew a line from each of these appliances, the resulting triangle would show how efficiently a kitchen is designed. The closer together they are, the smaller the triangle. Today, the triangle probably is the refrigerator, microwave, and sink. That's probably what makes an efficient kitchen. Fortunately, the size of your triangle doesn't seem to be related to your weight. It is, however, related to your Visa limit.

18. From Lisa Kaplan Gordon, from HouseLogic.com.

19. Here's why: You see the first food and ask yourself, "Do I want Fruity Pebbles today or don't I?" If you answer "No," you move to the next cereal that catches your eye, and you ask yourself again. This continues until you see the magically delicious cereal that makes you say, "Yes!" But you're a whole lot less likely to get to the fifth food because you would have already picked the first or second one you saw. Your most visible foods are usually the least healthy. We unknowingly tilt the scale toward our favorite indulgent foods by having them front and center. While you could rearrange your cupboard so the first things you see are the healthiest, you don't. The endnote below shows where to find more excruciating detail on this.

20. One of the most comprehensive manifestos on stockpiling and consumption is also one you don't want to read while driving or operating heavy machinery: Pierre Chandon and Brian Wansink, "When Are Stockpiled Products Consumed Faster? A Convenience-Salience Framework of Postpurchase Consumption Incidence and Quantity," *Journal of Marketing Research* 39, no. 3 (2002): 321–35.

21. The most conclusive color study that's been published in a major journal dealt with color contrast. It showed that the greater the color contrast, the less people served themselves. That is, the greater the contrast of food on a plate (red pasta on a white plate), the less they served themselves. Koert van Ittersum and Brian Wansink, "Plate Size and Color Suggestibility: The Delboeuf Illusion's Bias on Serving and Eating Behavior," *Journal of Consumer Research* 39 (August 2012): 215–28.

22. This is not a well-researched area; most of the best evidence, however, can be found in this review: Brian Wansink, "Environmental Factors That Increase the Food

Intake and Consumption Volume of Unknowing Consumers," *Annual Review of Nutrition* 24 (2004): 455–79.

23. The kitchenscapes and tablescapes concepts are detailed in Jeffry Sobal and Brian Wansink, "Kitchenscapes, Tablescapes, Platescapes, and Foodscapes: Influences of Microscale Built Environments on Food Intake," *Environment and Behavior* 39, no. 1 (January 2007): 124–42.

24. This study on the package sizes was the basis for the 100-calorie pack: Brian Wansink, "Can Package Size Accelerate Usage Volume?," *Journal of Marketing* 60, no. 3 (July 1996): 1–14.

25. We're all part of the Clean Plate Club, eating about 92 percent of however much we serve ourselves. Here's our latest on the topic: Brian Wansink and Katherine Abowd Johnson, "The Clean Plate Club: About 92% of Self-Served Food Is Eaten," *International Journal of Obesity*, forthcoming.

26. Twenty-two percent is an average number. We've done a dozen studies on this, and this is the general amount less a person serves and eats with plates that drop from 12 inches to 10 inches. Going from 11 inches to 9.5 isn't much different. Below 9.5 inches, people begin to realize they're tricking themselves and go back for seconds and thirds, defeating the purpose of using smaller plates. Get out your ruler!

27. More at Ellen Van Kleef, Mitsuru Shimizu, and Brian Wansink, "Serving Bowl Selection Biases the Amount of Food Served," *Journal of Nutrition Education and Behavior* 44, no. 1 (2012): 66–70.

28. Testing spoon size was done with experts—nutritional science professors at an ice-cream social. Brian Wansink, Koert van Ittersum, and James E. Painter, "Ice Cream Illusions: Bowl Size, Spoon Size, and Serving Size," *American Journal of Preventive Medicine* 145, no. 5 (September 2006): 240–43.

29. This is also known as the unit bias. Andrew B. Geier, Paul Rozin, and Gheorghe Doros, "Unit Bias," *Psychological Science* 17, no. 6 (2006): 521–25.

30. Read more at Doug Walker, Laura Smarandescu, and Brian Wansink, "Half Full or Empty: Cues That Lead Wine Drinkers to Unintentionally Overpour," *Substance Abuse & Misuse* 49, no. 3 (2014): 295–302. The *Wine Spectator* wrote a nice summary of this: http://www.winespectator.com/webfeature/show/id/49026.

31. This is one of those studies that fell off the tracks. While we'd gotten Institutional Review Board approval for the basic study, it didn't include the videotaping part, so the whole study was unpublishable. Pesky details.

32. See Collin R. Payne, Laura E. Smith, and Brian Wansink, "Dish Here, Dine There: Serving Off the Stove Results in Less Food Intake than Serving Off the Table," *FASEB Journal* 2 2010): 878.7.

33. The covered-bowl study was part of a series of desktop candy studies. While the covered-bowl portion is unpublished, the rest of these studies included: James E. Painter, Brian Wansink, and Julie B. Hieggelke, "How Visibility and Convenience Influence Candy Consumption," *Appetite* 38, no. 3 (June 2002): 237–38; and Brian

Wansink, James E. Painter, and Yeon-Kyung Lee, "The Office Candy Dish: Proximity's Influence on Estimated and Actual Candy Consumption," *International Journal of Obesity* 30, no. 5 (May 2006): 871–75. The same thing happened when researcher Herb Meiselman put a lid over an ice-cream freezer.

34. For foodies, this is cool. Check out the CBS YouTube video with Julie Chen, http://www.youtube.com/watch?v=mkWgYYnl170; the full paper is Brian Wansink and Collin R. Payne, "The *Joy of Cooking* Too Much: 70 Years of Calorie Increases in Classic Recipes," *Annals of Internal Medicine* 150 (2009): 291.

35. This is the world's shortest article, noted in ibid.

36. Let's take the candy dish you might have in the dining room or the candy on your desk. When we moved the candy dishes of office workers only 6 feet from their desk in the last chapter, they ended up eating 125 calories less each day. When we asked them if 6 feet was just too much of a hassle for a hit of chocolate, most said no, it was just that the distance gave them "pause" to ask themselves if they were really that hungry. Half the time they answered "No." Over a year, that candy dish would have added more than a few pounds of extra weight. What's a little bit scary is that none of them would have known where those three pounds came from.

37. Sara Wildman covered my makeovers for *O, the Oprah Magazine:* "One-Bite-at-a-Time Diet Makeovers," October 2008.

38. Ellen Van Kleef, Mitsuru Shimizu, and Brian Wansink, "Just a Bite: Considerably Smaller Snack Portions Satisfy Delayed Hunger and Craving," *Food Quality and Preference* 27, no. 1 (2013): 96–100.

39. Fat-proofing your kitchen and tablescape is pretty easy because there are a lot of standard principles that mess us up. When it comes to the rest of the house, things get personal. That strange habit that you or I might have grown into is probably different than your spouse's habits. At that point, one-size-fits-all solutions don't work. That's why knowing what your daily patterns are helps to personalize the more useful slim-by-design steps.

40. This research isn't about TV viewing, but it is a nice look at why people say they stopped eating dinner last night. Brian Wansink, Collin R. Payne, Pierre Chandon, "Internal and External Cues of Meal Cessation: The French Paradox Redux?," *Obesity* 15 (December 2007): 2920–24.

41. Way, way, way too much detail but a darn cool punch line in the Chandon and Wansink (2002) *Journal of Marketing Research* article noted above.

42. The National Mindless Eating Challenge was available from 2006 to 2009 as a free Web-based program and was the only online weight-loss program to report weight-loss results in a peer-reviewed scientific journal. Although the average of about two pounds a month for adherent participants wasn't amazing, it didn't involve dieting and it was more than most of them had been losing. See Kirsikka Kaipanen, Collin R. Payne, and Brian Wansink, "The Mindless Eating Challenge: Retention, Weight Outcomes, and Barriers for Changes in a Public Web-Based Healthy Eating and Weight Loss Program," *Journal of Medical Internet Research*

14, no. 6 (2012): e168. More can be found about early experiments with the original National Mindless Eating Challenge in this article: Brian Wansink, "From Mindless Eating to Mindlessly Eating Better," *Physiology and Behavior* 100, no. 5 (2010): 454–63. Visit SlimByDesignMethod.com for the newest version.

43. The article, written by my friend Dan Buettner, is titled "The Minnesota Miracle," in *AARP The Magazine*, January/February 2010.

44. Introverts are less tricked by bowl sizes than extroverted kids. More at Koert van Ittersum and Brian Wansink, "Extraverted Children Are More Biased by Bowl Sizes than Introverts," *PLoS One* 8, no. 10 (2013): e78224.

CHAPTER THREE: RESTAURANT DINING BY DESIGN

1. Our recent survey of waitstaff showed they estimated only about 18 percent of their diners asked for to-go bags. But it's getting easier to ask if they want one. Some nicer restaurants will even give you a coat-check-style tag you use to pick up the to-go box at the end of the meal. That way you don't have an untidy plastic bag of food waiting by your elbow while you finish your coffee.

2. This is detailed in Daniel Kahneman, *Thinking, Fast and Slow* (New York: Farrar, Straus & Giroux, 2011), and in Dan Ariely, *Predictably Irrational* (New York: Harper Perennial, 2009).

3. For wine lovers, this is a funny study in chapter 1 of *Mindless Eating*. This was done in our original research restaurant, which was the Spice Box in Urbana, Illinois. Brian Wansink, Collin R. Payne, and Jill North, "Fine as North Dakota Wine: Sensory Expectations and the Intake of Companion Foods," *Physiology and Behavior* 90, no. 5 (April 2007): 712–16.

4. Still a working paper: Racheal Behar and Brian Wansink "Would You Take Leftovers? A Test of the Endowment Effect in Restaurants," Cornell Food and Brand Lab Working Paper Series, 2013, 13–14.

5. One example of this is when wine is heavily promoted at such meals: Brian Wansink, Glenn Cordua, Ed Blair, Collin Payne, and Stephanie Geiger, "Wine Promotions in Restaurants: Do Beverage Sales Contribute or Cannibalize?," *Cornell Hotel and Restaurant Administrative Quarterly* 47, no. 4 (November 2006): 327–36.

6. A number of managers have told me that after accounting for food costs and labor, there's less profit in a lot of the low-cost, unhealthy items than there is in a lot of the healthier appetizers, sides, and entrées.

7. It's like the parents who say their child eats only macaroni and cheese because they long ago gave up trying to offer the kid anything else.

8. Of course, if a restaurant sells only chicken wings and onion rings, these same insights can be used to encourage people to overeat. Fortunately, most restaurants would rather make twice as much on a healthy food than make half as much selling anything else.

9. Still preliminary: Brian Wansink and Mitsuru Shimizu,"Exploring on Seating Location Relates to Restaurant Ordering Patterns," Cornell working paper, 2014.

10. Cool implications for both fast-food restaurants and for us . . . find the darkest quietest corner to eat! Brian Wansink and Koert van Ittersum, "Fast Food Restaurant Lighting and Music Can Reduce Calorie Intake and Increase Satisfaction," *Psychological Reports* 111, no. 1 (2012): 228–32. This study is catchy but has so many limitations, it's crazy. We don't know if it was the music or the lighting or whatever that made the biggest difference. The point is that something big happens when you make these changes.

11. Want to lead a concession stand makeover at your favorite high school? We'll tell you how at our website SmarterLunchrooms.org—just search for "Concessions" at that site. In the medical school tradition, this paper has an author list that's about as long as its whole first paragraph: Helena H. Laroche, Christopher Ford, Kate Anderson, Xueya Cai, David R. Just, Andrew S. Hanks, and Brian Wansink, "Concession Stand Makeovers: A Field Study of Serving Healthy Foods at High School Concession Stands," (2014), doi: 10.1093/pubmed/fdu015.

12. Two big reasons why people were happier: First, we kept the same foods. Second, we added healthier foods. Some people were happy because they could make it a meal and not have to go home or stop somewhere else. Here's the cast of characters: Helena H. Laroche, Christopher Ford, Kate Anderson, David R. Just, Andrew S. Hanks, Kathryn Hoy, and Brian Wansink, "The Ripple of Healthy Changes: Generating Long-term Adherence in Community-based Studies," forthcoming.

13. These results inadvertently leaked to restaurant and hospitality industry magazines long before the study was actually published. I was surprised to be giving a talk at a culinary institute in Florence, Italy, in summer 2003 and to see it on a reading list. The official version is Brian Wansink, Koert van Ittersum, and James E. Painter, "How Descriptive Food Names Bias Sensory Perceptions in Restaurants," *Food Quality and Preference*: 16, no. 5 (2004): 393–400.

14. There's juicy detail about this study in *Mindless Eating* (chapter 6, "The Name Game"), but here's the complete article, which focuses on how menu names influence sales and repeat dining intentions. See Brian Wansink, James M. Painter, and Koert van Ittersum, "Descriptive Menu Labels' Effect on Sales," *Cornell Hotel and Restaurant Administrative Quarterly* 42, no. 6 (December 2001): 68–72.

15. Ibid.

16. Brian Wansink and Anupama Mukund, "How Many Calories Is Crispy? An Analysis of Menu Names and Calorie Levels," working paper, 2013.

17. I did this at a truck stop when adopting my original Restaurant Pledge so it could be borrowed by the *Blue Zones* project. Find more about half-plate profitability in Brian Wansink, "Package Size, Portion Size, Serving Size . . . Market Size: The Unconventional Case for Half-Size Servings," *Marketing Science* 31, no. 1 (2012): 54–57.

18. Here's why half-size portions work: Although the average monthly unit sales of the large-size portions dropped 297 meals per month or 40.9 percent (p <. 001), the average sales of half-size portions went from 0 to 949 units per month. Furthermore, the purchase of selected side orders of salad increased 116.5 percent, from 374 units/month to 811 (p <. 001). This resulted in an average estimated sales increase of $3,474. After subtracting the decrease in full-size meals and adding the new sales from half-size meals and the new sales from side orders, the increase in side orders and the new sales from half-size meals, the net increase in sales was an estimated $6,974.

19. More about half-plate profitability can be found at Wansink, "Package Size, Portion Size, Serving Size."

20. Ibid.

21. From Matt Van Voltenberg, Trail's Restaurant manager: "Guest counts have increased since we modified our menu based on Brian Wansink's suggestions to strategically place half-size portions by their full-size option and to purposefully list side choices with the healthiest options first. In addition, sales are up and guest check averages are on the rise." From the Restaurant Pledge and Starter Kit from Healthyways/Blue Zones.

22. Follow-up interviews with diners at a similar location indicated that when full-size portions for $10 were offered in a half-size portion for $7, some couples that would have otherwise split a full-size portion now opted for two $7 half-size portions. Other diners reasoned that by spending a bit less on the entrée, they felt more inclined to buy another item they might not have otherwise purchased.

23. This is truly a win-win tactic for most restaurants. Others—especially the super-high-end ones—want to use a large plate as more of a canvas. The other 98 percent of all restaurants just need a smaller plate: Brian Wansink, Brian and Koert van Ittersum, "Portion Size Me: Plate Size Can Decrease Serving Size, Intake, and Food Waste," *Journal of Experimental Psychology: Applied* 19, no. 4 (December 2013): 320–32.

24. It's not just bartenders pouring alcohol; it's us pouring milk, and our kids pouring juice. Brian Wansink and Koert van Ittersum, "Bottoms Up! The Influence of Elongation and Pouring on Consumption Volume," *Journal of Consumer Research* 30, no. 3 (December 2003): 455–63.

25. This punchy difference between clever and stupid is courtesy of Nigel Tufnel, from the ingenious rockumentary spoof *This Is Spinal Tap*. It bears repeating because the world is full of people who love to take things to the extreme. This was a witty warning. (The only movie I've watched more than ten times.)

26. It's amazing how powerful this is. Brian Wansink and Koert van Ittersum, "Shape of Glass and Amount of Alcohol Poured: Comparative Study of Effect of Practice and Concentration," *British Medical Journal* 331, no. 7531 (December 2005): 1512–14.

27. Only 40 percent of the people drink water in restaurants, so in California the water conservation policy is to not put it on the table unless someone asks.

28. It was once thought that if you drank a lot of water before a meal, it would fill you up and you'd take in fewer calories. In general, that doesn't seem to hold, and the loss is less than believed. Our work with water and the National Mindless Eating Challenge showed that people who were given water-drinking tips and asked to track their weight lost only 1.2 pounds over the course of three months in the study. Kirsikka Kaipainen, Collin R. Payne, and Brian Wansink, "The Mindless Eating Challenge: Retention, Weight Outcomes, and Barriers for Changes in a Public Web-Based Healthy Eating and Weight Loss Program," *Journal of Medical Internet Research* 14, no. 6 (2012): 100–13.

29. In our experience this goes from about 25 percent requesting it to about 50 percent accepting it. More in Brian Wansink and Katie Love, "Slim by Design: Menu Strategies for Promoting High-Margin, Healthy Foods," *International Journal of Contemporary Hospitality Management*, forthcoming

30. It's a neat article with a terrible title: Brian Wansink and Lawrence W. Lindner, "Interactions Between Forms of Fat Consumption and Restaurant Bread Consumption," *International Journal of Obesity* 27, no. 7 (2003): 866–68.

31. On a recent trip down Palo Alto Memory Lane, I noticed this Burger King was no longer at the corner of University and Emerson, possibly because of their Vegetarian Whopper.

32. From *Mindless Eating*, chapter 9.

33. Happy Meals offer a lot of options. There's usually a choice of the main food—Chicken McNuggets, a hamburger, or a cheeseburger (about 70 percent get McNuggets). There's a choice of a side of French fries or apple slices (about 85 percent get French fries). There's a choice of a drink—soft drink, chocolate milk, or low-fat white milk (about 80 percent get a soft drink).

34. McDonald's change in their Happy Meal—adding apple slices, cutting French fries from 240 to 100 calories, and promoting milk—ended up cutting 104 calories out of what kids ordered—an 18 percent decrease. What's also cool is it even influenced what their mom or dad ordered—dessert sales dropped from 10.1 percent to 7.9 percent. See Brian Wansink and Andrew S. Hanks, "Happier Meals: How Changes in McDonald's Happy Meals Altered Food Choices," *Journal of Nutrition Education and Behavior* 45, no. 4 (July–August 2013): 45:4S, 39–40, and the full paper: Brian Wansink and Andrew S. Hanks, "Calorie Reductions and Within-Meal Calorie Compensation in Children's Meal Combos," *Obesity* 22, no. 3 (2013): 630–32.

35. This is a tortured area of research. One of the more recent studies on this is certainly not perfect, but I'd rather poke at our own flaws than at somebody else's: Jessica Wisdom, George Loewenstein, Brian Wansink, and Julie S. Downs, "Calorie Recommendations Fail to Enhance the Impact of Menu Labeling," *American Journal of Public Health* 103, no. 9 (2013): 1604–9.

36. Calorie labeling works a little (like at a Starbucks) for people who are already weight conscious and don't need a whole lot more prompting. See Brian Wansink and Aner Tal, "Does Calorie Labeling Make Heavy People Heavier?" forthcoming.

37. There are a ton of reasons that other restaurants aren't crazy about calorie labeling: Menus vary, ingredients and cooks vary, accurate calculations cost money, plus they might scare customers off or lead them to enjoy their experience less. Yet there are some easy ways that both we and our favorite restaurants can get what we want. We want to eat fewer calories, and they want to make more money. What we can encourage them to do is to only make the changes that they think will make them more popular and more profitable. For instance, they could start with a few favorites and present them on a table tent, insert, or special section, or simply supply it when asked. It's as simple as a phone call to a local dietitian.

38. This was conducted up at Rich Foods—a frozen food company in Buffalo, New York. Elisa Chan, Brian Wansink, and Robert Kwortnik, "McHealthy: Habit Changing Interventions that Improve Healthy Food Choices," under review.

39. I only know this because I was eating breakfast at a Burger King in Taipei, Taiwan, while writing this sidebar and the entrance featured a floor-to-ceiling wall decal stating this and showing the eighty most popular versions.

40. This is an incredibly easy technique. The article's short, but about 95 percent of what you need to know to use it you've already read: Brian Wansink, Mitsuru Shimizu, and Guido Camps, "What Would Batman Eat? Priming Children to Make Healthier Fast Food Choices," *Pediatric Obesity* 7, no. 2 (2012): 121–23.

41. Most of these changes we had made earlier in Trail's Restaurant. We had made a number of suggestions—offering half-size portions, offering healthy side dishes, and reengineering their menu to help people order healthier. Guest counts increased, sales increased, and check averages were on the rise Also, for the first time ever, they were awarded the top National Franchise Restaurant of the Year and the National Franchise Top Sales of the Year.

42. From "The Minnesota Miracle: The extraordinary story of how folks in this small town got motivated, got moving, made new friends, and added years to their lives," *AARP The Magazine*, January/February 2010, http://www.aarp.org/health/longevity/info-01–2010/minnesota_miracle.html.

CHAPTER FOUR: SUPERMARKET MAKEOVERS

1. The only remaining photo of the original Kleenex Cam is in this newspaper article below. By today's tech standards, it's pretty boring, but back then it was really souped up. Read about it at SlimByDesign.org/GroceryStores/.

2. One interesting category of items that are most likely to become cabinet castaways are unusual foods that people are buying for a specific occasion. When that occasion never happens, the food just sits and sits. This is a neat article on that: Brian Wansink, S. Adam Brasel, and Stephen Amjad, "The Mystery of the Cabinet

Castaway: Why We Buy Products We Never Use," *Journal of Family and Consumer Science* 92, no. 1 (2000): 104–8.

3. All of these studies are preapproved. Today—compared to twenty or even ten years ago—studies to be approved by a university's Institutional Review Board to make sure that they are safe and to make sure all of the data is collected anonymously and that no one will ever know about that day you bought that EPT kit and the two pints of Chocolate Fudge Swirl. Some studies—like many shopping studies—are observational, but others might ask a person to complete a questionnaire at the end of a trip in exchange for a small amount of money, free food, movie tickets, and so on.

4. That is, about 88 percent of this food will be eaten. The 12 percent that's wasted, however, isn't the candy, chips, and ice cream; it's typically the spoiled fruit and vegetables, leftovers, and cabinet castaways. Brian Wansink, "Abandoned Products and Consumer Waste: How Did *That* Get into the Pantry?," *Choices* (October 2001): 46.

5. A cool example of all of these hidden cameras in use can be found at http://www.youtube.com/watch?v=2B0Ncy3Gz24. It's not at a grocery store but in a lunchroom. Same approach.

6. Lots of people visit our Lab (even from way overseas) like it's some weird trip to Consumer Mecca. Something I've heard a number of times is "Wow . . . this isn't really very high-tech!" No, it isn't. What we'd like to think, however, is that insights trump glitzy technology every day of the week. We've got low-definition hidden cameras, hidden scales, counters, and timers, because we don't need holograms or brain-scan machines to nail down the reality—not the theory—of why people do what they do. You don't need infrared sensors to see someone eating twice as many Cheetos when you change what they're watching on TV.

7. Denmark Islands. Denmark actually has a number of little islands, but none like poor Bornholm. It never gets any peace. Strategically located in the Baltic Sea, it was occupied by the Germans during almost all of World War II and the Russians right after that. And probably by the Vikings way before that.

8. People—whether public health professionals or politicians—can often get very dramatic in what they tell grocery stores they should do. Dramatic, but not always realistic or right.

9. This is an interesting paper of unintended consequences: Brian Wansink et al.,"From Coke to Coors: A Field Study of a Sugar-Sweetened Beverage Tax and Its Unintended Consequences," May 26, 2012, available at http://ssrn.com/abstract=2079840 or http://dx.doi.org/10.2139/ssrn.2079840.

10. This is controversial for me to admit since I'm the immediate past president of the Society for Nutrition Education and Behavior and because I was the White House–appointed person (2007–2009) in charge of promoting the dietary guidelines for the USDA.

11. This was one focus of my book *Mindless Eating*. The basic idea is that making small changes around you that you don't even really notice has a tremendous long-term impact on changing behavior and weight.

12. We no longer use the Kleenex Cam but we still call it that. We now use our bottles, hats, and iPhones.

13. A number of years ago we gave secretaries dishes of chocolate Kisses that we either placed on their desk or 6 feet from their desk. We found that those who had to walk only 6 feet ate half as much candy (100 calories less; 4 each day instead of 9). Yet when we asked them if it was because the 6-foot walk was too far or too much of a hassle, their answer surprised us. They said instead that the 6-foot distance gave them a chance to pause and ask themselves if they were really that hungry. Half the time they'd answer "no." The key was that something—that distance—caused them to pause and interrupt their mindlessness: Brian Wansink, James E. Painter, and Yeon-Kyung Lee, "The Office Candy Dish: Proximity's Influence on Estimated and Actual Candy Consumption," *International Journal of Obesity* 30, no. 5 (May 2006): 871–75.

14. Anything that stops and makes a person pause—even for a split second—might be enough to knock them out of their mindless trance and rethink.

15. The average grocery shopper buys only 24 percent of fruits and vegetables. Simone French, Melanie Wall, Nathan R. Mitchell, Scott T. Shimotsu, and Ericka Welsh, "Annotated Receipts Capture Household Food Purchases from a Broad Range of Sources," *International Journal of Behavioral Nutrition and Physical Activity 6*, no. 37 (2009).

16. Brian Wansink, C. R. Payne, K. C. Herbst, and D. Soman, "Part Carts: Assortment Allocation Cues That Increase Fruit and Vegetable Purchases," *Journal of Nutrition Education and Behavior* 45 (2013): 4S, 42.

17. Brian Wansink, Dilip Soman, Kenneth C. Herbst, and Collin R. Payne, "Partitioned Shopping Carts: Assortment Allocation Cues that Increase Fruit and Vegetable Purchases," under review.

18. A really robust finding. A great reason why you should also pass around the salad and green beans to your kids at dinnertime before you bring out the lasagna. Brian Wansink and David Just, "Healthy Foods First: Students Take the First Lunchroom Food 11% More Often than the Third," *Journal of Nutrition Education and Behavior* 43 (2011): 4S1, S9.

19. You can just believe me, or you can read ponderous evidence of why this happens: Pierre Chandon and Brian Wansink, "When Are Stockpiled Products Consumed Faster? A Convenience–Salience Framework of Postpurchase Consumption Incidence and Quantity," *Journal of Marketing Research* 39, no. 3 (2002): 321–35.

20. This is a really neat finding, but it seems like it will take a miracle to get it published. In the meantime, you can find it on SSRN: Brian Wansink and Kate Stein, "Eyes in the Aisle: Eye Scanning and Choice in Grocery Stores," 2013.

21. Would this dashed green line work through the rest of the store? It could go down some of the healthier aisles—say canned fruits and vegetables or foods with whole grains—and around much of the perimeter of the store. Yet to use the quotation from *Spinal Tap* again, "It's a fine line between clever and stupid." This line might work well in the produce section, but don't take it overboard. It might be irritating or too strange in the rest of the store—particularly because these long aisles might make it look like a highway divider.

22. My good colleagues Collin Payne and David Just have early evidence that this works well when it's first laid out. See Collin R. Payne and David R. Just, "Using Floor Decals and Way Finding to Increase the Sales of Fruits and Vegetables," under review.

23. Wansink and Stein, "Eyes in the Aisle."

24. If you want a beleaguered researcher's view of how this works, here's an op-ed: Kate Stein, "Shop Faster," *New York Times*, April 15, 2009, p. A29.

25. One source for this is Brian Wansink and Aner Tal, "Correlates of Purchase Quantities in Grocery Stores," under review.

26. Of course this is less accurate than measuring people barefoot with a German-made stadeometer, but knowing someone's relative height is probably sufficient. Being able to document that a six-foot male is taller than a five-five female is close enough for this calibration. This issue of precision does raise to mind the comedian Ron White's quote "I'm a pretty big guy—between six and six foot six—depending on what convenience store I'm coming out of."

27. In this study with Kate Stein, we tracked what people put in their carts but we didn't track them to the cash register. Still, unless someone changes their mind when in the *National Enquirer* checkout line, we assume that what they took, they probably bought.

28. And 12 inches is even a stretch. Most purchased products were within a 6-inch range—higher or lower—of eye level for a particular shopper. This includes 37 percent of what women put in their cart and 44 percent for men. To stretch the range of products purchased even further, widen the shopping aisles. If an aisle is narrow—6 feet or less—61 percent of the products you buy will be within 12 inches of eye level. But if you're in a wider aisle, you look higher and lower. If it's only 2 feet wider, half of what you buy will be outside this eye zone. But wide aisles also have something else going for them.

29. Paco Underhill, *Why We Buy: The Science of Shopping* (New York: Simon & Shuster, 2000).

30. There's also an irritation factor with narrow aisles. If a person can't see a clear way through an aisle, they might be less likely to go down it. And if you keep getting interrupted by people as you're trying to shop because they're scooting by you, you're less likely to linger.

31. Kate Stein and Brian Wansink, "Eye Height and Purchase Probability," under review.

32. Here's the best proof of why you shouldn't shop when you're hungry: Brian Wansink, Aner Tal, and Mitsuru Shimizu, "First Foods Most: After 18-Hour Fast, People Drawn to Starches First and Vegetables Last," *Archives of Internal Medicine* 172, no. 12 (June 2012): 961–63.

33. This is a current working paper by Brian Wansink and Drew Hanks, "Timing, Hunger, and Increased Sales of Convenience Foods." Hopefully it will be published in time for our retirement.

34. One of the ways we've tested this is by intercepting grocery shoppers in the parking lot on their way into a store. We ask them to answer a couple of questions about the store and if we can talk to them after they shop. If they say yes, we tag their cart so we can catch them as they check out. At that time, we ask them a few questions about their experience and if we can have a copy of their shopping receipt. A second group of people get the exact same treatment, except that they're also given a piece of sugarless gum as a thank-you. We tag their cart with a different color tag, and again catch them as they check out.

35. This is a great study that shows surprisingly that either taxing bad foods or subsidizing good foods seems to backfire. When you subsidize healthy foods, people buy more of both healthy *and* unhealthy foods. When you tax unhealthy foods, shoppers by less of both unhealthy *and* healthy foods. John Cawley et al., "How Nutrition Rating Systems in Supermarkets Impact the Purchases of Healthy and Less Healthy Foods," under review.

36. This is an award-winning article that opened a lot of eyes with the health halo concept: Pierre Chandon and Brian Wansink, "The Biasing Health Halos of Fast Food Restaurant Health Claims: Lower Calorie Estimates and Higher Side-Dish Consumption Intentions," *Journal of Consumer Research* 34, no. 3 (October 2007): 301–14.

37. There's a ton of evidence here that's compelling, but way too detailed to talk about in the text. It happens with both low-fat foods and with foods with healthy names. Knock yourself out reading these two detailed (but award-winning papers): One's mentioned in the prior note and the other one is Brian Wansink and Pierre Chandon, "Can Low-Fat Nutrition Labels Lead to Obesity?," *Obesity* 14 (September 2006): A49–50.

38. Wansink, *Mindless Eating*, pp. 178–9+.

39. Check out the article Brian Wansink and Kathryn Hoy, "Half-plate Versus MyPlate: The Simpler the System, the Better the Nutrition," forthcoming, and Brian Wansink and Alyssa Niman, "The Half-Plate Rule vs MyPlate vs Their Plate: The Effect on the Caloric Intake and Enjoyment of Dinner," *Journal of Nutrition Education and Behavior* 44, no. 4 (July–August 2012): S33.

40. The more latitude we give, the more likely they'll follow our advice. When rules become just a little too complicated or vague, we find reasons to stop following them. This was an early problem with MyPlate. When somebody starts questioning "Where does my dessert go?" or "How am I supposed to eat fruit with dinner," the more likely they are to simply say "Whatever" and ignore it.

41. A recap of this done by Jane Andrews, Wegmans dietitian, can be found at http://rochester.kidsoutandabout.com/node/1901.

42. See more at Wansink and Niman, "The Half-Plate Rule vs MyPlate vs Their Plate."

43. Learn more about how Wegmans implemented our idea at http://www.wegmans.com/webapp/wcs/stores/servlet/ProductDisplay?storeId=10052&partNumber=UNIVERSAL_20235.

44. Wansink and Hoy, "Half-plate Versus MyPlate."

45. See Ulla M. Toft, Lise L. Winkler, Charlotte Glumer, and Brian Wansink (2014), "Candy Free Checkout Aisles: Decreasing Candy Sales in Bornholm Island Supermarkets," under review.

46. More at Ulla M. Toft, Charlotte Glumer, Lise L. Winkler, and Brian Wansink (2015), "Food Free Checkout Aisles: A Danish Field Study of Becoming Slim by Design," under review.

CHAPTER FIVE: OFFICE SPACE AND WORKPLACE

1. Yeah, I know, who would ever do a study on something as silly as this? Brian Wansink, Aner Tal, Katheryn I. Hoy, and Adam Brumburg (2012), "Desktop Dining: Eating More and Enjoying it Less?" *Journal of Nutrition Education and Behavior,* 44:4 (July-August), S62.

2. Just like when we order the hot fudge sundae without the cherry—because we're on a diet.

3. A great observation by my friend John C. Peters, a long-time executive for Procter & Gamble and now the chief strategy officer of the University of Colorado Anschutz Wellness Center.

4. Generally, the ROI for spending on worker health promotion is believed to be about three to one, not including improved employee morale and retention: Ron Z. Goetzel and Ronald J. Ozminkowski, "That's Holding Your Back: Why Should (or Shouldn't) Employers Invest in Health Promotion Programs for Their Workers?" *North Carolina Medical Journal* (November/December 2006), 429; Josh Cable, "The ROI of Wellness," *EHS Today: The Magazine for Environment, Health and Safety Leaders* (April 13, 2007); Katherine Baicker, David Cutler and Zirui Song, "Workplace Wellness Programs Can Generate Savings," *Health Affairs* (February 2010), 1–7.

5. These plans work a little bit for a few people. That is, they might lead some fit-minded folks to shift from their personal gym to the company gym, the cafeteria might sell a few more salads each day, or they might lead one fitness challenge team to lose 8 pounds each until it creeps back on over the winter. Some examples of financial incentives include a $250 cash bonus for a 10 percent weight loss, $150 for participating in programs, subsidies for gym and Weight Watchers memberships, and discount coupons for healthy foods.

6. Some modestly successful wellness programs in four very different industries include Johnson & Johnson (annual savings of $224.66 per employee), IBM (saved $2.42 for every $1 spent on wellness), H-E-B Grocery (health care costs increased only one-third of national average), and Lincoln Industries (cut workers compensation claims in down from $510,000 to $43,000 in one year).

7. This 60-30-10 breakdown Human Resources people throw around as a rough approximation.

8. Preordering also works great for children: Andrew S. Hanks, David R. Just, and Brian Wansink (2013), "Pre-Ordering School Lunch and Food Choices Encourages Better Food Choices by Children," *JAMA Pediatrics,* 167:7, 673–74.

9. One place to find free posters is from here: wellnessproposals.com/wellness-library/nutrition/nutrition-posters/

10. From Ricky W. Griffin and Gregory Moorhead, *Organisational Behaviour: Managing People and Organisations,* 9th ed. (Mason, OH: South-Western, 2010), 522–24.

11. A student whose dissertation committee I was on, Jessica Wisdom, took a job with Google in People Analytics and has helped keep this going. An account of our work can be found here: Cliff Kuang, "In the Cafeteria, Google Gets Healthy," *Fast Company,* April 2012. More at David R. Just and Brian Wansink, "Better School Meals on a Budget: Using Behavioral Economics and Food Psychology to Improve Meal Selection," Choices 24, no. 3 (2009): 1–6.

12. Read more at Brian Wansink, "Convenient, Attractive, and Normative: The *CAN* Approach to Making Children Slim by Design," *Childhood Obesity* 9, no. 4 (August 2013): 277–78.

13. The basic study was first shown in James E. Painter, Brian Wansink, and Julie B. Hieggelke, "How Visibility and Convenience Influence Candy Consumption," *Appetite* 38, no. 3 (June 2002): 237–38. The 9 percent drop was reported by Jennifer Kurkoski and Jessica Wisdom to Cliff Kuang, "In the Cafeteria, Google Gets Healthier," *Fast Company,* April 2012.

14. The general figure our research has discovered is closer to 22 percent for the average person, but this 32 percent increase was reported by Jennifer Kurkoski and Jessica Wisdom in ibid.

15. This is a great way to eat smaller snacks—eat only one-fourth as much and distract yourself for fifteen minutes returning phone calls or straightening up: Ellen Van Kleef, Mitsuru Shimizu, and Brian Wansink, "Just a Bite: Considerably Smaller Snack Portions Satisfy Delayed Hunger and Craving," *Food Quality and Preference* 27, no. 1 (2013): 96–100.

16. Michiel Bakker is Google's Director of Global Food Services and Michelle Hatzis, Ph.D., is Google's Director of Global Food—Health & Wellness Program Manager.

17. A major drawback with traffic signals is that some color decisions can appear subjective—is 1 percent milk a red light or a yellow light? When consumers think there is too much subjectivity, they either ignore it or react against it.

18. This was based on an Innovation Lab project between Stanford's Abby King and Google's Bob Evans called the Avatar of Future Me.

19. This is a cool study on lunch trays with unexpected results: Brian Wansink and David R. Just (2014), "Trayless Cafeterias Lead Diners to Take Less Salad and Relatively More Dessert," *Public Health Nutrition,* forthcoming.

20. The full list of all of the changes is available at SlimByDesign.org.

21. Always serve the healthy things first, even at home. Brian Wansink and Aner Tal (2014), "The Power of Healthy Primes When Selecting Meals," under review.

22. Here's the best reason to start at the healthiest part of the buffet line: Brian Wansink and Andrew S. Hanks (2013), "Slim by Design: Serving Healthy Foods First in Buffet Lines Improves Overall Meal Selection," *PLoS One,* 8:10, e77055.

23. One great solution to this is to have cards limited so they can only buy healthy items. More at Brian Wansink, David R. Just and Collin R. Payne (2013), The Behavioral Economics of Healthier School Lunch Payment Systems, under review.

24. I've heard this quote a number of times. Here's a secondary citation of it: http://www.instantdane.tv/ultimate-fitness-guru-taught-how-to-stay-fit/. This guy is truly a studly "Just do it" inspiration. Check him out on YouTube.

25. In the beginning, we held Consumer Camp for anyone who had participated in a study of ours over the prior year. When people are in a study, there's always some of them who want to know the results. Consumer Camp is a much more fun way to tell them what we've been doing than sending out a form e-mail. Over the years we've had people from 37 different states attend Consumer Camp. We've never limited now many people could attend. More information and registration details can be found at foodpsychology.cornell.edu/content/consumer-camp.

26. The same thing happens even if you ask people to just "think" about exercising. See Carolina O. C. Werle, Brian Wansink, and Collin R. Payne (2011), "'Just Thinking About Exercise Makes Me Serve More Food:' Physical Activity and Calorie Compensation," *Appetite,* 56:2 (April), 332–35.

27. This changed the whole way my Lab has viewed exercise . . . for the better: Carolina O.C. Werle, Brian Wansink, and Collin R. Payne, Werle (2014), "Is it Fun or Exercise? The Framing of Physical Activity Biases Subsequent Snacking," *Marketing Letters,* 10.1007/s11002-014-9301-6.

28. Described in *Steve Jobs* by Walter Isaacson New York: Simon & Schuster, 2011.

29. Reported in Brian Wansink and Carolina Werle, "Toning vs. Burning: Reframing of Weight Lifting Reduces Compensation," Cornell Working paper.

30. The basic design of the weight-loss portion of this was presented at the Experimental Biology conference in 2011: Brian Wansink, Aner Tal, and Mitsuru Shimizu (2011), "The Wichita 'One-Ton' Weight Loss Program: Community Weight Loss and the National Mindless Eating Challenge, *FASEB Journal,* 25:974, 2.

31. Details about the program can be found in the article in the next endnote along with this more general version: Brian Wansink (2010), "From Mindless Eating to Mindlessly Eating Better," *Physiology & Behavior,* 100:5, 454–63.

32. When *Mindless Eating* was published, we were indulged with calls and e-mails—maybe 800 a week—asking what would be the one or two biggest changes that a person could make in their life that would make the biggest difference in helping them mindlessly eat less. To help each of these people and not lose our lives, we developed the National Mindless Eating Challenge. We directed these people to a website that asked them eighteen different questions, and based on these questions, we presented them with the three small changes they could make that would cause them to lose weight. Not a lot of weight—just 1 or 2 pounds a month—but they would be doing it without dieting, and the number on the scale would be moving in the right direction. Learn more at SlimByDesignMethod.com.

33. We focused on those who adhered to at least one change they were given. See more at Kirsikka Kaipaninen, Collin R. Payne, and Brian Wansink (2012), "The Mindless Eating Challenge: Retention, Weight Outcomes, and Barriers for Changes in a Public Web-based Healthy Eating and Weight Loss Program," *Journal of Medical Internet Research,* 14:6, e168.

34. If you work in company wellness, you'll find this article useful. It shows what you can put in these contracts and what to leave out, Rebecca S. Robbins and Brian Wansink (2014), "Designing Employee Health Contracts to be Slim by Design," forthcoming.

35. Although this is an early article on this law, there's not a lot that's been reported since then that is of much note: Norimitsu Onishi (2008), "Japan, Seeking Trim Waists, Measures Millions," *New York Times* (June 13, 2008).

36. The exact number reported by the AFP agency is 12.3, but I conservatively rounded up because this strikes me strangely too low for such a disciplined country with such strong social norms. Here's the details: Jacques Lhuillery (2013) "Breaking the Law, one sushi roll at a time," *AFP* (AFP.com/en/node/804444), January 25, 2013.

37. This is radical thinking, so it's surprising so many managers seem to be behind it. Download this article at the Social Science Research Network, Rebecca S. Robbins and Brian Wansink (2014) "The 10% Solution: Tying Managerial Salaries and Promotions to Workplace Wellness Efforts," *Journal of Occupational Health Psychology,* forthcoming.

CHAPTER SIX: SMARTER LUNCHROOMS

1. Clip-on ties were invented for wounded vets who had difficulty tying a necktie because of hand injuries. Pajamas replaced full-length nightgowns, more closely mirroring the GI's need to sleep in underclothes. The full story of the history of hot lunches can be found at http://www.cracked.com/article_18703_5-inventions-you-wont-believe-came-from-war.html.

2. Specifically, "46% of African Americans and almost one-third of European Americans called for the draft were classified '4-F'—unfit for service." Mary Beth Norton et al., *A People and a Nation: A History of the United States*, vol. 2, *Since 1865* (Boston: Cengage Learning, 2011), p. 754.

3. Throughout this chapter I'll use the word "buy" instead of "select" or "choose." Some people have to pay for the things they take in the lunchroom (or their parents do). Other people get certain foods free as part of a free or reduced USDA reimbursable meal. Instead of continually qualifying this in the text, "buy" will basically mean "take." At any rate about the only people who really care about the distinction are reading this endnote, so at least we'll know the semantics.

4. We've seen this Domino's side-door delivery stunt a bunch of times. As someone who spent his summer delivering pizza in Sioux City, Iowa, I can say this is neither a nutritional win for the students nor a big tipping win for the delivery driver.

5. We'll be focusing on individual behaviors, but there are also excellent works that take a more macro look at lunches. These include Janet Poppendieck, *Free for All: Fixing School Food in America* (Berkeley: University of California Press, 2010), Marion Nestle, *Food Politics: How the Food Industry Influences Nutrition and Health* (Berkeley: University of California Press, 2002); and Ann Cooper and Lisa M. Holmes, *Lunch Lessons: Changing the Way We Feed Our Children* (New York: Collins, 2006).

6. Nice treatment of these new challenges are in Katherine Ralston, Constance Newman, Annette Clauson, Joanne Guthrie, and Jean Buzby, "The National School Lunch Program: Background, Trends and Issues," Economic Research Report; and D. W. Schanzenbach, "Does the Federal School Lunch Program Contribute to Childhood Obesity?," *Journal of Human Resources* 44, no. 3 (2007): 684–709.

7. Unfortunately for some kids, a ban on chocolate milk ends up being either "chocolate milk or no milk." See Andrew S. Hanks, David R. Just, and Brian Wansink, "Chocolate Milk Consequences: A Pilot Study Evaluating the Consequences of Banning Chocolate Milk in School Cafeterias," *PLoS One* (2014): 10.1371/journal.pone.0091022. It's importantly noted in this study that the 7 percent decrease in those eating school lunches is consistent with but not uniquely explained by the chocolate milk ban.

8. A number of these peer-reviewed milk studies are popping up at various economics, nutrition, and psychology conferences. Three of these include Andrew S. Hanks, David R. Just, and Brian Wansink, "Chocolate Milk Consequences: A Pilot Study Evaluating the Consequences of Banning Chocolate Milk in School Cafeterias," *PLoS One* (2014): 10.1371/journal.pone.0091022. Also see Drew Hanks, David Just, and Brian Wansink, "A Source of Contention or Nutrition: An Assessment of Removing Flavored Milk from School Lunchrooms," *Journal of Nutrition Education and Behavior* 44, no. 4 (July–August 2012): S21; and Laura E. Smith, David R. Just, Brian Wansink, and Christine H. Wallace, "Disrupting the Default Choice: The Contentious Case of Chocolate Milk," *FASEB Journal* 25 (2011): 781.24.

9. Some kids receive free or reduced-price lunches based on the income level of their parents. If their income is 180 percent below the poverty level, the meal is free. If it's below 130 percent, it's discounted.

10. While putting a colorful fruit bowl out in the open consistently increases fruit sales by about 100 percent in most of our studies, even simply using a colorful bowl boosts sales. This is useful for schools that think they can't bring the fruit out from behind the sneeze guard: Laura Smith, Brian Wansink, and David Jus, "SmarterLunchroom.org's Fancy Fruit Bowls Increase Fruit Sales by 23–54%," *Journal of Nutrition Education and Behavior* 42 (2010): 4S1, S116–17. There are also other approaches, such as those used by Simone A. French and Gloria Stables, "Environmental Interventions to Promote Vegetable and Fruit Consumption Among Youth in School Settings," *Preventative Medicine* 37 (2003): 593–610.

11. Most of these fruit-bowl-like changes can be made overnight for free. A few others might take a week and fifty dollars from the lunchroom slush fund. One way or the other, how the cafeteria is designed is going to influence how kids eat. It's either for the better or for the worse.

12. After this sixty-second move, we scoured lunchroom sales receipts and production records—how much lettuce, carrots, tomatoes, and little Barbie-size corn-on-the-cobs did they sell? Within two weeks of moving the salad bar, sales went up 200–300 percent, depending on the day: Laura E. Smith, David R. Just, and Brian Wansink, "Convenience Drives Choice in School Lunch Rooms: A Salad Bar Success Story," *FASEB Journal* 24 (2010): 732.11.

13. This even works great in both schools and homes and with both kids and adults: Brian Wansink, David R. Just, Andrew S. Hanks, and Laura E. Smith, "Pre-Sliced Fruit in Schools Increases Selection and Intake," *American Journal of Preventive Medicine* 44, no. 5 (May 2013): 477–80.

14. A nice visual of lunch-line redesign is titled just that: Brian Wansink, David R. Just, and Joe McKendry, "Lunch Line Redesign," *New York Times*, October 22, 2010, p. A10.

15. The specific show is the MTV-owned show called *Channel One*. It's a hip, almost too-cool-for-school program that actually is for school. It shows a ten-minute news feature every morning during homeroom to five million kids in America—typically those in the big cities.

16. The video of this can be found at SmarterLunchrooms.org. Thanks to the Ithaca Food Service director, Denise Agati, for making this happen and sticking with the changes.

17. This is a great two-part (before/after) video with a lot of energy, good lessons, and some modest laughs. You can find it at YouTube at healthymeals.nal.usda.gov/healthierus-school . . . /lunchd-part-one and the "after" version at healthymeals.nal.usda.gov/healthierus-school . . . /lunchd-part-two.

18. This works great in the lab, but that's when you have three vegetables in a row: Brian Wansink and David Just, "Healthy Foods First: Students Take the First

Lunchroom Food 11% More Often than the Third," *Journal of Nutrition Education and Behavior* 43 (2011): 4S1, S8.

19. These changes can be so easy even a high school kid could do them. We showed that by having a high schooler we never met implement a vegetable-naming program two hundred miles away from us. More at Brian Wansink, David R. Just, Collin R. Payne, and Matthew Z. Klinger, "Attractive Names Sustain Increased Vegetable Intake in Schools," *Preventive Medicine* 55, no. 4 (2012): 330–32.

20. Nothing makes it easier to choose the right food than when it's convenient. Here are some great tips: Andrew S. Hanks, David R. Just, Laura E. Smith, and Brian Wansink, "Healthy Convenience: Nudging Students Toward Healthier Choices in the Lunchroom," *Journal of Public Health* 34, no. 3 (2012): 370–76.

21. I'm pretty McBiased toward McDonald's. Each week I eat two breakfasts there. Each month my three girls eat two Happy Meals. Each year I meet twice with their Global Nutrition Council to work with them on making healthy win-win changes to their menu, their restaurants, and their promotions. (I'm also pretty biased toward all fast food—must be from seldom ever having it when growing up.)

22. We have been working with a number of soup kitchens to develop low-cost/no-cost changes that make them more inviting and attractive. There's more at our website SlimbyDesign.org.

23. A few years ago, a visionary governor from Arkansas, Mike Huckabee, sent BMI Report Cards home to parents. These reports told parents a child's height and weight compared to the other kids in the class. No lecturing, no A-plus or F. Simply a number and the average BMI of other kids. People went crazy. This was a violation of privacy, it was embarrassing, and it would scar the self-esteem of these kids. But it worked for many. In the early reports, Arkansas BMIs started dropping almost immediately.

24. These Lunchtime Report Cards—or Nutritional Report Cards—hold tremendous promise for changing the way kids eat and how their parents talk with them about lunch. The proof and the programming code can be found in Brian Wansink, David R. Just, Richard W. Patterson, and Laura E. Smith, "Nutrition Report Cards Improve School Lunch Choice," under review at *American Journal of Public Health,* and the initial stats on their effectiveness can be found at Brian Wansink, David R. Just, Richard W. Patterson, and Laura E. Smith, "Nutrition Report Cards: An Opportunity to Improve School Lunch Selection, *PLoS One* 8, no. 10 (2013): e72008.

25. If your school is interested in the computer program that does this automatically, we've designed one and it can be downloaded and used at no charge. It's available from the Nutrition Report Card article mentioned in the previous endnote, and it is also available at SlimByDesign.org.

26. Much of our earlier work on this is summarized in my book *Mindless Eating* and in Brian Wansink and Koert van Ittersum, "Portion Size Me: Plate Size Can Decrease Serving Size, Intake, and Food Waste," *Journal of Experimental Psychology: Applied* 19, no. 4 (December 2013): 320–32.

27. High color contrast between food and the plate leads people to serve less and eat less. If you want more detail on this than a person should have to endure, check out Koert Van Ittersum and Brian Wansink, "Plate Size and Color Suggestibility: The Delboeuf Illusion's Bias on Serving and Eating Behavior," *Journal of Consumer Research* 39 (August 2012): 215–28.

28. Branding works better for healthy foods than the indulgent ones—basically because indulgent ones sell well anyway. Check out Brian Wansink, David R. Just, and Collin R. Payne, "Can Branding Improve School Lunches?," *Archives of Pediatrics & Adolescent Medicine* 166, no. 10 (2012): 967–68.

29. Using real trays is not a reality for every school. Some schools have gone to disposable trays and others don't have the facilities to wash trays.

30. More details are available from Brian Wansink and David R. Just, "The Smarter Lunchroom Tray: Designing the Sustainable, Scientific Solution to Lunch," under review.

31. See Marla Reicks, Joseph P. Redden, Traci Mann, Elton Mykerezi, and Zata Vickers, "Photographs in lunch tray compartments and vegetable consumption among children in elementary school cafeterias," *JAMA* 307, no. 8 (2012): 784–85.

32. Simply putting this icon on the tray leads to a big initial boost in what kids take. Marla Reicks, Joseph P. Redden, Traci Mann, Elton Mykerezi, and Zata Vickers, "Photographs in Lunch Tray Compartments and Vegetable Consumption Among Children in Elementary School Cafeterias," *JAMA* 307, no. 8 (2012): 784–85.

33. One exception is van Ittersum and Wansink, "Plate Size and Color Suggestibility."

34. These are cool and everyone in my Lab has one. The price is $10.95 and you can buy them here: http://www.mcphee.com/shop/lunch-lady-action-figure.html.

35. The power of personal connection is unbelievable. That's why the big chefs "work the room" and ask how you like everything. It's the same with tater tots: Brian Wansink, Andrew S. Hanks, and David R. Just, "Server Affect and Patronage," under review.

36. Other great tools to help school cafeterias include Sarah Wu, *Fed Up with Lunch* (San Francisco: Chronicle Books, 2011), and Amy Kalafa, *Lunch Wars: How to Start a School Food Revolution and Win the Battle for Our Children's Health* (New York: Penguin, 2011).

37. Kathryn Hoy, R.D., manages our Smarter Lunchroom Movement along with communication support from Sandra Cueller and Katie Baildon. Find resources at SmarterLunchrooms.org.

38. The best one-stop source for how to do start a SNAC or to help change your lunchroom can be found at SmarterLunchrooms.org. There are also dozens of YouTube videos about how to do makeovers.

1. The lose-win policies don't much work because they generally don't happen. Like the teenager you send to their room without TV, you'll either be resisted or worked around.

2. Even schools get $5,000 or more in their budget for each student enrolled. If half a dozen parents decide to send their kids to a charter school or a private school, or to homeschool them, some teacher just lost half his or her salary.

3. Nothing makes it easier to choose the right food than when it's convenient. Here are some great tips: Andrew S. Hanks, David R. Just, Laura E. Smith, and Brian Wansink, "Healthy Convenience: Nudging Students Toward Healthier Choices in the Lunchroom," *Journal of Public Health,* forthcoming. See more at Brian Wansink (2013), "Convenient, Attractive, and Normative: The CAN Approach to Making Children Slim by Design," *Childhood Obesity,* 9:4, 277–78.

4. First, we change what *we* do to be more slim by design. Second, we ask the places around us to help us. Read more about the CAN Approach at Brian Wansink (2015), "Change Their Choice: Changing Behavior Using the CAN Approach and Activism Research," *Psychology and Marketing,* forthcoming.

5. These changes can be so easy even a high school kid could do them. As mentioned earlier, we showed that by having a high schooler we never met implement a vegetable-naming program three hundred miles away from us. More at Brian Wansink, David R. Just, Collin R. Payne, and Matthew Z. Klinger, "Attractive Names Sustain Increased Vegetable Intake in Schools," *Preventive Medicine* 55, no. 4 (2012): 330–32.

6. Brian Wansink, "Profiling Nutritional Gatekeepers: Three Methods for Differentiating Influential Cooks," *Food Quality and Preference* 14, no. 4 (June 2003): 289–97.

7. Brian Wansink, "Nutritional Gatekeepers and the 72% Solution," *Journal of the American Dietetic Association* 106, no. 9 (September 2006): 1324–26.

8. Doing things in a group or as an organized community can be good, but many community groups spend more time organizing than accomplishing. Also, the people who are the most active are often also the most extreme, and extreme approaches won't work with most restaurants, grocery stores, schools, and workplaces. It's too much like the neighbor who calls and screams at you to shut down your party or he'll call the police. Even if he gets some results, they will be begrudged and short-lived, and you can bet his neighbors won't be lending him any cups of sugar in the future.

9. For those who aren't feeling electronically predisposed, we can send you a free Actionism Kit that includes a set of hard copies and other goodies to get you started.

Index

Note: *Italic numbers* indicate illustrations.

tortilla chips, 92, 103

Trail's Restaurant (Minnesota), 87–88,
284*n*, 286*n*

Tufnel, Nigel, 284*n*

TVs (televisions)
  at home, 76
    dining rooms, *50*
    In-Home Slim-by-Design Self-
      Assessment Scorecard, 63
    kitchen, 39–40
    overeating while watching, 55
  in restaurants, *73*, 74, 76
  in school lunchrooms, 199
  in work break rooms, 157

Twitter
  reaching out to grocery stores via, 258
  reaching out to restaurants via, 254

Underhill, Paco, 124–25

unit bias, 280*n*

United States Department of Agriculture
    (USDA)
  cafeteria makeover (Washington, D.C.),
    162–64, *166–67*
  Dietary Guidelines, 3, 102, 132–33,
    162, 252

University of Colorado's Anschutz Health
    and Wellness Center, 178

USDA. *See* United States Department of
    Agriculture

value and price, 89, 91

Van Ittersum, Koert, 89

Van Kleef, Ellen, 54

vegetables. *See also* salads; salad bars
  in grocery stores, 288*n*
    half-cart option, 118–19
    Slim-by-Design Grocery Store Self-
      Assessment Scorecard, 142–43
    store layout, 121–23, *126–27*
  Half-Plate Rule, 132–34
  precut, 54

prep site for, 43
in school lunchrooms, 199–203,
    200–201
  Smarter Lunchroom Scorecard, 220
  Smarter Lunchroom Starter List, 204

vending machines, 156

visible foods, 36, *37*
  candy dish studies, 49, 52, 280–81*n*
  first seen vs. first eaten, 41
  in the kitchen, 36, *37*, 40–42
    breakfast cereals, 26, 36, 277*n*, 279*n*
    clearing counters, *37*

waitstaff (servers)
  half-plate portions, 70, 88
  Slim-by-Design Restaurant Pledge, 103
  Slim-by-Design Restaurant Self-
    Assessment Scorecard, 109
  suggestions from, 86
  table layout, 71

walking trails, 169–70

wanderers, 121

water, 92, 93, 285*n*

Wegmans, 132–33, 270

weight loss, 20–22, 276*n*
  counting calories, 23, 26, 276*n*
  goals of, 23, 26
  length of diet, 21–22, *22*
  National Mindless Eating Challenge,
    276*n*, 281–82*n*, 294*n*
  online programs, 174

weight-loss programs, 172–74

wellness programs. *See* corporate wellness
    programs

Werle, Carolina, 169

What Would Batman Eat?, 99–101

What Would McDonald's Do? (WWMcD),
    208–9

Why We Buy (Underhill), 124–25

willpower, 1, 6–7

wine, restaurant study, 68, 282*n*

wine glass size, 47–48, 87–88